The Turn-On

The Turn-On

How the Powerful Make Us
Like Them—from Washington
to Wall Street to Hollywood

Steven Goldstein

HARPER
BUSINESS

An Imprint of HarperCollins*Publishers*

HarperCollins books may be purchased for educational, business, or sales promotional use. For information, please email the Special Markets Department at SPsales@harpercollins.com.

FIRST EDITION

Designed by William Ruoto

Library of Congress Cataloging-in-Publication Data has been applied for.

ISBN 978-0-06-291169-8

19 20 21 22 23 LSC 10 9 8 7 6 5 4 3 2 1

To Loretta,
for whom an entire state
joins me in love

and in memory of
Senator FRL and Salena

CONTENTS

The Turn-On

Discovering
The Turn-On

At 9:00 a.m. on Friday, September 21, 2001, nearly ten days to the minute after two planes had crashed into the World Trade Center on the orders of Osama bin Laden, his half brother Abdullah interviewed me in midtown Manhattan to see if I could save the bin Laden name.

When a family intermediary called me earlier in the week, I thought it was a sick joke. I've spent decades working with some of the most likeable people in the world. Suddenly the bin Ladens?

I'd been running a communications and political consulting firm on Wall Street in Manhattan, a short walk to Ground Zero. Although I hadn't left my apartment in Brooklyn Heights that day, the stench of fire and atrocity would waft across the East River to engulf our neighborhood for days. I couldn't open my apartment window without sobbing.

Also working near the Trade Center were my father and my cousin Maxine. They were already at the office. Soon after the first plane hit, Dad and Max joined the petrified crowd on the street that funneled into a massive bunker under the Chase Manhattan Bank complex.

My relatives emerged all right, but like many other New Yorkers, I had family and friends who lost loved ones.

We were, all of us, a devastated people.

The call from Abdullah bin Laden's intermediary came a couple of hours before I headed to synagogue for Rosh Hashanah, during which we Jews recite prayers highlighting our millennia-long attachment to Israel. America's support for Israel had prompted bin Laden to declare war on the United States in 1996.

I told the intermediary to call me again after the holiday. As I sat in synagogue over the next couple of days wondering whether that first call was real, I considered what it would be like to meet a bin Laden at my office, which survived miraculously intact.

As bin Laden entered my office, he would be greeted by the watchful eyes of Theodor Herzl, the founder of Zionism, the movement that created the modern state of Israel; his eyes guarded the doorway from a portrait above my desk. On another wall hung framed copies of laws I helped to write that advanced the civil rights of women, people of color, and my own LGBTQ community.

It all begged the question: Why on earth would the bin Laden family seek advice from a gay Jewish Zionist? In its coverage of my encounter with bin Laden, the European edition of the *Wall Street Journal* described me as having "a track record of support for Israeli causes." As if I weren't improbable enough, I had begun preparation to attend rabbinical school, where I continue my studies to this day.

A friend of a friend told me he was friends with someone who was friends with Abdullah bin Laden. Only six degrees of separation lay between Osama and me.

With Rosh Hashanah over, Abdullah and I met that Friday morning not at my office but in the lobby of the InterContinental New York Barclay hotel on East Forty-Eighth Street in Manhattan. Abdullah, a student at Harvard Law School, had flown in from Boston. He brought two colleagues from the family conglomerate, the Saudi Bin-ladin Group, which uses a different English spelling of the surname.

All four of us were dressed in dark suits and conservative ties, blending in among the corporate types in the heart of midtown Man-hattan's business district. Abdullah had large, piercing eyes, impecca-ble manners, and seemingly Parisian elegance. As we sat down in the hotel dining room, none of the other diners realized a bin Laden was now among them.

Abdullah said he had met Osama only five times, most recently in 1989 at the funeral of one of their older brothers.

As Abdullah continued, I believed he had nothing to do with 9/11. He was pro-America and fully Westernized, and wanted Saudi Arabia to enter more egalitarian times.

And the circumstances supported him. First, Osama was one of an estimated fifty-three siblings and half siblings from various moth-ers across a family of hundreds scattered around the world. Second, the bin Ladens had repeatedly distanced themselves from Osama, in-cluding after the 1998 terrorist attacks on U.S. embassies in Africa just three years earlier.

After we had sized each other up for about a half hour, Abdullah got to the point. He had heard I was not afraid of big challenges. As a congressional staffer, I had taken on terrorists who bombed abortion clinics and helped to write a law instituting tough criminal penal-ties. I had taken on the National Rifle Association to stop convicted spouse and child abusers from owning guns. As a communications strategist, I had confronted Exxon by running the press operation for the fishermen and women in Alaska whose livelihoods ended with the Valdez oil spill that devastated the environment and the Alaska fishing industry.

"*Tzedek, tzedek, tirdof,*" the Torah instructs us in Hebrew. "Justice, justice, you shall pursue."

The day before I met Abdullah, I contacted the FBI to send agents to meet and debrief me after the breakfast. We arranged to meet at the office of my friend, Congresswoman Carolyn Maloney of Manhattan's Upper East Side, to which I took a cab from the InterContinental. Carolyn wound up telling the story of my adventure to the press.

"[Steven] would never consider working for them for a million years," Carolyn said of me to the Capitol Hill newspaper *The Hill*. "But I can understand why the bin Ladens went to [him]. If I had a public relations debacle on my hands, I'd go to him too."

Carolyn was right about whether I'd work for them. True, the family didn't have anything to do with 9/11. But even if Abdullah and other bin Ladens had modern views, they were too important to Saudi Arabia, a nation where women are oppressed and where my faith and others are banned from public practice.

At my breakfast with Abdullah, I did all I could to listen for details that might be useful to the FBI. Somehow I morphed into an amalgamation of Mike Myers characters: the spy Austin Powers and Linda Richman, the host of "Coffee Talk" on *Saturday Night Live*, with an accent as thick as buttah from Brooklyn, my birthplace.

Yet Abdullah grew more intrigued. He quizzed me further about my background, wherein I revealed I was not only a communications consultant but also a lawyer. He smiled and said if you need a lawyer, hire a cousin.

My goodness, he meant hiring a cousin from among the descendants of Abraham! He considered my religion to be a plus. In other words, I could be the counterweight to balance out the public's perception of the family.

Because Carolyn quickly gave the story to the press, I never got the chance to speak with Abdullah again. Nor did he extend a formal offer to me, obviously, after the publicity. When the news hit, the bin Ladens' preexisting flack said that was never the family's intention.

Two FBI agents took my information. What they didn't tell me—and what news reports later revealed—was that at least thirteen other bin Ladens had chartered a jet to leave the United States with the FBI's blessing. The FBI was satisfied that none of the bin Ladens in America, including Abdullah, the one who remained a bit longer, had connections to 9/11.

Clearly Abdullah had sought the FBI's help. But why mine? For the same reason others have during my career: Abdullah wanted his family to come across as publicly likeable. And—dare I say it?—I found him to be both likeable and credible.

To be sure, neither Abdullah nor I used the term "likeable." And remember, likeability had not yet emerged as the universal name for interpersonal currency. It would be three years before Mark Zuckerberg and his Facebook colleagues unveiled Facebook and elevated "like" to an emotion as popular as love. And it would be seven years before Barack Obama told Hillary Clinton during a 2008 Democratic primary debate in New Hampshire that she was "likeable enough."

What could I, of all people, teach the bin Ladens about winning over the American public post-9/11?

To answer the question, we need to look at two successive jobs early in my career.

In January 1993, at age thirty-one, I became a staff lawyer for the U.S. House Judiciary Committee working for Congressman Chuck Schumer, now the Senate Democratic leader.

I landed the job and landed on a dream. For as long as I can remember, I wanted to make a difference in the world. During the

1968 presidential campaign, I played hooky to volunteer for Hubert Humphrey at the local Democratic Party headquarters. I was six.

If I loved licking envelopes for Hubert Humphrey as a child, imagine how much I would love working for Congress so early in my career—and in one of the more influential staff jobs on Capitol Hill. My joy danced me to work every day.

The House Judiciary subcommittee Chuck Schumer chaired and for which I worked, the Subcommittee on Crime and Criminal Justice, had been assigned to write a big chunk of President Bill Clinton's domestic policy agenda. I worked on the progressive elements, including new laws to protect Americans from hate crimes and gun violence, and to advance women's rights.

As a lawyer for Congress, I organized subcommittee hearings on my bills, lining up witnesses to tell the stories of their imperiled lives to reinforce the positive impact of the legislation my team and I were proposing. I booked emotional witnesses who could move members of Congress to tears, astonishment, or both, and always got press coverage. That fit well with Chuck, famous for owning press coverage of any issue in which he was involved. In all fairness, the coverage was about more than his career. He also wanted to advance his causes. And in winning over hearts, likeable witnesses also won congressional votes—and helped pave the way for laws that would change our nation.

But my political radar told me we Democrats would lose control of the House in the November 1994 elections. Before that happened, I went on a job hunt and got an offer within a couple of weeks. My new boss also wanted me to start soon—and she was giving me a job as unbelievable as the one I was in. How could I say no?

I packed my bags, turned my head, and rushed out of Washington on the last Friday of July 1994. That Monday, I began my new job in Chicago.

I was a producer on *The Oprah Winfrey Show*.

As a producer for *Oprah*, I booked emotional guests who could move the audience to tears, astonishment, or both. Sound familiar? Like the other producers, I liked high ratings. But I had an activist's motive to achieve them. The more people I reached, the more I could persuade people—through Oprah—to act on the issues closest to my heart.

In one weekend I rocketed between two entirely different jobs in two entirely different careers, or so it may seem. But to me, the jobs were nearly identical. They required me to find and communicate the real stories of real people in real trouble who needed real help. Let me explain the parallels.

Over the course of the two jobs, first in Congress and then at *Oprah*, I took notes on the people I had booked who were the most successful in moving my target audiences. Which kinds of people were the best witnesses to persuade members of Congress at a hearing? Which kinds of people were the best talk show guests to affect Oprah in the studio?

Likeable people, of course. But what made witnesses and guests likeable? In both jobs, I began to jot down the traits. The lists I kept in each job began the same way.

In Congress: Witness has an entertaining or captivating story to tell.

On *Oprah*: Guest tells a story in an entertaining or captivating style.

I wound up compiling a list of dozens of traits during the two jobs, with a substantial overlap. Eventually, I combined and honed the list into eight likeability traits. The traits could be the start of a book.

But time passed, and I never wrote that book. Instead, I founded Garden State Equality, New Jersey's statewide organization for LGBTQ civil rights, in 2004 and served as executive director until 2013, the year we won marriage equality in New Jersey. Along the way, I built an organization of 150,000 members—my heroes—who won 216 other LGBTQ laws at the state, county, and local levels in just nine years.

Throughout my time at Garden State Equality, I was in the news almost every day. When reporters in the New York market needed a go-to person for a quote on a gay rights controversy, there I was, instantly available and quotable. That's what working for Chuck Schumer taught me and everyone else who has worked for him.

My approach to the press was different, and remains different, from that of most other leaders, elected or unelected. I didn't see my job as presenting issues. I saw my job as presenting stories that illustrated the issues I wanted to advance.

Once I found a story, I would build it into a cause célèbre that millions across the state and region would come to know and care about. That's how my organization wound up winning so many laws. We didn't advocate issues dryly. The stories I found were heartbreaking and became part of the emotional soundtrack of everyday lives.

As an activist, I insisted we have a dominant story in the news at all times that would provoke one of five emotions: one that would make people cry, scream, gasp, smile, or laugh. That came from my days as an *Oprah* producer. The smile or laugh would come through a triumphant resolution to our story, when the wrongdoers would cave in, our victims would prevail, and our legislature would pass a new law.

A year had passed since I founded Garden State Equality, whose goal was to win marriage equality. During our first year my colleagues and I found hundreds of couples willing to tell the press about the discrimination they faced because the state had refused to allow same-sex couples to marry. But none of the couples captivated me enough, nor would have captivated the state enough, to spur the sympathy of millions to advance our cause. Certainly, none of the couples had all eight traits of likeability.

One morning in November 2005, I received a phone call from Garden State Equality's vice chair, Karen Nicholson-McFadden. "Where are you?" she asked excitedly.

It was 7:30 a.m. and I was still behind the wheel of my car, having just pulled up to rabbinical school.

"Steven," Karen said, "I found our story."

She read me an article buried in the middle of a local newspaper, the *Ocean County Observer* (Toms River, New Jersey), which doesn't exist anymore. She was reading from her hard copy.

The article described the anguish of a dying police officer, Lieutenant Laurel Hester, who had worked for Ocean County and helped to protect the seven members of the county legislature, called freeholders. She was diagnosed with lung cancer that was spreading rapidly through her body. Doctors said she had months to live, at most.

Knowing she would soon die, Laurel asked the county to assign her death benefits to her domestic partner, Stacie Andree. The freeholders—the same county legislators whose lives Laurel protected—said no because Laurel and Stacie were a same-sex couple and thus didn't deserve the same rights as married opposite-sex couples. If New Jersey had marriage equality, Laurel could have assigned her benefits to Stacie as a matter of right.

Freeholder Jack Kelly later explained the freeholders' decision bluntly. Laurel and Stacie's relationship, in his view, violated the sanctity of marriage.

"That's it!" I screamed to Karen. "That's our story!"

During the first break in my Biblical Hebrew class, I called

Margaret Bonafide, the reporter who wrote the article, asking her to give my number to Laurel. I skipped the rest of my classes to drive to Ocean County to meet Laurel and Stacie at their home.

Laurel had all the likeability traits I had identified while working under Chuck Schumer and Oprah. Laurel and Stacie were the couple that would take New Jersey by storm. I didn't have to coach them. I just had to get them in the news.

That night and the following day, television stations across New Jersey, New York, and Philadelphia covered Laurel's fight for life and justice at or near the tops of their broadcasts. As I watched the stories, I checked off whether each portrayed Laurel with the traits of likeability you're about to read in this book. Each story did.

Every day the story was in the news, hundreds of new members, then thousands, joined Garden State Equality to support Laurel and Stacie. Many of our new members were straight, conservative Republicans who stayed with our organization over the long run to fight for marriage equality itself. Meanwhile, the polls showed that statewide support for marriage equality had grown dramatically because of the nonstop media coverage of the epic battle, fueled by daily rallies and protests that Garden State Equality had organized on Laurel's behalf all over the state.

In January 2006, a month before Laurel died, the freeholders voted to allow her to assign her death benefits to Stacie. The fight for Laurel Hester became a documentary, *Freeheld*, that went on to win the Oscar for Best Documentary Short in 2008 and become a full-length Hollywood movie in 2015 in which Steve Carell played me. I'll tell you how Hollywood simplifies the personalities of real-life people portrayed in fictionalized films to make those people more likeable, and sometimes less likeable, to fit preconceptions of what the American people want to watch.

At least Carell didn't play me as the 40-Year-Old Virgin.

When the Hollywood movie came out, I was a professor of law and political science at Rutgers University in Newark. That's when I found myself reviving the idea for this book, nearly a quarter century after I began jotting down notes as a congressional staffer and a producer of *Oprah*.

Five minutes into my first class in Campaigns and Elections, I was comparing the likeability of presidential candidates with that of Hollywood stars. I knew the first task of teaching was to capture students' attention, for captivation is my likeability trait #1.

When I mentioned Morgan Freeman and Sandra Bullock in the same breath as Barack Obama and Hillary Clinton, students' eyes lit up like fireflies at night. With several undergraduate business students in the course, I'd soon add names from the business world, such as Warren Buffett, Tim Cook, and Sheryl Sandberg. I'll tell you about all those folks and dozens more.

In the classroom, I wasn't merely dropping boldface names. I was teaching my students in the style that would become my hallmark—as a Professor Robin Williams who ran around with a manic energy and was willing to do anything to hold my students' attention for a three-hour class.

Ideas raced through my head as I bounced around from row to row. I'd write a book that would cover my traits of likeability for public figures in the three fields I was mentioning to students: politics, entertainment, and business.

I taught Campaigns and Elections again in the fall of 2015. This time I included Donald Trump as likeable.

That's right. Having been a delegate at Democratic National Conventions for both Hillary Clinton and Barack Obama, I was still objective enough in late 2015 to understand how Trump's plain-speaking appeal stood out in the crowd of the seventeen Republican candidates for president. So did my students, nearly all of whom were far-left Democrats on a campus ranked by *U.S. News & World Report* as the most diverse in the country.

But one student wasn't buying it. Trump makes a mockery of morality and he isn't even nice, she said. But as I explained to the class, likeability doesn't require morality, as much as all of us wish it were otherwise. News organizations had run dozens of investigations casting doubt about Donald Trump's ethics by the time he ran for president in 2016. Nearly half the electorate found him likeable anyway.

As for Trump's not being nice? I don't equate likeability with being nice, either. I define "likeability" as the traits we perceive in another person that welcome us into a satisfying emotional relationship. They're also the likeability traits we present to others when we want to come across as likeable.

Over twenty-five years, I wound up jotting down dozens of likeability traits before I consolidated them into eight. Those eight traits have remained constant over the past few years and form the basis of this book. They are captivation, hope, authenticity, relatability, protectiveness, reliability, perceptiveness, and compassion. Each of us presents the eight traits to others and perceives them in others, in four stages in which we present or perceive one pair of closely linked traits at a time. I'll tell you more about each trait and which other trait I pair it with, and why, in the pages ahead.

Some of the traits, such as hope and compassion, are related to niceness. But other traits, such as protectiveness and reliability, revolve around toughness—the opposite of being nice. Like chicken soup, being nice doesn't hurt, but it's not a requirement if you can captivate people and present other likeability traits. Think about the people you and everyone else like. They don't have strong opinions or personalities. They're milquetoast. They piss no one off. Their like-ability is a mile wide yet a centimeter deep, for no one likes them intensely.

Although this isn't a how-to book—such as *How to Become More Likeable in Eight Easy Steps*—you're bound to compare your level of likeability to those of the entertainers, politicians, and business leaders whose likeability secrets I will now reveal. And it's completely fine if you do! I won't discourage it.

The intention behind what's to come, however, is to help readers develop a deeper understanding of how, exactly, some public figures become likeable, while others don't. Let's call it "likeability literacy": the ability to identify and articulate, beyond a vague instinct or feeling, the specific features and characteristics that make certain CEOs, politicians, athletes, singers, and actors so appealing to the masses.

As we'll soon discuss, there's power in popularity. It's nice to be admired and respected, of course, but most public figures who seek to cultivate their likeability do so for far more than just the sake of being admired and respected. Likeability grants the likeable among us a certain degree of clout and influence. People listen to them. They follow their lead. Likeable public figures tend to sell more tickets, garner more votes, and build better relationships with their employees. Likeability affects what we do, whether we're aware of it or not. Likeability is leverage.

CHAPTER 2

Wear Your Hard Hats: Likeability Is a Construction Industry

Benjamin Franklin was America's first celebrity, renowned across the thirteen colonies for his mesmerizing erudition that helped to unify our national culture. Like Ronald Reagan and Bill Clinton centuries later, Franklin had the genius and an instinct for telling stories in a conversational fashion that captivated others from all walks of life.

As if he were a performer on *Saturday Night Live*, Franklin played dozens of characters, all with rich identities and stories, that made every character likeable in different ways. The characters were aspects of Benjamin Franklin himself.

When Ben was twelve, he worked for his older brother James, who founded the *New-England Courant*, one of the colonies' first newspapers. Denied the chance to contribute articles, at age sixteen Franklin began writing under the pseudonym Mrs. Silence Dogood, a fictitious middle-aged widow for whom Franklin had created an entire backstory. Franklin, you might say, was the original *Tootsie*. Mrs. Dogood's letters were so popular, it's believed that male readers sent marriage proposals to the newspaper.

Franklin went on to run the highly successful *Pennsylvania Gazette* and *Poor Richard's Almanack*, making him both very rich and a voice of authority on life in the colonies. If either Twitter or cable news had existed then, Franklin would have become even more prominent than he already was.

While Franklin's voice was quintessentially American, it translated beautifully around the world. As a diplomat in France from 1776 to 1785, he catalyzed Franklin-mania among the intellectual elite. Women courted him, and his face was put on porcelain plates for people to collect. In France, where Franklin negotiated the Treaty of Paris that ended America's Revolutionary War, he became known for the accoutrements for which celebrities are still known today. Franklin's fur hat became as popular in France as John Wayne's cowboy hats and Jacqueline Kennedy's pillbox hats centuries later in America.

Franklin was also the first American to break down likeability into traits, which he called "virtues." In his autobiography, which took him nearly two decades to write before it was published in 1790, Franklin outlined the thirteen virtues he had developed as a young man to live his most self-actualized life: temperance, silence, order, resolution, frugality, industry, sincerity, justice, moderation, cleanliness, tranquility, chastity, and humility. Some of those virtues are goofy in the context of today's world. Others are evergreen and play a role in how I dissect likeability traits.

Having worked for racial justice, I cannot pass over that Franklin was a slave owner, despicably normal at the time. But later in life he became an abolitionist, freeing his own slaves and critiquing the slave trade. He knew the power of publicly acknowledging his own imperfections, a quality that would become a permanent bulwark of celebrity in America. He wrote his autobiography as a collection of personal stories to inspire others toward self-improvement. He was, in that sense, the Oprah of his time.

Franklin described imperfections, both his own and others', as a new kind of personal perfection. With peerless emotional intelligence, he knew the populace would find the quest for perfection to be exasperating because of its unattainability. "A benevolent man should allow a few faults in himself," he wrote, "to keep his friends in countenance."

Franklin told stories with a common trajectory. He went from troubled times to better times, from self-doubt to self-confidence. He knew that people wanted to hear rags-to-riches stories, not riches-to-rags.

He also knew that the most likeable stories from public figures are not only uplifting but also simplified. Simplification is the equalizer that allows everyone in the audience to understand the stories and to retell the stories themselves. Few of us want the burden of processing the complexity of strangers' lives. It's hard enough for us to process the complexity of our own.

Maintaining a catalogue of positive stories, and balancing simplicity and realism in telling them, is central to how public figures transmit likeability. President Reagan's stories were rooted in the truth but had simplifications that made the stories feel like the movie-marketing caveat: "Based on a true story." His audiences didn't object because they loved his charm. His simplification also empowered them to repeat his stories and become more likeable themselves.

Unlike Reagan, a number of other public figures, including Franklin, have used physical items to become more likeable—props, if you will. An inventor, among his other roles, Franklin produced creations that improved the lives of thousands throughout an emerging nation, no doubt making him more known and more likeable with each invention. Before American independence, he invented the Franklin stove, as well as the armonica (the glass harmonica) and the lightning rod. Shortly after independence, he invented bifocals.

Franklin's lightning rod emerged from his experiment with a kite. That famous kite would become a forerunner of the sky-bound machines from a couple of public figures today. Virgin founder Richard Branson, building his likeability brand as a visionary, has promised the world he would begin space tourism through a space-travel company he has branded Virgin Galactic. Tesla founder Elon Musk, another CEO focused on vision, has been developing a reusable rocket he expects will dramatically reduce the costs of space travel to make it possible for millions.

Traveling from space to biblical times—perhaps in Michael J. Fox's likeable time machine from *Back to the Future*—we arrive in circa 1300 BCE to examine one of the first props of likeability. God, through a burning bush, encountered Moses with a rod in his hand. Apparently so taken with the rod, God gave it magical powers. When the Israelites had to cross the Red Sea in their exodus from Pharaoh, God told Moses to lift up his rod and hold out his arm over the sea to recede the waters so the Israelites could march on dry land.

Whether we believe the Bible was written by divinely inspired people or by God directly, or if it is a work of literature that includes myth to some extent, the author or authors of the Bible knew the power of a prop to help make Moses a leader whom the Israelites would follow. They also knew the power of a prop to make Moses unlikeable, at least to God. When God told Moses to speak to a rock to get it to produce water and Moses instead used his rod to hit the rock for water—which had worked once before—God prohibited the disobedient Moses from entering the Promised Land.

Over thousands of years, from Moses's rod to Ben Franklin's kite to business leaders who dream of spaceships and rockets to catapult humanity into the galaxy, society has judged, and will continue to judge, public figures by their likeability.

Likeability is something to which each of us can relate instinctively. Every day we make decisions about whom we like and whom we don't, be they in public life or in our personal lives, and have a sense of who likes us and who doesn't. Likeability is also an instrument of democracy that empowers people from all walks of life to assess public figures from an equal starting point.

But in our sweep of public figures who have used props to become more likeable, I don't want you to think props are necessary. My point is to illustrate that likeability is a construct.

By "construct," I mean that likeability—or, more exactly, likeability as presented to the public—is a quality public figures can and do indeed manufacture, sometimes with the help of likeability gurus you'll meet soon.

Today, likeability constructs are everywhere. When Ruth Bader Ginsburg wears her famous "dissent collar" as she reads dissenting opinions from the bench, she comes across as independent and, to millions of Americans, courageous. When NBC's *Today* show wanted to transform Hoda Kotb and former cohost Kathie Lee Gifford into likeable party animals, producers put glasses filled with wine in front of them and relabeled Tuesday as Boozeday and Wednesday as Winesday. When Warren Buffett opened the 2018 Berkshire Hathaway shareholder meeting in Omaha, Nebraska, he quickly sat down and made a show of passing a box of peanut brittle to his vice chairman Charlie Munger. Sure, Berkshire Hathaway owns See's Candies, but the gesture doubled down on Buffett's likeable reputation as a warm and just-folks kind of guy.

How far will celebrities go to protect what they consider to be their likeable attributes? According to reports, Bruce Springsteen has insured his voice for $6 million, Julia Roberts has insured her teeth for $30 million, and for $27 million, Jennifer Lopez has insured her derriere. That's a long way from Dolly Parton's insuring her cleavage for a reported $600,000 in the 1970s.

Make no mistake: Likeability is not just a construct; it is also an entire business by which companies can profit.

Perhaps you remember the 2014 Academy Awards. It was among the most memorable Oscar telecasts in recent years and more highly rated than Oscar ceremonies since. The host, Ellen DeGeneres, provided the world with one of television's all-time most likeable moments. It's hard to forget how she glided effortlessly into the audience to take a selfie amidst a constellation of other Hollywood stars, including Meryl Streep, Bradley Cooper, Julia Roberts, Brad Pitt, Angelina Jolie, Jennifer Lawrence, Lupita Nyong'o, and Jared Leto.

How likeable was the moment to the world? One hundred thousand people retweeted the photo instantaneously, crashing Twitter. Within a half hour, 780,000 people retweeted the photo, breaking the previous all-time retweet record President Obama set on Election Night 2012 when he tweeted "Four More Years" to caption a photo of him and Michelle in a jubilant embrace.

Ellen's selfie was a produced construct, obviously. No one happens to gather some of the most famous people in the world on a moment's notice for a seamlessly herded group selfie without missing a beat—on a broadcast under a microscope that wouldn't tolerate a missed beat.

But that wouldn't fully explain the construct. ABC had signed a $20 million deal to provide Oscar night advertising and product placement to Samsung, maker of the Galaxy smartphone she used for the selfie—or more exactly, that which Bradley Cooper used after Ellen handed him the phone. Wittingly or not, he meticulously held the phone so as not to obscure the Samsung name near the phone's camera as it made love to another camera—the one broadcasting the Oscars to a billion potential consumers.

Samsung's contract with ABC guaranteed ten celebrity selfies to be tweeted throughout the Oscars. Apparently the contract didn't prohibit Ellen from using non-Samsung phones. From backstage, Ellen tweeted away photos of herself and other stars from her personal smartphone—an iPhone.

Those backstage photos, like those she sends year-round from her daytime talk show, were marked as "Twitter for iPhone." Given the on-air/off-air dichotomy, could there have been better proof that Samsung, ABC, and Ellen had dreamed up the ultimate likeability construct? In fact, during Oscar rehearsals, Samsung employees were on set showing Ellen how to use a Samsung phone—notwithstanding the company's claim after the Oscars that the famous group selfie had happened "organically."

The construct didn't stop at the Oscars. Ellen and her team, anticipating that the celebrity group photo would be a likeability sensation, extended the goodwill to the next day, when she gave away free Samsung Galaxy Note 3 phones to the entire studio audience on her daytime talk show. This made everything feel more organic. In other words, Ellen's handlers did not construct her use of Twitter from whole cloth. Ellen had been a Twitterholic since Twitter's earliest days. As of June 2019, her 77.8 million Twitter followers make her Twitter's eighth most popular user in the world.

Now let's pivot from Ellen's moment of likeability to another one: the time presidential candidate Bill Clinton played a saxophone in

1992 on *The Arsenio Hall Show*. Analysts have called it the gig that changed political campaigning forever—the first television appearance, supposedly, in which a president or presidential candidate transformed him- or herself into a full-fledged entertainer. But it wasn't the first at all.

When Dwight Eisenhower ran for president in 1952, his friends worried whether his formal communication style, which worked on the battlefield, would translate as likeable enough for the new television era. To his credit, Eisenhower did not reject the criticism, whereas others in his shoes probably would have. He was, after all, beloved across America for being a World War II hero.

At his friends' urging, Ike hired the first political likeability guru of the television era, Rosser Reeves from the Ted Bates ad agency. Reeves told Eisenhower to ditch the idea of buying thirty-minute or one-hour blocs on television to address the nation. Instead, Reeves had the campaign produce commercials of twenty to sixty seconds that included voters and soft touches to the candidate's biography. In one commercial Eisenhower says: "My Mamie gets after me about the high cost of living. It's another reason why I say, 'It's time for a change!'" Roy Disney, brother of Walt, even produced a commercial that turned the slogan "I like Ike" into a full-fledged jingle.

In 1960, Senator John F. Kennedy inched closer to entertainment by appearing on a non-news program, *Tonight Starring Jack Paar*. But in a buried, bizarre twist of history, it was Kennedy's opponent in 1960—the dour Richard Nixon, of all people—who became the first presidential hopeful to entertain America outright. In 1962, Nixon appeared with Jack Paar to play the piano as part of a self-conceived campaign to make himself more likeable after losing the 1960 campaign.

Paar wound up introducing Nixon to a writer on the show, Paul

Keyes, whom Nixon put on his payroll throughout the 1960s. Keyes helped to construct the "New Nixon," a more likeable Nixon, whose successful 1968 campaign for president included his appearance on *Rowan & Martin's Laugh-In* shortly before the election to say the show's signature words: "Sock it to me."

Both Nixon and his opponent in 1968, Hubert Humphrey, credited Nixon's *Laugh-In* appearance with having won Nixon the election. Likewise, from the moment Bill Clinton wore his Elvis-cool sunglasses to play "Heartbreak Hotel" on *Arsenio Hall* in 1992—an appearance pushed by Clinton adviser Mandy Grunwald as part of a larger strategy to reach younger voters through vehicles reflecting their pop-cultural preferences—Clinton's likeability numbers among young voters rose and kept rising through the rest of the campaign.

Clinton's appearance on *Arsenio* was rooted in reality. Clinton had been a star saxophone player during his days at Hot Springs High, winning the position of first chair in saxophone in Arkansas's statewide student band. It's not as if he went on *Arsenio* to dance, as Barack Obama did years later on *Ellen*. Clinton has never considered himself a great dancer. In his post-presidency, he turned down the opportunity to be a contestant on *Dancing with the Stars*, believing he needed way too much training to be credible.

Likeability constructs, such as those channeled by Ellen DeGeneres through her Samsung and Bill Clinton through his saxophone, abound in entertainment, politics, and business. Take the black turtlenecks Steve Jobs wore nearly every day—and always during his iconic public announcements of new Apple products.

Jobs's personal uniform exuded a natural quirkiness and ultimate cool that buttressed the justified image of his irascible, eminently appealing genius. That his clothes were a national likeability construct was not lost on entrepreneurs outside Apple. Several created knockoff Steve Jobs clothing lines replete with black turtlenecks, Levi's jeans, and even nonprescription versions of Jobs's glasses.

The uniform had to be a construct to Jobs himself. What, exactly, would have been natural to a lifelong Californian about always wearing a long-sleeved black turtleneck, even in the summer?

The black turtleneck had been an icon of 1940s and '50s Beat Generation writers in downtown Greenwich Village and uptown Morningside Heights, the neighborhoods of NYU and Columbia in a city and on a coast where Jobs had spent no appreciable time in his life. When the poet Allen Ginsberg moved from New York to San Francisco in 1954 and brought his clothes and other writers with him, Steve Jobs would not be born for another year. The black turtleneck was the symbol of creativity and anti-materialism.

Jobs provided biographer Walter Isaacson a lengthy explanation for the outfit. When the young creator of Apple visited Japan in the 1980s, the then head of Sony, Akio Morita, had spoken about the benefits of employees wearing corporate uniforms, particularly in bonding workers to their company. Jobs then approached the designer of Sony's uniforms, Issey Miyake, to design one for Apple employees. When the employees rebelled, Jobs said he had his new friend Miyake simply make him some turtlenecks.

To be sure, the story had the benefit of making Jobs seem sensitive to, and democratically overruled by, his employees. But other stories had leaked from Apple over the years in which employees said Jobs was far from a dream to work for, with a vile temper and unpredictable temperament. The truth would make him no less likeable to the many of us who've worked for genius bosses ourselves, but Jobs, a barometer of mass appeal, apparently felt otherwise. Had he been alive, one could imagine him flipping out watching Oscar host Ellen DeGeneres take photos on the air with her Samsung.

Before the 2011 Isaacson biography, Jobs had a different story about his black turtlenecks, demonstrating that one or both of his stories were constructs. In a 2005 interview in the *Financial Times* with his longtime friend John Lasseter—the founder of Pixar who would later apologize for sexual harassment during the #MeToo movement—Jobs said that when he had seen an Issey Miyake black turtleneck he liked, he called Miyake's company to ask them to make another one. The company refused. Jobs asked how many black turtlenecks he'd have to buy to get more. When the answer was one hundred, he bought one hundred—and thus his signature look was born.

Steve Jobs, of course, was the most design-savvy industrialist of his lifetime and ours. If anything, Jobs's switch to sleek designer wear was a move toward his true self. Jobs's clothes had finally caught up to his unrivaled sense of industrial design.

Likeability: From Construct to Impact

My focus in this book is on what makes public figures in politics, business, and entertainment likeable, with a look at the behind-the-scenes players who make them popular. But in case you're wondering, why should any of us care about the likeability of public figures in the first place?

When we perceive public figures as likeable, they influence our daily lives. When we perceive politicians as likeable, we allow them to shape the course of America. Let's take a moment to look further at the impact of political likeability and then the impact of likeable CEOs and celebrities.

The Impact of Political Likeability

Television had been around for years by the time General Eisenhower ran for president in 1952, but it was not until the 1950s that television became commonplace in American life. By the 1952 election, an estimated 40 million Americans owned a television.

Throughout the television era, the more likeable candidate has usually won the general election. In 1952 and 1956, Eisenhower, the war hero who learned to present himself as warm as he was courageous, defeated the patrician Adlai Stevenson. In 1960 the young and hopeful John F. Kennedy, emphasizing the future, defeated the dour Richard Nixon. In 1964, Lyndon Johnson, who could be alternately charming and brutal on the turn of a dime, faced a less likeable opponent in Barry Goldwater, whom Americans feared as an extremist.

In 1968, an exception to the rule, Richard Nixon faced the more likeable Hubert Humphrey, the Happy Warrior. But Nixon had addressed enough of his likeability issues to prevail. In 1972 he faced in George McGovern an opponent whose campaign was so weak—McGovern had to replace his own vice presidential running mate in the middle of the general election campaign—that Nixon, in comparison, projected likeability traits based on strength.

In 1976, Jimmy Carter based his entire campaign on likeability—specifically on trust, as he told Americans "I'll never lie to you"—to defeat Gerald Ford, who had likeability qualities of his own.

In 1980 and 1984, one of the most likeable public figures of all time, Ronald Reagan, defeated Carter and then Walter Mondale. The election of 1988, between George Bush and Michael Dukakis, was a likeability standoff until Bush's campaign eroded Americans' confidence that Dukakis was tough enough to lead the nation. As you'll see in the pages ahead, likeability is not only different from being perceived as nice, but also tough people can be perceived as likeable. Think John Wayne, Clint Eastwood, and—at least to Democrats—Speaker Nancy Pelosi when she takes on the opposition.

No other candidate could come close to Bill Clinton's likeability in 1992 or 1996. In 2000, down-home George W. Bush of Texas, the stylistic opposite of his more formal dad with Connecticut roots, beat the smarter but stiffer Al Gore. In 2004, Bush had become the tough war hero from 9/11 who faced another war hero, John Kerry, without Bush's appeal.

In 2008 the Democrats nominated their own Reagan of likeability in Barack Obama. Not even John McCain, a beloved American patriot, stood a chance. The McCain campaign was so frustrated, it ran an ad that attacked Obama for his celebrity—in essence, Obama's likeability. The ad didn't work.

By no means am I suggesting likeability is the only factor, or the one that prevails over all else, to win elections. I posit that likeability is a vital force, but not the exclusive force, in voting behavior. It's too glib to ignore the state of the economy or whether the country is at war or enjoying peace. Those issues are powerful election issues in their own right, and help to shape a candidate's likeability in voters' minds regardless of the candidate's personality traits.

But the world had changed by the 2012 presidential election. We had entered a social media world. In 2012, Twitter had grown to 185 million users from just 54 million in 2010. Facebook had reached slightly more than 1 billion users, up from 350 million users as 2010 began.

The rise of social media exponentialized the power of likeability in politics—and in every other realm of public life, for that matter. Politicians and many other public figures, or the social media gurus behind them, were now packaging likeability for social media in real time. And opponents were trying to destroy others' likeability in real time. It was a bigger revolution than the jump from three networks with sporadic news coverage to twenty-four-hour news coverage when Ted Turner founded CNN in 1980. This time public figures themselves had full control of their likeability constructs on social media, skipping the intermediary reporters in traditional media.

If we look closely at national elections since the first social media election—that of 2012—we can certainly see a pattern in which likeability prevails over the economy.

By the 2012 election, President Obama had turned around the economy from that which he had inherited, the worst economy since the Great Depression. The collapse of Lehman Brothers in 2008 and its resulting earthquake upon the entire financial sector accelerated unemployment to 10 percent in October 2009. In October 2012, unemployment was 7.9 percent.

Nonetheless, 7.9 percent unemployment should have tilted the scales toward Obama's prospective defeat. Americans vote in national elections according to where their lives stand at election time, rather than factor in trends. But Obama, whose personal likeability ratings always remained high, faced Mitt Romney, who didn't connect with voters. Because of Obama's likeability advantage, voters reelected him with the benefit of the doubt.

By the 2014 midterm election, the economic recovery had kicked into high gear. Unemployment had fallen to 5.7 percent, approaching half of what Obama had inherited. Nonetheless, Obama's Democratic Party suffered a staggering defeat. Democrats lost nine U.S. Senate seats and handed control of the Senate to Republicans. And the Republicans increased their majority in the U.S. House. It wasn't that Obama became unlikeable. Democrats faced another likeability trend: Voters get bored by the sixth year of a two-term president's time in office, and vote for the opposition party. Voters want to be captivated anew. Here, likeability, or the lack of it, on the part of Democrats prevailed over the economy again.

The 2016 presidential election between Hillary Clinton and Donald Trump was, of course, the biggest upset victory in presidential election history. Clinton was running as the candidate of the incumbent presidential party that had turned a severe recession into a full-fledged economic recovery. Unemployment had dropped to 4.9 percent, and other economic indicators were corroborating that it was morning again in America. But the election largely hinged on likeability—a faceoff between Clinton, who had always polarized voters and produced legions of Hillary lovers and haters, versus Donald Trump's likeability, marred by financial and personal ethics scandals the likes of which no other nominee could ever surmount. No previous nominee had had three wives, flaunted his infidelity, had as many questions about his business propriety, or boasted he could grab women "by the p**sy."

To the extent Trump won the election—he had help from Russian operatives who manipulated social media, and Clinton still won the popular vote by 3 million—Trump's base turned out in droves because they found him likeable. He spoke his mind and came across as authentic. He was also entertaining, particularly on social media and often in a shocking way, and that, too, was an attribute for his base. Talk about an election where likeability proved not to be the equivalent of nice! It didn't hurt Trump that enough Americans could not bring themselves to vote for Clinton under any circumstance under the sun.

Ultimately, the 2018 election was a classic triumph of likeability over the economy. On Trump's watch, unemployment in November 2018 was a startlingly low 3.7 percent. Yet the Democrats captured forty new seats and sudden control of the U.S. House. They lost only two seats in the U.S. Senate, which was one-third or one-fourth the loss experts once predicted, given that twenty-six Democratic senators and only nine Republican senators were up for reelection. But Russiagate and other scandals in the Trump administration and in Trump's past, many of which had been brought to the fore by Special Counsel Robert Mueller, had destroyed Trump's likeability except with the hardest core of his base. Yet that core has remained devoted to him in the face of increasingly troubling facts about his behavior in and out of the nation's highest office. Why certain public figures remain likeable to some members of the public even as the majority feels differently is one of the paradoxical qualities of likeability. We'll delve into these dynamics later.

The Impact of CEO Likeability

Just as a candidate's likeability, the economy, and war and peace have all played a role in how we vote—with a candidate's likeability mattering more in the social media era—so, too, reasons exist for a CEO's likeability other than his or her personality. If a CEO is leading a company whose stock values are on the rise, no doubt shareholders will view the CEO as likeable even if investors don't really know the CEO at all—or perhaps know the CEO superficially from shareholder meetings or occasional appearances on CNBC. What if the warm, folksy, and accessible Warren Buffett were, instead, a horror from hell? Would 40,000 shareholders not show up to Berkshire Hathaway's annual shareholder meetings in Omaha, Nebraska, and not cheer for Buffett as a rock star? Of course they would, because he's making them truckloads of money. Consider this: An investment of

$1,180 on Berkshire Hathaway's initial public offering date, May 9, 1996, would have generated $6,295 after a stock split on January 21, 2010.

In recent years, studies have sought to pinpoint the impact of likeable CEOs on their companies and the world at large. In 2015 the global public relations conglomerate Weber Shandwick conducted an online survey of 1,700 senior executives from around the world about the impact of CEO reputation. The survey heavily weighted personal likeability in assessing reputation. The survey also excluded CEOs themselves from participating, so as not to skew the outcome.

The results:

- The 1,700 executives estimate that 44 percent of their company's market value is attributable to the reputation of their CEO.
- Eighty-seven percent of the executives believe that a CEO with a positive reputation attracts investors.
- Seventy-seven percent of the executives believe that a CEO with a positive reputation attracts employees.
- Seventy percent of executives believe a CEO with a positive reputation retains employees.

The likeability of CEOs is also intertwined with how much good they and their companies do in the world. CEO likeability goes far beyond bottom-line profitability. In the Weber Shandwick survey, 64 percent of the executives surveyed believe CEOs must be active in the local community to have an "admirable" reputation. In turn, 40 percent of executives say corporate responsibility efforts influence a company's reputation a great deal. At least within the business world, when a CEO and his or her company spend time and money trying to do good in the world beyond the bottom line, the CEO and the company become more likeable.

Indeed, there's a correlation between likeable CEOs and corporate social responsibility. In 2019, in a ranking *Forbes* calls the "Just 100," the magazine lists the one hundred corporations it deems are the best corporate actors. The criteria do not come down simply to philanthropy, understandably, given that actors in the corporate world could buy better reputations through charitable giving. The criteria include involvement in local communities, doing right by the environment, and treating workers well.

Let's take the top ten companies on *Forbes*'s "Just 100" and compare them with their CEOs' likeability scores on Glassdoor, by which employees evaluate their CEOs. A 90 percent Glassdoor rating for a CEO means 90 percent of employees like the CEO. In the chart on the next page, the years note the most recent year by which a Glassdoor ranking is available for the CEO.

Except for Robert Swan, the interim CEO of Intel for whom there are not yet Glassdoor results, nearly every CEO in these top ten socially responsible companies earns a Glassdoor likeability score of 90 percent or more. The one exception is Ginni Rometty, CEO of IBM. For that matter, her rating is significantly below 90 percent, at 68 percent. What else might you have noticed? Rometty is the only woman among these ten CEOs. We'll discuss the double standards of likeability for public figures from oppressed communities, including for women in public life.

The Impact of Celebrity Likeability

What if I told you Robert Downey Jr. is a more effective ambassador of American power around the world than Donald Trump? I can see

CEO Likeability and
Corporate Social Responsibility

FORBES "JUST 100" RANKING	COMPANY	CEO	GLASSDOOR RATING AND YEAR
#1	Microsoft	Satya Nadella	96% (2018)
#2	Intel	Robert H. Swan	(not yet rated)
#3	Alphabet (Google)	Sundar Pichai	96% (2017)
#4	Texas Instruments	Rich Templeton	93% (2017)
#5	IBM	Ginni Rometty	68% (2018)
#6	Nvidia	Jen-Hsun Huang	99% (2017)
#7	VMware	Pat Gelsinger	90% (2017)
#8	Procter & Gamble	David Taylor	90% (2017)
#9	Adobe Systems	Shantanu Narayen	96% (2017)
#10	Cisco Systems	Chuck Robbins	91% (2018)

many of you Democrats smirking now. Anyone would be better than Trump, you're thinking. But a movie star?

In 2004, Joseph S. Nye Jr., a professor at Harvard's John F. Kennedy School of Government, wrote a book, *Soft Power: The Means to Success in World Politics*, that attributes the power of nations to more than force or the potential to use force. Nye calls that traditional kind of power "hard power." "Soft power," he says, is the indirect power nations have to influence other nations rather than to coerce them. According to Nye, every nation's soft power in the world falls into three categories: "Its culture (in places where it is attractive to others), its political values (when it lives up to them at home and abroad), and its foreign policies (when others see them as legitimate and having moral authority)."

Under President Trump, the United States is no longer the world's leader in soft power, according to the Soft Power 30, an annual ranking of soft power from the Center on Public Diplomacy at the University of Southern California in conjunction with Portland Communications in London. In 2016 the United States ranked #1 in soft power. In 2017, the first year of the Trump administration, the U.S. fell to #3. In 2018, the U.S. ranked #4. The United Kingdom, France, and Germany now hold first, second, and third place, respectively.

But during all three of those years, in the subcategory of cultural soft power, the U.S. ranked #1. Indeed, no other nation around the world exports its culture, including through movies, television, and music, as powerfully as the United States does. Movie stars especially are America's ambassadors of goodwill, no matter the fluctuations in global perceptions of America linked to U.S. presidents.

Hollywood, more than any other movie capital in the world, is the clear leader in movie exports. In 2018, sixteen of the top twenty grossing films worldwide came out of Hollywood. The others were *Fantastic Beasts and Where to Find Them*, a *Harry Potter* spinoff film coproduced by Warner Bros. and a smaller British studio, and three films from China.

Among the various ways to measure the likeability of movie stars, their performance at the box office is certainly a strong measurement. Are moviegoers around the world willing to put their money where their mouth is to see the stars they like best?

Here's a ranking of the top ten movie stars through March 2019 in international box office receipts. In terms of ambassadors for their home countries, seven of the ten are American. Emma Watson and Daniel Radcliffe, both of *Harry Potter* fame, are British. Chris Hemsworth is Australian.

Lifetime Box Office, Worldwide, for Actors in Leading Roles

RANKING	ACTOR	TOTAL BOX OFFICE	FILMS	MONEY PER FILM
#1	Robert Downey Jr.	$11,347,906,177	43	$263,904,795
#2	Scarlett Johansson	$10,786,869,239	28	$385,245,330
#3	Johnny Depp	$10,292,180,982	50	$205,843,620
#4	Tom Cruise	$10,013,446,441	42	$238,414,391
#5	Samuel L. Jackson	$9,908,090,427	59	$167,933,736
#6	Vin Diesel	$9,656,383,827	22	$438,926,538
#7	Tom Hanks	$9,498,831,861	49	$193,853,711
#8	Emma Watson	$9,093,129,400	15	$606,208,627
#9	Daniel Radcliffe	$8,233,524,904	20	$411,676,265
#10	Chris Hemsworth	$8,155,464,381	20	$407,773,219

Likeable entertainers also have the power to save lives. Consider Angelina Jolie. In May 2013, she wrote an opinion piece for the *New York Times* explaining the reasons behind her decision to have a preventive double mastectomy. "My doctors estimated that I had an 87 percent risk of breast cancer and a 50 percent risk of ovarian cancer," she wrote, revealing that she carries a rare mutation of the BRCA1 gene. "Once I knew that this was my reality, I decided to be proactive and to minimize the risk as much I could."

The article went viral. According to one survey conducted a few weeks later, researchers from the University of Maryland and Johns Hopkins University found that nearly three in four American adults were aware of Jolie's double mastectomy.

After Jolie's announcement, the number of women getting tested for breast cancer spiked. A study led by Harvard Medical School researchers published in the *BMJ* (formerly the *British Medical Journal*) revealed that daily BRCA test rates among American women ages eighteen to sixty-four increased from 0.71 tests per 100,000 women in the fifteen business days before Jolie's article to 1.13 tests per 100,000 women in the fifteen business days following. Researchers concluded that "celebrity endorsements can have a large and immediate effect on use of health services." Media outlets reported increased rates of testing in Canada, Australia, and the UK, too.

Research from Cornell University found the number of women getting a risk-reducing mastectomy nearly doubled in New York State, climbing from an average of 3.3 bimonthly cases per 1 million women twenty months prior to Jolie's announcement to 6.3 cases per 1 million women twenty months after. A similar trend occurred in New South Wales, Australia.

Entertainers certainly have the ability to drive other behavior. In October 2018, as the midterm elections neared, Taylor Swift encouraged her fans to participate. "Please, please educate yourself on the candidates running in your state and vote based on who most closely represents your values," she wrote to her 115 million followers on Instagram. "Go to vote.org and you can find all the info."

According to Kamari Guthrie, director of communications for Vote.org, the site received 65,000 registrations in the twenty-four hours after Swift's post. At about forty-eight hours, the figure topped 240,000. Throughout the entire month of September 2018, by comparison, 190,178 new voters had registered through the site. In August 2018, 56,669 had registered.

If all that's not convincing enough, approach likeability from the opposite perspective. Unlikeable celebrities also have influence, but negative influence.

After multiple men accused actor Kevin Spacey of sexual misconduct, Netflix dropped Spacey from its hit series *House of Cards* and also dropped a completed film in which Spacey played Gore Vidal. The decisions cost Netflix a reported $39 million. In late 2017, producers of Ridley Scott's *All the Money in the World* were willing to spend a sudden $10 million extra to allow Scott to reshoot scenes in which Christopher Plummer replaced Spacey. The film turned out to be a mild hit, grossing $57 million against a total production cost of $50 million.

Smart decision. In the summer of 2018, Spacey's crime drama *Billionaire Boys Club* earned $126 on opening day. You read correctly: One hundred and twenty-six dollars.

With those case studies from politics, business, and entertainment on the impact of likeability on the world, let's now turn to the behind-the-scenes likeability gurus who make the impact happen.

CHAPTER 3

America's Food Chain of Likeability, Starting with Marion in Iowa

T hink back to when our elementary school teachers taught us how all living beings on earth are interconnected and interdependent. You remember the food chain. For the rest of our lives, it became a scientific fact and a multipurpose metaphor. Let's start with the third-grade fact.

A rabbit eats the grass and grows. Then the rabbit becomes food for the fox. Then the fox dies, or poops, and becomes fertilizer for the grass.

With our refresher course out of the way, let's turn to my food chain of likeability. The chain has three characters who work behind the scenes to shape the likeability of politicians, entertainers, and business leaders for public consumption. I call them the Trainer, the Evaluator, and the Presenter. The relationship among the three in constructing, assessing, and sustaining likeability, from the most public of public figures to the local television weather forecaster, reveals the circle of life in the likeability industry.

The Trainer

Our food chain of likeability begins with the Trainer. Think of the Trainer as the grand master Yoda from the *Star Wars* movies who helps Luke Skywalker unearth his dormant Jedi powers. Now transfer that image to the likeability industry: the politician, actor, business leader, or other media personality is Luke Skywalker, and the trainer Yoda taps into the well of likeability, intrinsic to each of us, to make individuals more likeable to the public.

Once these media personalities, politicians, and CEOs get in touch with their likeability traits and learn how to project them, all sorts of positive outcomes emerge. Likeable politicians win elections. Likeable actors draw more people at the box office. Likeable CEOs can become icons to help increase sales.

In 1957, Frank Magid, a professor of social psychology, anthropology, and statistics, combined all those fields when he founded a company that would become our national command center for likeability. Bet you didn't know we had one, did you? Frank's company, Frank N. Magid Associates—now simply called Magid—invented training to make people more likeable.

Frank based the company in Marion, Iowa, population 40,000, where the company maintains an office today. Why Marion? Frank received his bachelor's and master's degrees in sociology at the University of Iowa, one of the two institutions where he'd go on to teach. The other was Coe College in nearby Cedar Rapids. Understanding the sociology of television viewers, he began to coach the on-air newscasters at a CBS affiliate in Cedar Rapids, KGAN, to become more likeable. As his consultancy became a full-fledged business, he based it in Marion, a suburb of Cedar Rapids.

To be sure, neither Frank nor the coaches and analysts at his company have marketed their services as likeability training, but that's what they've done to remarkable effect. For more than forty years they've trained people to communicate with several of the likeability traits I've mentioned, including captivation, hope, authenticity, and relatability.

As Frank achieved success at KGAN—certainly measured by an increase in the newscast's ratings—he and his company coached television anchors and reporters in other markets to communicate more likeably to viewers. They didn't coach on a hunch. Frank would conduct survey research in each market to find local viewers' opinions of that particular market's newscasts and their on-air "talent," the term in the television news business for anchors, reporters, and anyone else who appears on air.

For decades, the company focused almost totally on coaching television talent, whereas today it coaches all sorts of public figures. In television, Magid's clients are not typically the talent themselves but local stations and the national networks that hire the company to see how to make their newscasts more likeable and increase their ratings. That's why people across television called Frank Magid, and today his company, the "news doctor." Frank himself died in 2010, but Magid the company continues to grow. Today it has hubs in Marion, New York, Los Angeles, and Minneapolis, from which Brent Magid, Frank's son, runs the company.

I heard about Magid in the early 1990s when I worked for a local station in Washington, D.C. At first, I thought the name Magid was a play on a Hebrew word. In Hebrew, *Magid* means "to tell"—the perfect coincidence.

Beyond coaching talent, Magid shapes newscasts for its clients by researching what kind of presentation viewers in a particular market would most prefer. In the 1970s, Magid helped to transition news away from a format in which a camera throughout the broadcast focused largely on the anchor—in the old days, usually a white man—toward newscasts that feature engaging graphics, diversity among anchors and reporters, and live reports at the scene of breaking news. Magid picked up the pace of presenting news in a compelling fashion decades before social media did the same.

Magid also developed ABC's *Good Morning America*. When it premiered in 1975, folksy anchors spoke conversationally to the audience from a living room set rather than a news desk, taking advantage of a vacuum in the early mornings that the *Today* show and CBS's many hard-news morning shows had left.

The first time I visited Magid was in 1999. I brought one of America's most powerful people at the time: Jon Corzine, who had just left his position as CEO of Goldman Sachs and was now running for U.S. Senate from New Jersey. I had signed on as his co–campaign manager upon the recommendation of Senator Frank Lautenberg, who had announced his retirement and recommended a few of his staffers for Jon to hire. Frank regretted his retirement and wound up running for—and winning—New Jersey's other U.S. Senate seat just two years later.

I didn't know Jon and had no preconceptions when I met him. He was the last person in the world with the demeanor of a Wall Street CEO. With his beard, sweater vests, soft-spoken demeanor, and riveting eye contact, he was great at connecting one-on-one. But he showed his communication talents only one-on-one. To larger audiences, his unemotional, low-key demeanor came across as a lack of passion. It was easy to interpret him as just another rich guy wanting a Senate seat as his latest toy. Fact is, Jon had a huge heart for others. He just didn't show it in his public speaking.

Soon after I joined the Corzine campaign, Jon and I sat down quietly. I suggested he do some training at Magid. He questioned why anyone would go to Cedar Rapids, Iowa, for media training rather than to Manhattan.

I clarified that it was Marion.

Who's Marion? he asked.

So Jon and I flew to Chicago and then took a prop jet to Cedar Rapids. That thirty-minute leg of the trip was the same that the television host and producer Dick Clark had taken for years. Longtime Magid staffers fondly remember how Clark would fly to Magid incognito, wearing an oversized Hoppy baseball cap over his eyes, to evaluate tapes of talent as he searched the next generation of stars for the shows he produced.

After Jon and I drove about twenty minutes from Cedar Rapids to Marion, we came upon America's control center of likeability.

As Jon and I sat down with Magid coaches, they began by showing us a videotape of the most likeable politician in America. It wasn't Bill Clinton or Ronald Reagan.

The tape was of the fast-talking, peerlessly energetic U.S. senator from Minnesota, Paul Wellstone. Wellstone died tragically in a plane crash in 2002 when he was fifty-eight, but in 1999 he was serving his second term in the Senate as a progressive leader. To be sure, Magid is nonpartisan, and the coaches' choice of Wellstone had nothing to do with Wellstone's being a Democrat. It was only years later that I learned one of our two chief Magid coaches was a Republican and the other a Democrat. Their politics didn't matter. They were invested in our success.

As we watched Wellstone, we saw his voice, hands, and entire body communicating with electric passion as if he were a nonstop fireworks display. You couldn't take your eyes off him. You couldn't stop smiling, either, as he bubbled over with authenticity and hope. I was awed by the brilliance of the Magid philosophy and Magid coaches. They didn't choose some inoffensive, bland, nonethnic middle-aged man to show Jon what a likeable communicator looked and sounded like. In presenting Paul Wellstone, the Magid coaches chose someone unlike any other public figure in America at the time, and indisputably authentic. The message: Magid was going to coach Jon but not turn him into someone else. He would become the most engaging version of his most authentic self.

Over two days I saw the trainers work with Jon's body language and calibrate his vocal style to speak more quickly or more slowly, higher or lower, as the subject warranted. He had it in him. He was improving by the hour.

Because of Magid, Jon went from a grade C– communicator to a frequent B+ or A– communicator who sometimes hit an A+ out of the park. He won the Senate seat and served there for six years before becoming governor of New Jersey. What he learned at Magid made all the difference in the world.

Years later I returned to Iowa to talk to Magid's coaches and analysts for this book. As they told me about the company's success stories, one stood out: how the team enhanced the likeability of a weather forecaster at a station in Shreveport, Louisiana, a city besieged by megastorms. In Shreveport and other television markets with wild seasonal fluctuations, the weather is often hard news that begins a newscast. A popular weather forecaster can be as important as the two main news anchors in increasing a newscast's ratings. Conversely, if the weather forecaster is not optimally connecting with viewers, a newscast's ratings suffer.

Such was the challenge facing KSLA, Shreveport's CBS affiliate for the Ark-La-Tex, the area where Arkansas, Louisiana, Texas, and even Oklahoma meet. With just over 1 million residents, it ranks as the ninetieth largest television market among all 210 in the United States.

In 2007, KSLA brought in a new chief meteorologist, Stephen Parr, a thirty-four-year-old weatherman from the neighboring town of Tyler, Texas, where he had become a star. He took the science of weather seriously. He was no weather entertainer. Parr looks as if he could be Stephen Colbert's younger brother: genial good looks, rimless glasses, and a sturdy jaw.

When the station announced Parr's arrival, the promotion materials said: "Stephen's experience tracking storms in our region is reassuring to our viewers. He knows this area and will live up to our commitment to provide weather coverage you can count on." In the Ark-La-Tex, where storms could level people's homes and change their lives forever, reassurance was key.

Earlier Magid research had shown that viewers ranked KSLA's weather coverage as #1 in the Ark-La-Tex. Not so in 2010, and KSLA wanted Magid to tell the station how to fix it.

Magid's four-hundred-person phone survey of regular news watchers in the area ranked Parr fifth among seven meteorologists tested. No one questioned Parr's knowledge. But as Magid and KSLA dug deeper into the findings, one common critique surfaced: Parr didn't come across as liking his job and therefore didn't project the infectious energy that would make viewers want to turn to him.

That ideal on-air persona has a name. Pete Seyfer, the Magid vice president who worked with KSLA and Parr, described it to me as "the joy of performance." And that's when it clicked: The foundation for captivating others is the joy of performance. Seyfer would know. Like many other Magid consultants, he had once been an on-air newscaster who proved successful in captivating viewers and increasing a newscast's ratings.

Think about the stars who always look and sound as if they love what they do. Here's what they telegraph: I wouldn't want to do anything else in the world but to entertain or inspire you as I'm doing now. Dolly Parton is the epitome of such a star. If you mention her name to people across every diverse walk of life in America, I promise a uniform reaction. Everyone will smile as he or she thinks of Dolly smiling at us. That's the joy of performance. It is the opposite, Seyfer said, of being "plain vanilla."

Stephen Parr, upbeat and charismatic when we spoke, came across differently when he joined KSLA, according to Seyfer. Parr didn't smile as often as he could, he didn't banter much with the news anchors, and he didn't present each weathercast with the enthusiasm of someone who believed he had the best job on the planet. Viewers couldn't relate to him at all, and that is not someone from whom anyone seeks reassurance. The big question now was whether KSLA would keep Parr or replace him.

Pete Seyfer was tasked with delivering the news to Parr. As Seyfer recalled, "Most people would have told us, 'Go to hell.'" But rather than challenging the findings, Seyfer said, Parr "rolled up his sleeves" and said, "So tell me how I'm going to get better."

Not that it was easy for Parr to hear. It wouldn't be easy for anyone.

"I remember going into the meeting where Pete delivered his findings," Parr told me. "He met with me, my news director, and her boss. You think to yourself, This is not going to be good. And then they start just showing you the numbers. And they wouldn't show me all the numbers. They showed my name and left blanks where everybody else was. But what I got out of that meeting was that no one knew who I was, and even those who did didn't like me.

"As I asked what I could do better, they said they still believed in me, and that was nice to hear. I had come in dead last but they wanted to stick with me. They said they had a plan. In my head, I was praying, Anything but a dog. Please don't give me a dog. That was when stations gave forecasters dogs."

For all the quantitative research Seyfer had presented to KSLA and Parr, Seyfer understood the numbers don't mean everything. Magid's coaches base their recommendations not only on the numbers but also on their own mastery of captivation from having worked in television and other fields of public presentation.

Brent Magid, Frank Magid's son, has served as president and CEO of the company since 2002. "Sure, we use big data and all the behavioral research we've developed," Brent told me, "but we never forget the human side of the equation. My dad, going back to the mid-1950s, understood that emotions drive behavior, because he was a student of social sciences. And that's central to our company's work today. The emotional connection with the audience is still the bottom line."

True to form, rather than dropping a truth bomb and fleeing the scene, Pete Seyfer got into the trenches with Parr to make visible improvements to Parr's on-air likeability.

As Parr himself would tell me, during his previous gig in Tyler, Texas, he personalized his weather forecasts by speaking directly, in his mind, to a friend's wife, a woman he felt accurately represented the region's target audience. In Tyler she was a teacher and mother. However, following his move to Shreveport, Parr admits he somehow lost this personal approach.

In the months after the survey results, Magid trainers examined Parr's engagement with the camera and his nonverbal expressions. What was his body language like when he displayed maps? What was his bedside manner during severe storms? How did he share news about good weather with the audience? The show often featured the same graphics, so the weatherman needed to be able to connect directly to the community.

After Magid's coaching, Parr began to exude more joy of performance through body language, facial expressions, and colloquial conversation. If you think that's phony, Parr told me Magid's recommendations brought out his more authentic self—the real Stephen Parr off camera.

It was as if Magid gave Parr the advice I've given students in my political communication course. Don't take figurative "fancy pills" before you speak publicly. You'll sound like a movie star from the 1940s and '50s, and no one today would find you glamorous—simply impersonal and unrelatable. Back then, actors delivered their lines with a formal, nearly Shakespearean cadence even in everyday on-screen conversations with their costars. Why natural communication wasn't the coin of the realm, who knows? Remember, people once dressed up to travel on airplanes.

As Parr became his more authentic and relatable self, Magid also recommended to KSLA that the station rebrand him. Consistent with Pete Seyfer's recommendation, Parr morphed from being the formal and bureaucratic chief meteorologist to everyone's friendly protector: "Stormtracker Steve."

When Seyfer mentioned the name to Parr in the meeting about Magid's findings, Parr recalls thinking: I can live with that.

The label took off immediately. Everywhere Parr would go, people would call him Stormtracker Steve. He understood how it made him human and accessible—or at least most of the time he did.

"I pushed back on Pete's recommendation that I never show a map with cold fronts and warm fronts," Parr recalled. "He said nobody at home knew what those were. Then I realized I was presenting one map every show, whether or not it had anything to do with the weather story—like, 'Look, here's a cold front that's not going to affect us.'"

I had never heard anyone else in the television business, of which I'm a veteran, use the term "weather story." But of course communicating about the weather is about communicating a story.

"It wasn't only about telling people they could wash the car or go to the store," Parr said. "I just wasn't good at working that into the conversation. So I talked about how the weather would make people feel, departing a bit from the structure of the story I was communicating. One of the things I've learned about storytelling is that structure is good, but too much structure is too rigid and not a conversation."

I asked Parr whether he had to end his forecasts—his weather stories—on a note of hope.

"Magid suggested that a couple of times," he said. "When we had a storm, the one thing I didn't want people to do was to panic. Even when things were horrible, I made clear to people there is no need to panic. And so I think staving off panic ended up giving people hope."

In 2012, Magid repeated its survey of the market. Among weather forecasters, Stormtracker Steve climbed from #5 to #1. On-air, he was engaging, energized, and watchable. By 2012 the ratings for KSLA's newscasts climbed to #1 in the Ark-La-Tex.

Just as sending Jon Corzine to Magid was one of the best decisions of my career, so, too, was sending Stephen Parr to Magid one of the best decisions a television station could ever make.

The Evaluator

If the construct of celebrity were a full-time job, what kind of job would it be without a performance evaluation? Enter the Evaluator. In my food chain of likeability, the Trainer—such as Magid—works with public figures to draw out their most likeable traits. The Evaluator then examines whether the training has worked.

For decades the one tool for evaluating celebrity likeability was the Q Score. In 1964, Marketing Evaluations, a company on Long Island, unveiled Q Scores to equip television networks and local stations with numbers that measured the extent to which the public was familiar with, and liked, individual stars whom the networks and stations might want to hire or retain.

By 2006 the field had expanded. A Hollywood talent company, Davie Brown Entertainment, created its own metric, the Davie Brown Index. Davie Brown Entertainment had started in 1982 as the Pepsi-Cola Entertainment Group, an agency that worked exclusively for Pepsi and helped it evaluate which celebrities to hire for its advertising wars against Coca-Cola.

The Pepsi-Cola Entertainment Group changed its name to Davie Brown Entertainment, after founders Jim Davie and Brad Brown, when it took on other clients and focused on product placement, matching celebrities to brands. Then the global communications company Omnicom bought Davie Brown and another agency, The Marketing Arm. Omnicom retained The Marketing Arm, which absorbed the Davie Brown Index and renamed it the Celebrity DBI. In 2019, The Marketing Arm shortened its name to TMA.

The creators of the Celebrity DBI, Jeff Chown and Matt Delzell, are still with TMA today. At their company's headquarters in Dallas, Chown and Delzell explained how the Celebrity DBI works.

The Celebrity DBI database includes likeability numbers for 4,500 notable people, give or take a couple hundred at any given time. Most of the celebrities are entertainers from movies, television, sports, music, and general pop culture, along with a few dozen of the best-known leaders from the political and business worlds. Working from a pool of 1.5 million consumers, TMA surveys 1,000 different respondents a week.

Although it wasn't the first to assign likeability numbers to public figures, TMA's Celebrity DBI has revolutionized the methodology to provide more comprehensive analyses of celebrities than the rudimentary numbers that would have satisfied business clients just a few years ago. Given the frequency with which it goes into the field, its massive pool of respondents, and the various categories in which it ranks celebrities, the Celebrity DBI is, in my view, the gold standard of quantitative measurement of celebrities.

Chown, CEO of the company's entertainment division, described the evaluation process: "Once a brand approaches us or we approach a brand, we brainstorm to find the right celebrity. That's the first stage. At the second stage, we use the Celebrity DBI to make sure we're casting the right person, and once we're sure, we then approach the celebrity and the celebrity's agent. The third stage is managing the relationships between the talent and the brand. We're the intermediary between the talent and the brand throughout the life of the relationship."

TMA also allows companies to subscribe to the Celebrity DBI, which can start at $20,000 a year. That cost is minimal compared to what's at stake. If a company chooses the wrong celebrity endorser, tens of millions of dollars go down the drain. The Celebrity DBI is insurance against marketing disaster.

Once a respondent indicates he or she is aware of a celebrity, the survey asks the respondent to measure the celebrity across eight key attributes: awareness, appeal, breakthrough, endorsement, influence, trendsetter, aspiration, and trust. TMA develops a score of 1 to 100 for each celebrity in each of the eight categories.

"Appeal" is TMA's number for a celebrity's likeability. Therefore, when I provide Celebrity DBI numbers for celebrities' likeability in the pages ahead, the numbers are for their appeal unless I note otherwise. TMA's other seven attributes are different from my traits of likeability. After appeal, the Celebrity DBI categories measure the celebrity's marketing potential, which makes sense for TMA's mission.

Breakthrough, for instance, measures a celebrity's ability to break through all the media clutter. Trendsetter measures up-and-coming celebrities who have particular appeal to Americans younger than thirty-five, which invariably produces an outsize number of musicians among trendsetters. Trust is particularly important to measure for public figures whose likeability rests on their image of our being able to trust them. Trust is an important category in assessing television news reporters and anchors, as well as entertainers who play authority figures.

When NBC anchor Brian Williams spiraled into professional crisis for having lied about his role in a wartime battle, TMA helped to assess how deeply Williams had damaged his brand. As the *New York Times* reported on February 9, 2015: "Before Mr. Williams apologized for exaggerating an account of a forced helicopter landing during the Iraq war, he ranked as the 23rd-most-trusted person in the country—on par with Denzel Washington, Warren E. Buffett and Robin Roberts. On Monday, he ranked as No. 835."

In addition to appeal and the other seven categories in the Celebrity DBI database, TMA assigns each celebrity an overall Celebrity DBI score. The overall score is a combination of awareness and appeal, with 60 percent of the score based on awareness. Why so much emphasis on awareness? As Matt Delzell, TMA's managing director, told me: "Five years ago, Brooke Burke and Oprah Winfrey had similar appeal. Brooke had won a season on ABC's *Dancing with the Stars* and then cohosted the show (from 2010 to 2013). Oprah was known by 98 percent of the population, as she is now, and Burke was known by about 10 percent. But of the 10 percent that knew her, they liked her to the same degree that people who know Oprah like Oprah. But that doesn't tell the whole story, and the Celebrity DBI takes it into account."

As of early 2019, here, courtesy of TMA, are the public figures with the ten highest scores for appeal—in other words, the top ten most liked individuals in America:

Whom Americans Like Best

RANKING	PUBLIC FIGURE	PROFESSION	APPEAL SCORE
#1	Malala Yousafzai	Social justice activist	85.88
#2	Betty White	Television actor	85.03
#3	Tom Hanks	Film actor	84.12
#4	Sandra Bullock	Film actor	82.91
#5	Lupita Nyong'o	Film actor	82.82
#6	Dwayne Johnson	Film actor and pro wrestler	82.78
#7	Lauren Daigle	Christian music artist	82.76
#8	Emilia Clarke	*Game of Thrones* actor	82.68
#9	Denzel Washington	Film actor	82.52
#10	Chris Pratt	Television and film actor	82.33

Now that we've made stops along the food chain of likability to meet the Trainer and the Evaluator of likability, let's proceed to the final stop to meet the Presenter.

The Presenter

After the Trainer has shaped a public figure's skills to communicate more likeably and the Evaluator has measured the extent of that success, enter the Presenter.

The Presenter holds much of the final power in delivering the substance of the public figure's message to the rest of us. The Presenter can be a behind-the-scenes player who shares power with the public figure in communicating the public figure's message. Political speechwriters and Hollywood screenwriters fit the bill. They prepare the words and the principals speak them.

Sometimes the Presenter can have the sole power to communicate the public figure's message. That happens when a press secretary, publicist, agent, or manager speaks to the press on behalf of a public figure who isn't even there.

In 1997, I became press secretary to United States Senator Frank Lautenberg, the senior senator from New Jersey, who had been the top Democrat on the Senate Committee on the Budget. In that position, he worked together with President Bill Clinton and his administration to produce the first balanced budget for our country in a generation. A national balanced budget seemed impossible in the years before 1997, and it seems just as impossible to achieve today.

But Senator Lautenberg showed how an unapologetically liberal Democrat—as liberal as Elizabeth Warren is now—could get our nation's financial house in order while fighting successfully to provide more for the poor, the middle class, and those who have endured discrimination.

When I joined Frank's staff in 1997, he had become a titan of the United States Senate who had authored landmark laws to advance civil rights, our environment, and our national transportation

infrastructure. But the relationship between Frank's glorious achieve-
ments and his anemic public profile was inverse, and it was shocking.
His name recognition even in New Jersey was low, and his positive
rating was lower than it should have been, given his laws that have
shaped America. Because of Frank Lautenberg, smoking is banned on
airplanes, America has a national standard to combat drunk driving,
and convicted spouse and child abusers cannot own guns.

But Frank Lautenberg didn't grow up in the modern television era.
He did not know how to stop a sentence, continuing as he often did
for five or ten minutes after he had made his point. When he sensed
reporters were dozing off, he did the opposite of what most of us
would do. He added whatever additional explanation he considered
necessary. Most reporters stopped going to him altogether, choosing
to quote other senators who hijacked his signature issues

It hurt Frank. It hurt me, too, because he had become a father
figure to me. He had no choice but to change—not who he was but
his presentational skills so he could come across to journalists and the
public as the engaging, passionate person he was in real life.

My solution? Social media.

Wait a minute: I worked for Frank Lautenberg in the late 1990s,
yet I'm claiming to have used social media ten years before it was invented? Who am I, Al Gore?

Using the conventional communications of the time, which still
included faxes but with email taking over, I wrote with the brevity
and the grab-you-by-the-throat language that would later become the
hallmarks of social media.

I stopped writing press releases, the one- to two-page composi-
tions that press secretaries fill with dense, homogeneous writing to
convey news and spin. Few journalists had the time or patience to
read them. Instead I wrote what I internally called "scream sheets."

They consisted of a headline and a subheadline with the story underneath. That gave me space to feature 72-point fonts compared to the typical 12-point size for snoozy press releases.

The scream sheets elevated Senator Lautenberg's press profile instantly and dramatically.

On March 9, 1998, the Associated Press did a story called "The Selling of Sen. Lautenberg." Here's how AP reported it:

> The selling of Frank Lautenberg over the past year has been entertaining, to say the least. On July 10, when R.J. Reynolds announced the end of its trademark advertising campaign, a Lautenberg fax declared, "JOE CAMEL DEAD."
>
> And in August, when tobacco companies reached an out-of-state settlement with Florida, a Lautenberg fax cried, "FLORIDA, SCHMORIDA: BIG TOBACCO IS STILL HIDING THE TRUTH."
>
> The press area of Lautenberg's Washington office has the look of a war room, with grids on the wall to plot speeches, interviews, and television appearances. At the center is a fax machine. If it could talk, it would probably plead for a nap.

The boldness stunned some others. In an article titled "The Senator and the Showman," here's what the *New York Observer* reported about my scream sheets in its political gossip column on November 10, 1997:

"Bob Schieffer, CBS's chief Washington correspondent and host of the Sunday morning public-affairs show *Face the Nation*, keeps a file of them in his cubicle at the Capitol. 'They're just so bizarre,' he told The Transom, adding that he's become strangely addicted to the missives . . .

" 'It has kind of been like collecting baseball cards,' said the CBS newsman."

Schieffer was right. The techniques *were* bizarre compared to the communications strategies of the time. I often wrote in fewer characters than Twitter would allow years later, and that was before Twitter raised its limit from 140 to 280 characters.

I even sent out faxes with a headline and a photo—such as my fax featuring packs of Camel cigarettes with cancer warnings for a news conference on fighting the tobacco industry. Seems simple by today's standards, but using photos in press materials was a shock before Instagram. Today we know that Facebook posts and tweets with photos get a higher response. That's how Instagram came about.

Like others of the Greatest Generation who served in Congress, such as former Senator Bob Dole, Frank Lautenberg had a public formality rooted in a sense of respect for the institution. But in private he was not only passionate but also funny as hell. Dare I say, he was as entertaining as my scream sheets. And when he saw their instant effect, he told me, "Killer, I'm ready. What more have you got?"

That's when I taught Frank Lautenberg how to craft and deliver a sound bite, the coin of the realm for all public communication, written or spoken, in any medium. Sound bites are the catchy quotes, often with pop-cultural metaphors like the many you've read so far, that stand out as memorable for their boldness, humor, or creativity.

For his legislation to counter drunk driving, I had Frank practice this sound bite: "Jim Beam has no place in your Beemer."

To protest a potential infusion of guns into the United States from Iran, Frank practiced: "Eighteen years after he took Americans hostage, the Ayatollah is laughing again—this time from his grave."

And when the state of Florida reached a modest settlement with tobacco companies in the aftermath of decades of deaths caused by cigarettes, Frank delivered this line with humor: "Florida, Schmorida! Big tobacco is still hiding the truth." I wrote "Florida, Schmorida" as a sound bite with Jewish flavor. Florida has the third largest Jewish population among U.S. states, which increased the chances Frank's sound bite would appear all over Florida television. I knew that Frank, the former national chairman of United Jewish Appeal, would deliver the words "Florida, Schmorida" perfectly.

After a couple of months, Frank was in the news constantly, both locally and nationally. His name recognition and approval ratings jumped, and remained high for the rest of his career.

My strategy with Frank was to give him the tools to be the engaging person in public that he was in private. To that end I wrote a speech guaranteed to make him laugh. During practice, he couldn't get through a third of the speech without chuckling.

I knew Frank would laugh just the same—with giggles and a mischievous gleam in his eye that took twenty years off his age—when it came time to deliver the speech to the Washington press corps. I was thrilled about the prospect. Whenever any of us laugh at ourselves publicly, we become more vulnerable and therefore more likeable.

Frank began his speech. He burst into laughter at the moment I had expected, one-third into the speech. Journalists laughed with him as if they were his fans—possible in those less adversarial days. Afterward one reporter asked if Frank Lautenberg was as likeable in real life as he seemed to be in public. Mission accomplished. Reporters never covered Senator Frank Lautenberg the same way again.

May his memory be a blessing.

CHAPTER 4

How We Fall in Like
Is How We Fall in Love

ow do we decide whether we like public figures—including politicians, entertainers, and CEOs—when they are not part of our personal worlds? Actually, they're strangers. But that doesn't stop us from saying how much we like them, love them, or hate them.

Falling in like with a public figure is like falling in love with a romantic partner. In both cases, we view them through the eight traits of likeability. So here we go. Just what are the eight likeability traits, and in what order do we humans present them?

- First, we present *captivation* and *hope* as symbiotic traits.
- Second, we present *authenticity* and *relatability*.
- Third, we present *protectiveness* and *reliability*.
- Finally, we present *perceptiveness* and *compassion*.

Now imagine going on a blind date. You don't know anything about the guy—and I'm calling him a guy because that's my experience—but a mutual friend tells you he's one of the good ones. You're not really in the mood to go on another date, but you have nothing else going on next Thursday night, so why not? If he's a dud, you never have to see him again. It's one Thursday in your life. The stakes are low.

Thursday comes and you head to the restaurant. You're two blocks away when he texts you saying he's already inside, near the back. You enter the front door and scan the room. You have no idea what to expect, and you're nervous. You know from past dates that it will take you ten seconds to assess whether there's chemistry, and although you convinced yourself it's just one Thursday night of your life, forget logic now. Is there anything worse than being on a date with someone from whom you immediately wanted to escape?

Someone near the back of the room puts his hand in the air and waves you over. It's him. You force a smile onto your face, walk toward his table, and sit down. He says hello and jumps right into the small talk. It's a blind date, so the two of you have to start somewhere.

Two minutes into the date, the first trait of likeability becomes a looming question. You're asking yourself: Is my date *captivating*?

This includes his physical appearance and style of dress, yes, but it's fuller than just those surface-level attributes. Does he grab and keep your interest? Does he draw you in with his words and gestures? Is he charming and witty? Fun and exciting? An active listener? Is he . . . not boring?

Shiny objects get people to notice. They might not have anything else beyond the flash of light, of course, but the flash achieved the first step for any successful relationship to take root. It got you to look.

Whatever it may be—his hair, his facial expressions, his playfulness, or his interest in you—he's got you captivated. You're impressed. You're enthralled.

But what's next? Your date can do his entertaining song and dance for a while, but what happens when the music stops and the lights go dim?

That's where *hope* enters as the likeability trait closely linked to captivation. Captivation alone is not enough to like someone. After all, who doesn't love to hate reality-show villains? Hope asks these questions: Does your captivating date give you confidence in yourself and your future? Does he make you just a bit more optimistic about the world? Is there something about him that offers a promise of better days ahead?

By going beyond the surface, however shiny it might be, hope touches on something more lasting. We all need hope, and without it captivation is unsustainable, even grating. If your date's words, ideas, and passions strike you as ambitious, but he's just as encouraging about yours, he's displayed the likeability trait of hope.

By now the dinner with your blind date is going well. You've each had a drink and your meal should be arriving any minute. He's shown you captivation and hope, and you're hooked—hooked enough to prevent you from going to the restroom to tell your best friend to call in ten minutes with a work emergency. You're beginning to invest some emotional energy into the man sitting across the table from you.

This is where some cold, hard reasoning kicks in. Do you really know this guy? He was, after all, a stranger twenty minutes ago. What if he's merely a charismatic psychopath, gifted at saying what you want to hear? In other words, you ask yourself: Is this person for real?

Enter the third trait of likeability: *authenticity*. If the guy is a phony, the deal is off. His captivation and hope mean little if they're not coming from a place of sincerity. If he's one person in public but another in private, the two likeability traits preceding authenticity crumble into dust.

The bottom line: Your date has got to be genuine for your fondness to grow. One artificial ingredient—whether it's a laugh, an anecdote that doesn't ring true, or a mannerism that seems borrowed and should be returned—can leave a rotten taste in your mouth. And nobody wants that. It's the extra dose of MSG that sends off alarm signals throughout your body.

Once your date proves that his words are credible and his motives trustworthy, he's conveyed the trait of authenticity. You breathe a sigh of relief and sip your wine—in my case, Manischewitz—knowing you're not dining with a sociopath.

You've leaped over a huge obstacle. Now it's time to find out more about what you have in common. Indeed, if there's any chance of turning this blind date into a second date, never mind an eternal love, he needs to show the likeability trait of *relatability*.

Can you connect with the guy when it comes to major things like your families, your work, and your values? Can you connect with him on less weighty matters such as movies, books, travel, and food? Do you like the same stuff? Hate the same stuff? Are you both the children of divorced parents? Does his perspective of life overlap with yours? Does he "get" you?

Those are a lot of questions, but they're important ones. Although you might both be captivating, hopeful, and authentic individuals, that doesn't mean you'll click as a couple. It's crucial that you relate to one another for the relationship to move forward.

The food has arrived. The conversation is humming. You're connecting on multiple levels as everyone else in the restaurant slowly starts to fade away into the background. You order another drink because it's Thursday night and you're having fun. You feel yourself leaning in closer and closer to the man a couple feet away from your face.

So far your date has walked successfully through the first four traits of likeability. You feel the flutter that he will make your life better, more interesting, more enjoyable.

You also find yourself letting down your guard. Without realizing it, you stumble across a memory that brings up unexpected pain. The event from your past hurt you, and suddenly you feel comfortable, or comfortably vulnerable, to share it with your date. You're about to take a risk.

At this moment, your date will pass or fail the fifth trait of likeability: *protectiveness*.

As you put yourself out there, warts and all, for the first time, you wonder if your date has the capacity to keep you safe. Is he tough in a way that makes him your fighter? Will he stay strong when things get rough, or will he be the first out the door? Fight or flight?

Don't get me wrong: Protectiveness has nothing to do with men shielding women. Sexism and heteronormativity have no part in my thinking or in this book. Protectiveness is when you confront what's wrong for the sake of what's right.

If your date can convince you he has a strong moral backbone capable of keeping his head high for the both of you during adversity, he's got protectiveness.

But your date's protectiveness—and every other likeability trait, for that matter—must also be consistent. If the guy's good side isn't constant—allowing for the occasional bad day, of course, because he's human—then how good is he, really? Here I'm referring to the sixth likeability trait of *reliability*. Trust and accountability are must-haves for any healthy relationship. Your partner must be stable and not a myriad of personalities from one day to the next. Another word for "reliability" is "character," because it gets to the core of his being.

It's getting late, especially for a Thursday. The restaurant is empty.

When you look around, you see way more staff wiping tables than you do customers enjoying their desserts. Without asking for it, your server puts the check on your table and tells you both to have a good night. Your feelings for your date are heavy, but not heavy enough to tip the scales in your heart. He's still short two likeability traits, and he's running out of time.

The first of these final two tender traits is *perceptiveness*. He might be willing to protect you from future hurt, but does he understand your past pains? Does he even try? Think about it: In long-term relationships that end up falling apart, haven't we all heard our friends say their spouses don't understand them anymore? That their spouses don't get how your friends have changed?

Perceptiveness is emotional intelligence. It's the ability to detect the subtlest of shifts in the atmosphere. If your date can show this advanced level of sensitivity, you're one trait away from falling for him hook, line, and sinker.

The companion trait to perceptiveness is *compassion*. Both traits tell you about your date's sensitivity to the world, which begins with how he perceives you and culminates in how kind he is to others. Does he care about humanity in general? Was he kind to your server and generous in spirit when another customer accidentally bumped into his chair? Does he volunteer, donate to charities, or have a deep-seated goodness in his heart? Would he be patient with your brother with disabilities and remain devoted to you should you develop disabilities in your old age?

If so, congratulations. You're in love.

And that's how we fall in like with public figures. They need to possess all eight traits, from captivation and hope, to authenticity and relatability, to protectiveness and reliability, to perceptiveness and compassion.

Let's talk more, for a moment, about the order. The eight traits of likeability work similarly to those in the late psychologist Abraham Maslow's hierarchy of needs, which argues that humans have a list of needs arranged in a highly specific order.

The lowest, most basic tier is our physiological needs, such as food, air, water, and warmth. The elements that keep us alive. The next tier up is safety, which consists of security from violence, illness, and financial ruin. Up yet another level is a need for love, meaning friends, family, and a sense of connection. Love is followed by esteem. Think prestige, respect, and confidence. The final tier in Maslow's hierarchy of needs is called self-actualization. This top of the pyramid involves a sense of achieving one's full potential. Our ultimate purpose and meaning.

My eight-traits theory, like Maslow's, has a structure of one pair building upon the other. For example, you can't relate to someone if you haven't figured out how to captivate the person first. Likewise, no one would feel fully protected by a partner who didn't seem in the slightest bit authentic. Phonies, after all, don't elicit a feeling of safety.

It's time at last for our eight traits of likeability and for me to explain which public figures from politics, business, and entertainment shine the most in some traits but not others.

CHAPTER 5

The Gateway Traits: Captivation and Hope

aptivation and hope, as you know, are the first two traits of likeability. Captivation yells, "Hey! Look over here." Hope follows with "Now that you're looking, I can make your life better." Before any relationship can begin, a public figure must capture your attention. Once the public figure has it, she must give you a reason to stay before you move on to someone or something else that competes for your precious time.

Modern life, after all, is overpopulated with interests competing for our attention, from ads at bus stops to news alerts on our smartphones. The distractions are endless. If public figures don't provide captivation and hope, forget it. There's no way you'll like them because you won't even know they exist.

CAPTIVATION:
Passion + Presence + Erudition

Let's go back to my teaching days—specifically, to the first class in my legislative advocacy course at Rutgers Law School in Newark. I begin the course not by introducing myself, but by lowering the lights. In the dark I announce there will be a diagnostic quiz immediately after the video I'm about to play. I hear groans and gasps.

The video begins. It's a scene on a ship. Are the nation's ports under attack? Is admiralty law a course prerequisite? The music blares and the star of the video appears.

It's Cher! My students are watching her prance around a ship in fishnet stockings, singing and dancing in the music video for "If I Could Turn Back Time." Believe it or not, I once hired a Cher impersonator to come to a New Jersey state Democratic conference in hopes of diverting public officials and their staff to see her—actually him—to be followed by our pitch for legislation to ban discrimination against transgender people. Hundreds showed up, "Cher" performed, we made our pitch, and a few weeks later the bill passed both houses of the state legislature and became law.

At the conference, the state party director wasn't happy. She said the appearance was "undignified" and instructed me to ask "Cher" to leave. But "Cher" wouldn't leave. It got heated in the lobby, a crowd grew, and the press came over to report it all.

And the coverage spread like wildfire. For the story it placed on page one, the *Star-Ledger*, the state's largest-circulation newspaper, wrote a headline for the ages: "He Was No Cher, and Democrats Were Not Sunny."

Some labeled the story "Cher-gate," while others gave it a catchier name: "Cher-nobyl." The national attention helped us pass the bill within weeks.

To be sure, a public figure doesn't have to be Cher or an approximate facsimile to be captivating. If someone is a celebrity in any field, at one time or another she has captured the public's imagination—or at least the imagination of a large core constituency, such as the business world, the electorate at hand, or an audience of millennials.

Bruce Cohen is one of Hollywood's most prominent producers. Before going on to produce his own movies, including *American Beauty*, *Big Fish*, and *Milk*, Bruce was the first assistant director to Steven Spielberg on the 1991 movie *Hook*.

I visited Bruce at his apartment in the West Village in Manhattan, where I asked him about the role that captivation plays in likeability. Bruce responded immediately with Steven Spielberg's view.

"Steven used to talk about this all the time," Bruce said. "You have to entertain first, even when you have a film like *Schindler's List* with the potential to change the world. The second that an audience feels they're being preached to, they're out the door. That stayed with me and is constantly in my head during the production of a film, especially films about important issues. *Milk* could've gone off into the didactic path, but we were constantly trying to make sure we were captivating people first, because that's the only way they're ever going to learn anything or hear anything."

When I told Bruce I had used a Cher video as a teaching tool, he started to laugh. "Exactly!" he said. "You have to be captivating right off the bat if you want to captivate the American public to any lasting degree."

He then mentioned the legendary *Star Wars* creator George Lucas. "George says you have the first eighteen minutes of a movie to lock people in. He's right. But you really must captivate people from the first frame. You have only a brief window of time once you've caught the audience's attention to lock them in, to make them feel invested [in] discovering what the movie is really about."

Hollywood could be considered the Los Alamos National Laboratory for captivation. Every aspect of an entire industry is established around this one concept. It is the moment when something clicks, and it had better click fast.

Bobby Florsheim, a friend of mine, is a screenwriter in Hollywood. According to Bobby, screenwriting courses in film school teach students to strive for immediacy.

"A friend who went to UCLA film school told me they have a class where the entire assignment was to write the first page of a script," Bobby told me in his Studio City home. "The professor graded the assignment based solely on whether page one was enough to make you want to read more."

As I have told my students, and you, captivation need not be entertainment in the showbiz sense; many public figures do indeed put on a show to captivate. Obviously musical artists do so, and not just through their music. The most beloved musicians of our time also go to great lengths to captivate us visually, from Michael Jackson doing the moonwalk and Madonna writhing seductively on a bed to Prince and David Bowie in many aspects of their too-short lives.

Speaking of captivating musicians, did you know that Goldman Sachs CEO David Solomon moonlights as a DJ under the stage name D-Sol? If you read the business pages, you probably do. Why? Because the combination of finance with electronic dance music is a strange and ultimately captivating characteristic that makes Solomon stand out. The media loves it and emphasizes this fact whenever possible.

His Instagram account, @djdsolmusic, has almost 20,000 followers. In the summer of 2018, D-Sol dropped his first single, titled "Don't Stop," a remix of Fleetwood Mac's 1977 hit. It entered the *Billboard* dance charts. He's played gigs in New York, Miami, and the Bahamas.

"David's always believed that having a wide range of outside interests leads to a balanced life and makes for a better career," a Goldman Sachs spokesperson told the *New York Times* in July 2017, prior to Solomon's ascent to CEO. "He's preached that regularly to younger employees in the firm and tries to lead by example."

In putting on a show, Virgin founder Richard Branson long ago set the standard for business leaders. My bringing "Cher" to a state Democratic conference was nothing compared to most of Branson's stunts.

In 1987, Branson crossed the Atlantic in a hot-air balloon to promote his airline. He dressed up as a giant soda can in 1994 to launch his cola. He jumped off a hotel in Las Vegas in 2007 wearing a tuxedo and bungee cord to promote his airline's expansion. And in 2013, when he lost a bet with AirAsia's CEO over a Formula One race, Branson dressed in drag to serve as a flight attendant on an AirAsia flight.

"If you are willing to make a fool of yourself and make people smile—as long as you do it with a sense of fun—you can get away with it," Branson once said, according to *Entrepreneur* magazine. There it is again: the joy of performance.

When business leaders like Richard Branson put on a show, their objective is not only to increase their personal popularity for the sake of it, although Donald Trump might well be the exception. They also want to draw attention to their companies in a ruthlessly competitive marketplace. And no business leader today works harder to put on a show with a competitive edge than John Legere, the CEO of T-Mobile.

Legere uses every medium at his disposal to put on a circus, with Twitter in the center ring. From there, he operates as ringmaster—or, rather, ringmaster turned superhero. An homage to Batman fills the background of Legere's Twitter account as if to morph the two, reinforcing Legere's tweets and speeches that T-Mobile will shield the world from dangerous other mobile carriers.

Add Legere's shoulder-length hair, right there in the profile photo, and *Sock! Pow! Bong!* It's Hipster Batman, albeit three times older than many of the real hipsters of Williamsburg, Brooklyn. Those hipsters are part of Legere's target demographic. They'd probably like Hipster Batman.

At a T-Mobile press event in June 2014, Legere took to the stage in his signature hipster outfit: sneakers, a hot-pink T-Mobile T-shirt, and, yes, the hair. Amidst his mentions of energy drinks, doobies, kicking ass, and not giving a sh*t, he called his most frequent targets, AT&T and Verizon, "greedy bastards." At another point he attacked them as "these high and mighty duopolists that are raping you for every penny you have. The fuckers hate you."

For that one, Legere wound up apologizing on Twitter: "The drawback to having no filter when I speak . . . [S]ometimes I need a filter. Genuinely apologize to those offended last night."

Personalities like John Legere and, less benignly, Donald Trump have something in common with Howard Beale, the fictional, psychologically unhinged anchorman played by Peter Finch in the film *Network*. Beale exploited the darker side of a society, always looking for scapegoats with reckless abandon, screaming "I'm mad as hell and I'm not going to take this anymore!" Beale understood the moving power of his anger, just as Legere does today: Their anger reflects that of their audience and foments it. As Legere described himself to Business Insider in 2014: "I don't walk closely up against the line. I ignore it. It's who I am. I may be a little rough and crude, but I'm more like my customers and employees than I am an executive."

Legere, Trump, and the fictional Howard Beale articulate a similar belief—namely, that people will forgive out-of-bounds behavior if it is a result of utter outrage, simply because the public yearns for authentic individuals who speak their mind. In a similar vein, Legere explained to CNBC that he can tell the truth because he's not like other CEOs—because he's not one of the "suits," as he put it. Host Jim Cramer agreed, describing Legere as the "Che Guevara of the cell-phone business."

But here's the catch: Photos of Legere taken as late as 2010 prove just the opposite. He was indeed a suit. He wore tailored suits and dress shoes and kept his hair cut short. In a few images he can even be seen leaning over a chessboard in a stately corporate office—the epitome of a CEO on fancy pills.

But remember: Likeability is a construct. Nowadays it's as if Legere exchanged his fancy pills to run T-Mobile on Che Guevara weed, or so you'd think from reading some of the CEO's tweets.

In July 2015, Legere launched a merciless Twitter attack against Sprint CEO Marcelo Claure over Sprint's consumer pricing plan. Less adept than Legere at waging wars on social media, Claure eventually exploded, tweeting "bullshit" to Legere and throwing his hat into the Twitter ring. Legere replied with a casual "You mad, bro?" before tweeting: "Isn't it cute that Marcelo's been following me on Twitter since joining? Now he's starting to sound like me to get attention—it's working!"

CAPTIVATION Subtrait: Passion

Captivation, of course, is one hell of a broad concept. So enter another concept: I am going to boil down each of my eight likeability traits into a formula of subtraits.

For captivation, my formula involves a combination of the three subtraits of passion, presence, and erudition. When I equate being captivating with being entertaining, that doesn't mean business and political leaders must break out into song and dance as Hollywood stars do.

Entertaining means having the passion that compels the public to listen to what the public figure has to say. Passion, more than any other quality, is the key to what pop culturalists would come to call the "It" Factor. The late Paul Wellstone had the It Factor. Magid chose him as its ideal speaker because his passion made him pop out of the television screen and grab you by the neck as if to scream, "Listen to what I believe! Our lives depend on it!"

Although he has shown a softer side on NBC's *Shark Tank*, Mark Cuban, a venture capitalist, rode to national fame through his passion. Images of Mark Cuban are ingrained among the rest of us: his raving from the stands, choosing to cheer for his team with the fans rather than from a secluded luxury owner's box. Cuban throws his entire voice, body, and heart into these displays. He'll rush onto the court—yes, in the middle of a game—and won't hesitate to lambaste referees with whatever curses or insults come to mind.

Since he bought the Dallas Mavericks in 2000, Cuban has faced $2 million or so in fines for outbursts and remarks to referees, including the time he said he wouldn't hire NBA referee Ed Rush to manage a Dairy Queen, for which Cuban paid a cool $500,000. Dairy Queen invited Cuban to work at one of their restaurants for a day, and he said yes. He spent two hours at a Dairy Queen franchise making cones and Blizzards for the hundreds of patrons and oglers who came to see him.

Mark Cuban is willing to pay the price for his passion and enjoys doing so. Talk about the joy of performance. Talk about a man who never takes "fancy pills" to relate to the rest of us. Mark Cuban proves that fancy pills kill passion. Every time I teach advocacy skills in politics or the law, I jokingly tell my students to hand over their fancy pills to the DEA. But Mark Cuban wouldn't have to.

In 2015 he confronted the U.S. Securities and Exchange Commission as directly as he's been known to attack officials on the basketball court. The good folks at the SEC were "idiots," Cuban proclaimed, for overregulating financial markets.

Even when you disagree with his opinions, Mark Cuban engages in passionate normalspeak that makes it easy to like him. Beyond that, he is adept at conveying a sense of genuine, heartfelt passion through skillful storytelling that reaches people on a personal level.

Speaking at an innovation conference in 2015, Cuban said: "I've got a 5-year-old son. By the time he's 25, the idea of going to a drugstore and buying over-the-counter medication will seem barbaric. He's going to say, 'Dad, what do you mean? You bought this medicine and on this over-the-counter medicine there was a warning that said you might be the one unlucky schmuck that dies from this. And you actually bought it and paid for it?'"

Mark Cuban's passion has been evident since the beginning of his career, when he showed an astounding amount of initiative without any encouragement at all. After he joined Mellon Bank for his first job out of college, Cuban sent pages and pages of notes, all brimming with ideas, to the CEO. Cuban organized happy hours for senior executives to meet and mentor younger employees, himself included. He quoted his boss's reaction—"Who the fuck do you think you are?"—in an article he wrote for *Forbes*. When he moved to Dallas, Cuban got fired from his new job for showing too much passion. Bosses simply didn't know what to do with him.

Passion, however, is not simply being energetic. Passion is about being energetic in presenting your convictions.

If you're looking for passion in a cable news pundit, look no further than Republican strategist Ana Navarro. She was one of the first Republican pundits on television to denounce Donald Trump—and she did it starting with the Republican primaries.

In one spirited exchange with former Trump campaign adviser Michael Caputo on CNN just prior to the 2016 general election, for example, Caputo called Navarro "outrageous" for suggesting that Trump was a racist. Navarro's response? In her passionate, authentic, fast-talking manner that she spent not one minute tamping down for television, she said: "Well, let me do it again, and let me do it in two languages: Es un racista. He is a flat-out racist and it's what he's played on for 16 months. He is a bigot. He is a racist. He is a misogynist. He has said horrible things about women. He has said horrible things about immigrants, about Hispanics . . . and for you to shake your head and say that I'm the outrageous one is what outrages me."

All Caputo could do was roll his eyes in silence.

But even in Navarro's case, passion doesn't mean emotions gone wild and a reckless abandonment of thought. Passion is still focused. Consider one of her tweets from early 2019, when controversy surrounded newly elected Democratic congresswoman Rashida Tlaib for saying, "We're going to impeach the motherfucker," in reference to President Trump. Navarro writes: "I fully understand urge to cuss in public to describe Trump. But there are circumstances—like, say, being in Congress or being employed by a major news network, that make it inappropriate. May I suggest 'President Loco' or 'racist, misogynist, 72-year-old man-baby' instead?"

CAPTIVATION Subtrait: Presence

My definition of "presence" is more egalitarian than handsomeness or beauty. Presence is when a public figure radiates energy that creates a glow. Good looks don't hurt, but they aren't necessary, and don't need to be conventional, to have presence.

Presence, like captivation in general, is something the public must perceive immediately for a public figure to strike us as relevant. In his classic text *How to Win Friends and Influence People*, Dale Carnegie rattled off an anecdote about how Charles Schwab once told him his smile had been "worth a million dollars," under the section entitled "A Simple Way to Make a Good First Impression."

Indeed, a central argument of Carnegie's is that the best way to become likeable is to pursue people: Be interested in them, talk about their interests, ask questions, make them feel important, listen, and, yes, smile. In other words, take initiative to show people you care and respect them, and they will return the favor. In social psychology, the concept is known as reciprocity. In our paradigm, it's the key to captivation and its subtraits of passion and presence.

Now back to physical attractiveness. Who could deny that Sofia Vergara's beauty plays a role in how we feel about her the moment we see her? That doesn't mean she isn't smart, talented, funny, or hard-working. It means that her presence is felt when she walks into a room or enters the scene of a sitcom. Same for *People*'s 2018 Sexiest Man Alive, Idris Elba. He's tall, dapper, and downright sexy. No wonder the Internet wants the English actor to be the next James Bond.

The unfair reality is that physical attractiveness will tip the scales in our perception of another's presence. I know this from my own shocking experience.

The organization I founded, Garden State Equality, annually held a fund-raising gala attended by as many as 1,000 people, including stars from stage, screen, politics, and the business world who'd enter on a red carpet.

Producing "Legends," the shorthand by which New Jerseyans would call the event, required me to make several advance visits to each year's venue. In June 2011 we held Legends at the Jersey City Hyatt, facing the Manhattan skyline. That May, I entered an elevator at the Hyatt and saw the most beautiful woman I'd ever seen in my life.

Diminutive but statuesque, she was wearing white jeans and a fitted white shirt. Her jaw was strong, her hair long and glossy, but her bone structure was one of perfection. She was a world-class beauty of a certain age. My age, more or less.

I make no secret of my absolute, unambivalent, thoroughbred gayness. On a Kinsey Scale of 0 to 6—with 0 being totally straight and 6 being totally gay—I score a perfect 1600. But I couldn't stop looking at this woman. She was dazzling.

When she left the elevator, the rest of us followed her into the lobby. Words tumbled uncontrollably from my lips as I stammered and blushed.

"I just love you!" I exclaimed. My God. I hadn't been so excited since I was an adolescent taking advantage of my body's coming of age as I looked at photos of David Cassidy of *The Partridge Family* in *Tiger Beat* magazine.

Back at the Hyatt lobby, the object of my affection smiled broadly. She was utterly gracious. The others asked if they could take pictures of her. They'd also never met her before but had the same rush from her presence, the same desire to be close. And she couldn't stop obliging with kindness each time. Talk about the joy of performance.

This famous woman—a politician—captivated all of us through her physical presence. When she left us, I asked the other gawkers about their politics. Like me, they were all Democrats. Like me, they said they wouldn't vote for her in a million years. And yet we were all captivated.

After I said goodbye, I called one of my BFFs and told him I just saw the most beautiful woman I'd ever seen. I gave him three guesses, upon which he rattled off my trinity of gay icons: Barbra Streisand, Bette Midler, and Liza Minnelli.

No longer could I contain my fan-boy excitement. "I just met . . . Sarah Palin!"

"Are you having a migraine?" he asked.

But it was true. I had run into Sarah Palin, making a stop in Jersey City on her "One Nation" bus tour of whatever dreck she was advocating that I opposed. Yet there I was, a gay man and a Democrat, entranced by her beauty, just as the other Democrats in the elevator were. Don't tell me beauty doesn't matter.

Physical attractiveness doesn't have to be conventional so long as it has presence. The stunning Melissa McCarthy is as full-figured as Sarah Palin was surprisingly diminutive. But McCarthy's presence is equal to, and perhaps even surpasses, any runway model's. Her ability to dart her eyes, contort her face, wave her hands in the air, throw her body around—all the hallmarks of physical comedy—is utterly captivating.

Presence can also come through the voice. Scarlett Johansson is a Hollywood sex symbol and one of the industry's top moneymakers, both in terms of personal income and box office revenue. The *New Yorker* once noted that Johansson is, "evidently, and profitably, aware of her sultriness, and of how much, down to the last inch, it contributes to the contours of her reputation."

Yet in 2013's critically acclaimed film *Her*, we don't even see Johansson. In the science-fiction drama about a man who falls in love with his artificially intelligent operating system named "Samantha," Johansson provides the computer's voice—and that's it. *Rolling Stone* called Johansson's performance a "vocal tour de force" that was "award-worthy." Samantha was originally voiced by actor Samantha

Morton, but she was replaced by Johansson in postproduction. Writer and director Spike Jonze didn't think the character was coming across as captivating enough.

Johansson delivered. "Her voice—breathy, occasionally cracking—warms the entire film," said a review in the *Atlantic*.

That could also describe the voice, speaking or singing, of Lady Gaga in the 2018 remake of *A Star is Born*. But that's not the only way we've known her. Remember when, about a decade ago, she generated a ton of press for her outlandish fashion choices? Her plastic bubble outfit? Her cloak made entirely out of Kermit the Frog puppets? Then there's the unforgettable meat dress—with matching shoes, hat, and purse—that Gaga wore to the 2010 MTV Video Music Awards. *Time* called it one of the year's top fashion statements.

Fashion can be presence, too, because it communicates to everyone around you *something* about yourself. It either grabs someone's attention or it doesn't. Obviously, what someone wears is not the totality of a person's identity, but first impressions do linger—sometimes longer than we'd like.

CAPTIVATION Subtrait: Erudition

When I reentered the dating world in my fifties, I tried online dating and saw others use a term I hadn't known: "sapiosexual." It refers to anyone who finds intelligence to be the most sexually attractive characteristic of another person.

Whenever Warren Buffett appears on CNBC, his most frequent cable home, people from all walks of life, including the anchors, are in a trance. Money is an aphrodisiac, to be sure, but Buffett is also an oracle—the Oracle of Omaha, as he's known, for his guru-like status within the investing community. Buffett has written op-eds that include lines such as "Be fearful when others are greedy, and be greedy when others are fearful," and, in a letter to his top managers, "We can afford to lose money—even a lot of money. But we can't afford to lose reputation—even a shred of reputation."

Lest these homilies seem simplistic, they're not. Clichés don't start out as clichés. They start out as originality so compelling, everyone repeats them to make them clichés. Warren Buffett created many of America's present-day maxims of business savvy, and therein lay his erudition.

Buffett is a self-declared bookworm. He read up to 1,000 pages per day, he says, when he began his career in investing. "I insist on a lot of time being spent, almost every day, to just sit and think," Buffett once said. "That is very uncommon in American business. I read and think. So I do more reading and thinking and make less impulse decisions than most people in business."

He still lives in the same Omaha house he bought in 1958 for $31,500. He says he's sent only one email in his life. *Ever.* During a 2013 CNN interview with Piers Morgan, Buffett revealed that he still uses an ancient Nokia flip phone. "This is the one Alexander Graham Bell gave me," Buffett joked. "I don't throw anything away until I've had it twenty or twenty-five years."

It's this prudent judgment and calm composure that's made Buffett rich—and likeable. It's also helped him craft clever quotes of wisdom that apply to both business and life, such as this one: "No matter how great the talent or efforts, some things just take time. You can't produce a baby in one month by getting nine women pregnant."

Award-winning actress Helen Mirren also repackages complicated topics into understandable summaries. In 2015, during an appearance on NBC's *Today* show, for example, Mirren explained to host Matt Lauer that she doesn't like the word "sexy" because she thinks it's overused and restrictive.

"It limits human qualities into this very narrow, rather mundane and banal little place," she said, "and human beings are so much more complex and interesting and deep and everything than that." Earlier, when Lauer asked Mirren if she's conscious of being seen as a sex symbol, she responded, "No, of course not. You can't be conscious about that. That would be terrible. You know, we all have two people in us: we have the person that other people see us to be and the person that we are."

That's arousing for us sapiosexuals.

Equally erudite is Amal Clooney. An acclaimed international human rights lawyer and activist, she is among the smartest and most effective advocates in the world. She's worked to free a Canadian journalist detained in Egypt, along with two reporters jailed in Myanmar. She's defended a former president of the Maldives who was sentenced to thirteen years behind bars following what Clooney called a "politically motivated show trial." It's impossible to deny her intellect.

From the time she married an actor named George in 2014, members of the media have tried to force her into the role of a starlet perpetually walking down the red carpet, spouting vapid responses to banal questions. She's appeared on the cover of *Vogue*, but in the accompanying interview she also said this: "I hate the idea that you somehow, as a human being, have to be put in a box. There's no reason why lawyers can't be fun—or actresses can't be serious."

In 2015, while Clooney was representing Armenia in a genocide denial case at the European Court of Human Rights in France, a reporter raised the familiar question asked of most celebrities attending award ceremonies: Who was Clooney wearing? Was it Versace? Chanel? Dior?

"I'm wearing Ede & Ravenscroft," Clooney retorted, referring to the maker of her rather plain black robe that lawyers wear in international court.

Captivation isn't always smart, but smart is always captivating.

Of course, there are other ways to demonstrate one's erudition. Over the past decade or so, Compton-born rapper Kendrick Lamar has established himself as one of hip-hop's biggest stars for his insight and social commentary on topics such as police brutality and gun violence. In 2017 the *Economist* wrote that Lamar's "intellectual heft delights university-educated music critics," while his "fondness for quoting scripture . . . would surely put the current Republican president to shame." He's won thirteen Grammy Awards and six *Billboard* Music Awards, and sold millions of albums along the way.

In 2018, at the age of thirty, Lamar achieved the unprecedented: His fourth studio album, *Damn*, won the Pulitzer Prize for Music, making him the first artist in the prize category's seventy-five years who didn't win for jazz or classical music. The Pulitzer Prize board described *Damn* as a "virtuosic song collection unified by its vernacular authenticity and rhythmic dynamism that offers affecting vignettes capturing the complexity of modern African-American life."

HOPE: Optimism + Resilience + Goal-Oriented Thinking

Captivation without hope does nothing to contribute to a public figure's likeability. Naked captivation creates the star we love to hate. Hope is the additive necessary to turn captivation into the foundation of likeability. Captivation plus hope produces chemical reaction. We might as well not take calcium supplements without vitamin D.

Hope is the promise of a better tomorrow.

As always, likeability—and its second trait called hope—center on a story. Michael J. Fox has waged a fierce yet graceful battle with Parkinson's. In 1998, seven years after being diagnosed, Fox made his condition public in a *People* cover story. He projected hope and helping others, but as the embodiment of dignified hope without the artifice of over-sentimentality. His likeability, as much as that of any other figure in public life, is rooted in reality.

"It's not that I had a deep, dark secret," said Fox of his until-then-private struggle. "It was just my thing to deal with. But this box I had put everything into kind of expanded to a point where it's difficult to lug around. What's inside the box isn't inhibiting me. It's the box itself. I think I can help people by talking. I want to help myself and my family."

Fox also embodies humor as a tool of both captivation and hope. If you're a public figure who's funny, no doubt you have a head start on both traits. After Fox had brain surgery, his most noticeable symptom of Parkinson's, the shaking of his left arm, decreased dramatically. Before the surgery, Fox told *People*, "I could mix a margarita in five seconds."

No matter the opportunity for tears that *People* gave Fox and his wife, Tracy Pollan, neither gave in. "I'm not crying 'What a tragedy,'" he said, "because it's not. It's a reality, a fact." Although emotion is the fulcrum of passion, Fox knows his ability to generate hope for others with Parkinson's rests on his ability to symbolize an otherwise normal, functioning life.

"I've realized I'm vulnerable," Fox told *People*, and "that no matter how many awards I'm given or how big my bank account is, I can be messed with like that. The end of the story is you die. We all die. So, accepting that, the issue becomes one of quality of life."

In 2006, eight years after the *People* profile, Fox starred in a television ad for Claire McCaskill, the Democratic nominee for U.S. Senate in Missouri. He looked straight into the camera to endorse McCaskill for her support of stem cell research—and she wound up winning in a Republican state. Fox was pointedly critical of incumbent senator Jim Talent for opposing further stem cell research and wanting to "criminalize the science that gives us a chance for hope," as Fox put it.

The camera angle caught the whole upper body of Fox as it, along with his head, shook back and forth rapidly and dramatically.

Conservative Rush Limbaugh accused Fox of exaggerating his symptoms for emotional effect. Limbaugh shook his body and flailed his arms in an attempt to mimic Fox. "This is really shameless of Michael J. Fox," Limbaugh explained on his radio show. "Either he didn't take his medication or he's acting."

Fox responded during an interview with Katie Couric on CBS. She asked him whether he saw the opportunity to educate Limbaugh. "I could give a damn about Rush Limbaugh's pity," Fox said. "I'm not a victim."

Like Michael J. Fox, Robert Downey Jr. makes us feel hope in a straightforward way we can almost touch, several steps down from the Hollywood pedestal. Downey's story, unlike Fox's, inspires hope notwithstanding its roots in Downey's drug addiction. To be sure, Downey's resilience may ignite compassion in your heart depending on the kind of person you are or what you've been through in life.

Downey's story is that of a second chance, or even of a third and fourth, to which many of us can relate in one way or another. Plenty of us fall down in life—though thankfully not in such a public way—and see the opportunity soon enough to get back up again and keep going. We all love a comeback story and embrace it in our public figures.

Few public figures have risen from the depths of life as Downey has, repeatedly. And it's impossible to think of anyone else who has done so with such spectacularly brilliant humor, perhaps unrivaled in public life, and no less than at his own expense. Robert Downey Jr.'s mind is the perfect-storm combination of erudition and humor.

Robert Downey Jr. is so likeable, he's the only recovering drug addict on earth who could inspire an article titled "21 Reasons Robert Downey Jr. Is the Most Perfect Man in the Universe." That's what BuzzFeed called him in 2013.

No wonder. He is captivating and inspires hope.

Together, three subtraits generate hope: optimism, resilience, and goal-oriented thinking.

HOPE Subtrait: Optimism

Optimism is as easy as any other human quality to understand. It's our confidence that the future will be better than the present—and better than the past, to be sure.

That's why so many political leaders and their campaigns have slogans or sound bites based in optimism. In 1992, Bill Clinton ran for president as "the Man from Hope." In 2008, Barack Obama ran to bring us "Change We Can Believe In." In 2016, Bernie Sanders promised "A Future to Believe In."

When we're not looking to our leaders to provide us a better tomorrow, we're often looking to our potential spouses. Indeed, few institutions evoke more optimism than marriage. No wonder 29.2 million Americans watched Meghan Markle marry Prince Harry on Saturday, May 19, 2018, when it was 7:00 a.m. on the East Coast of the United States and 4:00 a.m. on the West Coast.

To see a black woman and her mother, also African-American, celebrated by the pomp and circumstance previously reserved for British white people was unforgettable. As the *Guardian* put it, "For all the talk about whether Markle is *really* black, for all the critique of her being 'white-passing' or ambivalent about her black heritage, there are certainly black women in America who feel one of their own has entered British royalty."

The wedding itself included a black preacher, a black choir, a black cellist, and a royal guest list of unprecedented diversity. The royal family now looks more like a modern family, and the world is better off.

Although he sometimes comes across as a bit off-kilter and arrogant, and makes unforced errors on Twitter that attract the attention of the SEC, there's something undeniably optimistic about Elon Musk. While we have ample reasons to question whether technology is making us a soulless society, Musk is unafraid. Save our planet with electric cars! Dig tunnels to cut down on that terrible commute! Travel to a hotel on Mars in a rocket ship! Time and time again Musk has railed against the notion that the future is set. His life's work, it seems, is to convince humanity that we choose our own fate.

Musk himself has suggested that you *have to* be optimistic about the future. "There's no point in being pessimistic," he once said. "I'd rather be optimistic and wrong than pessimistic and right."

HOPE Subtrait: Resilience

We all want a happy ending, both in our own lives and in the entertainment we embrace. Hollywood acts accordingly. *Fatal Attraction* gathered its entire cast and crew nine months after filming had ended—but before the movie was released—to film a different ending. It would be a happier ending to make the movie more likeable.

I asked Richard Fischoff, one of the producers of *Fatal Attraction*, what happened. Richard was also one of the producers of *Kramer vs. Kramer* and *Steel Magnolias*.

"We showed *Fatal Attraction* with its original ending to test audiences," Richard said. "Glenn Close's character, who had an affair with Michael Douglas while he was married to Anne Archer, committed suicide. She was in her apartment lying on the bathroom floor in a pool of blood with a knife right next to her. The police come to Michael Douglas and Anne Archer's house, and they tell him Glenn Close has been found dead. Michael asks, 'Did she kill herself?' And the police officer said, 'In our experience women do not kill themselves by slitting their own throats with a butcher knife."

As Richard was telling me the story, I said, "But Glenn Close's character was crazy. Of course, she could have done that."

"Yes, but the police don't know that. So they arrest Michael and take him away and he tells Anne Archer to call his lawyer. Anne goes running upstairs to find the phone book to call the lawyer and discovers in the drawer a cassette tape that Glenn Close had made, in which Glenn tells Michael that if he abandons her, she is going to kill herself. And then we cut to Anne Archer, who has an enigmatic, opaque look on her face. Is she going to go to the police with this tape or not? Or is she going to let Michael Douglas fry for having had the affair with Glenn Close in the first place?"

"That would have been such an unsatisfying ending," I said.

"Exactly," Richard agreed. "The audience hoped Anne Archer would tell Glenn Close, 'If you come near me or my family again, I'll kill you,' and for Anne to kill Glenn if she did. And that's what we wound up doing. When Glenn was in the couple's bathroom, Anne shot her dead. It took three weeks to film the new ending but audiences loved it."

Anne Archer's character, now revised, had become resilient.

In 2010 three scholars at Arizona State University published a compendium of academic papers as the *Handbook of Adult Resilience*. In their introduction, the three erect a model of resilience, composed of two equally important parts: recovery, as in a response to stressful events and the ability to regain equilibrium; and sustainability, as in the ability to continually recover, and perhaps even grow, in response to the stressful experience. In other words, resilience is the ability to adapt to adversity.

Some public figures dispense hope from their positions of authority, based in formal training or their universal respect, that make us believe in a chance for a better life. Others inspire hope with their personal stories. They create hope living by example, as people who have overcome the circumstances they inherited. That's how Oprah Winfrey became America's leading symbol of hope in the modern television era.

Malala Yousafzai is the epitome of resilience. In 2012, while riding a bus home from school at the age of fifteen, she was shot in the head by a member of the Taliban for promoting the idea that women deserved the right to an education. After making a miraculous recovery, Yousafzai went on to graduate from high school. And write an international best-selling book. And found a nonprofit organization. And win a Nobel Peace Prize. She's currently pursuing her education at Oxford, studying philosophy, politics, and economics. Now that's a rebound.

In March 2018, while appearing as a guest on Netflix's *My Next Guest Needs No Introduction with David Letterman*, Yousafzai said of her attackers, "I forgive them because that's the best revenge I can have."

Resilience does not always need to be a matter of life and death. In 2003, Ohio native LeBron James became the hope of his entire state when the Cleveland Cavaliers drafted him straight out of high school. The city of Cleveland was undergoing a sports drought. None of its major-league teams—baseball, football, or basketball—had captured a championship since 1964, and James was supposed to change that.

Soon enough, the team started winning. In 2007, James even led the Cavaliers to their first NBA Finals appearance, although they ended up losing to the San Antonio Spurs. Still, James persisted. "I got a goal, and it's a huge goal, and that's to bring an NBA championship here to Cleveland," he said during an interview on NBA TV. "And I won't stop until I get it."

After a few more seasons of being great, but not quite great enough to secure the trophy, James announced during an infamous ESPN special dubbed *The Decision* that he was leaving. "This fall I'm going to take my talents to South Beach and join the Miami Heat," James said, to the heartbreak of people across Ohio.

Hope vanished. His decision to pack his bags and join fellow all-stars Dwyane Wade and Chris Bosh in Miami felt like betrayal to many of his fans. Some even burned his jersey. In a letter posted on the team's website, Cleveland Cavaliers owner Dan Gilbert referred to James as "our former hero."

After four seasons in Miami, where James appeared in the NBA Finals each year and won twice, he announced that he was returning to Cleveland. "In Northeast Ohio, nothing is given," he wrote in an article published by *Sports Illustrated*. "Everything is earned. You work for what you have. I'm ready to accept the challenge. I'm coming home."

Then, in the 2016 NBA Finals, after overcoming a 3–1 series deficit against defending champions the Golden State Warriors, the Cleveland Cavaliers won. The drought was over. James had delivered. "Cleveland, this one's for you!" yelled a teary-eyed James after the final buzzer sounded. James, now a member of the Los Angeles Lakers, demonstrated what it means to persevere, and his popularity, once damaged, has soared because of it.

Jane Fonda also embodies resilience. Who else could be so successful for so long in so many fields, moving from award-winning actor to top-selling aerobics instructor to political activist and back again? To not only survive but thrive from decade to decade in the world of show business is uncanny.

It hasn't all been without controversies, though. Not even close. When in Vietnam in 1972, for example, a photo of Fonda surfaced showing her smiling and laughing with enemy troops. She publicly apologized many times, and the public has embraced her. She persevered and has triumphed time and time again.

HOPE Subtrait: Goal-Oriented Thinking

The late Charles Richard "Rick" Snyder, who died in 2006, was a scholar at the University of Kansas and editor of the *Journal of Social and Clinical Psychology*, a publication most closely associated with the theory of hope. Snyder was a pioneer in positive psychology, a branch of psychology that aims to enhance people's experiences of love, work, play, and life by focusing on humanity's strengths over its weaknesses.

For Snyder, hope requires goal-oriented thinking—our need to set goals and our belief we can achieve them, thereby having the motivation to achieve them. Hope, then, is more than just a happy feeling. Hope helps us navigate life through its hardships and uncertainties. Citing numerous studies, Snyder posits that hope leads to higher academic and athletic success, not to mention better psychological and physical health.

Among history's most goal-oriented public figures was President John F. Kennedy. On May 25, 1961, he stood before a joint session of Congress and announced, "This nation should commit itself to achieving the goal, before this decade is out, of landing a man on the Moon and returning him safely to Earth."

As Morten T. Hansen wrote in the *Harvard Business Review* in

2011, Kennedy's "Man on the Moon" goal has become "one of the most compelling, unifying goals ever articulated by a leader." Hansen cites the argument between Kennedy and then NASA chief James E. Webb that was transcribed and released years later.

Webb insisted that NASA's goal for the country should be "preeminence in space," broadly speaking.

But Kennedy stood firm. "Everything that we do ought to really be tied into getting onto the Moon ahead of the Russians," he told Webb. "If you're trying to prove preeminence, this is the way to prove preeminence."

Kennedy understood the power of a clearly defined goal. On July 20, 1969—ironically during the presidency of Richard Nixon, whom Kennedy defeated in 1960—the United States landed men on the moon shortly before the decade ended. To this day the U.S. is the only country ever to have landed on the moon with people versus with merely robotic spacecraft.

The most inspiring leaders set goals and make the progress toward reaching them transparent. Objectives give the mission focus and purpose, and it's much easier to cheer people on when you know where they're trying to go. Without goals, we're treading water out at sea, just existing—barely.

Plenty of Silicon Valley companies pride themselves on working to make the world a better place. That's great and all, but it's also a bit vague at best and downright misleading at worst. Without clear, goal-oriented thinking, things can go horribly wrong for everyone.

Recently, Twitter CEO Jack Dorsey has been hearing it from all sides of the political spectrum. Some accuse him and his platform of being too lax, which allows bullying, hate speech, and Russian election interference to flourish. Others, meanwhile, accuse him and his team of being too involved on the site, leading to bias, censorship, and the appearance of a rigged system. Still others assume Dorsey is doing whatever it takes to attract more users, generate more ad revenue, and boost share prices—healthy functioning democracy be damned.

No one, in other words, seems particularly fond of Dorsey because no one seems to know where he wants to take his social network. Does he have a plan? As a *HuffPost* headline bluntly put it in early 2019, "Jack Dorsey Has No Clue What He Wants."

In a 2018 interview with CNN, Dorsey admitted that his sinking favorability was, in part, due to a lack of clear goals. "I haven't done enough of articulating my own personal objectives with this service and my own personal objectives in the world," he said.

Hence all the confusion and doubt about Twitter ultimately making the world a better place.

If anyone has used communication to make the world a better place, it's *Black Panther* director Ryan Coogler. He made the movie with a clear goal: empowerment of the African-American community.

Coogler has told the story of when he started reading comic books as a kid. He'd devour all the regulars—X-Men, Spider-Man, Batman—but started to wonder if there were any superheroes that looked like him. One day an employee at Coogler's local comic book shop in Oakland introduced him to Black Panther. That moment impacted his life in a way he never could have anticipated.

Black Panther, with its predominantly African-American cast, became one of the biggest films of 2018. In an interview with *Time* that short-listed Coogler for its 2018 Person of the Year, the director explained his thinking behind the film by comparing the film industry to the National Basketball Association: "At some point, someone thought it's risky to put a black person on the court, that people wouldn't buy tickets. Now owners are like, 'I just want to win games, and I want the best player.' What I hope, for this industry, is we're transitioning from it even being a question that movies made by people of color or minorities are a risk."

Miley Cyrus: When Hope Rescues
Too Much Captivation

Miley Cyrus is a captivation machine who has reinvented herself with every spin cycle of her life.

If you're a parent who had daughters in elementary school thirteen years ago, you met Cyrus, no doubt, as her alter ego Hannah Montana in the Disney Channel series and feature film. Cyrus played the wholesome, infectiously cheery Miley Stewart, who led a whole other life she was keeping from her schoolmates. Miley Stewart was a famous pop star—famous on the show before the real Miley found fame—named Hannah Montana. The fiction became a take on reality when Miley Cyrus did live concert tours as Hannah Montana.

Cyrus based her persona on who she was in real life. The real Miley wore a purity ring to declare to the world she would not have sex before marriage. In the video for "The Climb," her biggest single from *Hannah Montana: The Movie*, she sang amidst mountains that seemed to reach the clouds, in a not-so-subtle reference to her faith. The religiosity was there for parents who wished to see it. Miley in the mountains shared the DNA of Julie Andrews singing "The Sound of Music" in the Alps. The wholesomeness was inescapable.

That was not by accident. Helping Cyrus craft her persona was her management team, the Morey Management Group, recommended by family friend Dolly Parton. "Dolly said the Moreys are people you can trust around your daughter," Miley's mother, Tish, told the press, "and she said they have good morals, which is not always the case in this business." Miley Cyrus as Miley Stewart as Hannah Montana provided parents triple insurance in three packages of artificial sweetener. But being a child star by no means guarantees career longevity.

Hello Miley Cyrus, sex siren. For some parents of her fan base, it must have seemed as if Miley dissolved her sugary image as fast as Lot's wife turned into salt in the Bible. In March 2013, eight months before she turned twenty-one, Cyrus hired Larry Rudolph, the manager who had masterminded Britney Spears's transition from child star to vixen.

The New Miley Cyrus made her world premiere a few months later in the video for "We Can't Stop." She writhed in bed with her fingers in her mouth or nearly between her legs and revved up one guy in the video so much, smoke came out of his zipper.

In the official music video for her single "Wrecking Ball," close-up shots of Cyrus show her crying out of emotional agony. Later, she's seen licking a sledgehammer and sitting naked on a wrecking ball. For those not following along, this was an entirely new form of captivation for the young singer.

From there, Miley walked farther into a Plato's Retreat from her former image. On the MTV Music Awards in August 2013, she metaphorically stepped out of a teddy bear costume into a nude-colored two-piece latex outfit and grabbed singer Robin Thicke's crotch. She twerked up against him and stuck her butt *right there*. As Rudolph described the scene to *Us Weekly*: "It could not have gone better."

The Old Miley was so dead, my grandmother of blessed memory might have sat an honorary shiva. Perhaps Miley herself would have come by to give her condolences. As she said when she hosted *Saturday Night Live* in October 2013: "I'm not going to do Hannah Montana, but I can give you an update on what she's been up to—she's been murdered."

As transparent as Miley was about her evolving constructs, other stars have been equally transparent. Madonna has reinvented herself with every album. Olivia Newton-John went from G-rated country crooner, as some of you remember, to sexy Sandy in the movie *Grease*. Then Olivia recorded *Physical*—quaint now, but another sensual leap for her original fan base. Lady Gaga has also shifted personas throughout her career.

The public, for sure, places more pressure on women public figures to reinvent themselves than it does on men. When that's not the case, it's often because our male icons, such as Rob Lowe and Robert Downey Jr., have messed up and we root for them to clean up—the opposite of the pressure many women face to become, well, dirtier.

Miley Cyrus has never hesitated to explain the evolution in how she executes captivation. In a December 2013 interview with the *New York Times*, she described the year she had just had. "I went from people just thinking I was, like, a baby to people thinking I'm this, like, sex freak that really just pops molly and does lines all day," she said. "It's like, 'Has anyone ever heard of rock 'n' roll?' . . . Well, *that's* a character. I don't really dress as a teddy bear and, like, twerk on Robin Thicke, you know?"

Miley's metamorphosis was bordering on a captivation train wreck. Her polar-opposite constructs couldn't both be rooted in reality. We, the public, had every right to wonder whether we were watching the New Nixon of pop music. On the one hand, few adolescents, even the most squeaky-clean among them, are as pure as Miley Cyrus presented herself in her Hannah Montana years. On the other hand, few teenagers rebel with such premeditated camp. How could anyone not have wondered: Will the real Miley Cyrus please stand up?

But the question would have been unfair. What young person doesn't go through significant changes from adolescence to the teenage years? Certainly Cyrus did, too. That makes her public extremes, but not the fact of her change, the construct. In 2013, Cyrus told *Billboard* she wished she could erase Hannah Montana's music. Haven't we all known teenagers who yearned to erase the image of their earlier years?

In recent years Miley Cyrus has evolved again. To her credit, she made another change rooted in reality. Now an adult in her late twenties, she exudes the newfound maturity and groundedness that are the hallmarks of her age. She has ditched the performative extremes that would have become outdated teen-star constructs had she kept them. These days she captivates us through songs of greater emotional complexity and a personality stripped of artifice but just as compelling, distinguished by both its force and warmth. Miley, indeed, is a master of the captivation construct: when to change it, how far to go, and how far not to go—all based on who she is at that point in her life.

In her maturity, she's added hope to captivation. By becoming a coach on NBC's *The Voice*, she smartly gave herself a showcase to give encouragement to others. She also founded the Happy Hippie Foundation, a charity to rescue and empower homeless LGBTQ youth and other young people from at-risk communities. By 2016, in just its first two years, Happy Hippie and another charity supported by Miley, My Friend's Place, had donated 40,000 meals, 20,000 snacks, and 40,000 pairs of underwear and socks to homeless children.

Today, Miley Cyrus is among the most prominent philanthropists and activists in public life. Infusing captivation with hope, she has taken on the gravitas of an adult. She has worked the constructs to position herself for a long career.

Summary: Captivation and Hope

Without captivating an audience and communicating enough hope to inspire people so they stay engaged, public figures will find their likeability dead on arrival. Even if they excel in the six subsequent traits, it won't matter. No one will stick around long enough to see.

How can the rest of us apply the lessons of captivation and hope to our own likeability? To be captivating, think about what makes you the most passionate. If it's your family or a favorite cause, set that level of passion as a goal for as many other daily interactions as you can.

To come across as more present, focus like a laser beam on whomever you meet and put your smartphone aside. Don't be that jerk who acts as if he always has somewhere better to be or someone more important to talk to. To share your erudition, think about which areas of expertise allow you to enrich the lives of others, free of pomposity, with knowledge they didn't have.

To present yourself as hopeful, don't be afraid to be the only optimistic voice in the room so long as you can back it up with evidence for business settings. Remind other people of their own resilience, or your organization's resilience, during tougher times. And, based on your goal-oriented thinking, offer a road map for recovery that compels others to join your bandwagon of hope.

CHAPTER 6

The Foundation Traits: Authenticity and Relatability

A ny public figure who has achieved proficiency in the first two likeability traits, captivation and hope, completed a mighty task. In 2018 the public figure had to grab our attention as each of us was bombarded by a record-breaking 495 scripted original shows on broadcast, cable, and various streaming services, 871 films released in the U.S. and Canada, and an estimated 2.6 billion social media users around the world. Amidst all that competition for our time, the public figure also gave us hope.

Once a public figure passes through captivation and hope, it's natural for us to seek confirmation of that good impression. We ask: Is this public figure for real? And is he or she someone to whom I can relate?

Authenticity and relatability are the foundation of any lasting relationship. Likeability can't survive without them.

AUTHENTICITY: True to Origins + Coolness and Self-possession + Self-disclosure

By now you know the likeability traits of public figures are constructs rooted in the appearance of likeability that public figures and their advisers shape for public consumption.

But if all eight traits in my likeability model are constructs, and the eight traits include authenticity, don't we have a problem? How could I call authenticity a construct? "Authenticity" conjures up everything we consider real, and "construct" does not.

Authenticity is the most complex of our likeability traits. To understand it better, we must differentiate between authenticity in real life—the lack of phoniness we respect in others—versus the version of authenticity that public figures show us.

No public figure has ever, or will ever, present him- or herself to the public with the kind of authenticity that reflects how nearly 330 million Americans understand the concept—except, of course, children at the early stages of development. When those children are old enough to use a dictionary, any dictionary they choose will reinforce society's understanding of the word: Authenticity is about being genuine. Authenticity is the opposite of phoniness. It follows, therefore, that even the smallest amount of phoniness can turn authenticity into inauthenticity.

Let's be clear: When public figures try to convince us of their authenticity, they and their advisers incorporate more than the smallest amount of phoniness.

For starters, all public figures withhold information about their personal lives and about their families. If the rest of us were public figures, we, too, would also withhold such information from the public. Our choice would be the moral one so long as it doesn't infringe on the public's right to information about public matters. The zone of privacy should never become zero for any human being, whether a public figure or any of the rest of us.

It raises the question: When public figures withhold personal information from us, do they deserve to be called phony? Most of us would consider that to be too harsh an assessment. But no matter how we look at it, a decision to withhold information from the public—even when it is not vital to the public interest—permanently changes the extent of a public figure's authenticity nonetheless.

As we saw in our food chain of likeability, another construct of authenticity arises through the publicity decisions that public figures and their teams make every day to produce positive spin. Notwithstanding how all those publicity decisions shape or reshape the truth, another construct of authenticity arises that is more pervasive.

It is structurally impossible for public figures to be authentic in public life as we understand authenticity to be in real life. Even when public figures want to show us the real versions of themselves, they face immovable obstacles.

Consider this: When a public figure communicates with the rest of us, it's nothing like the real-life conversations we have with our families and friends. Public figures usually read copy written by staff members. That's a sacrifice of authenticity no matter how talented the writer is at capturing the boss's voice. In real life, most of us wouldn't think of writing scripts, or asking others to write scripts, for our everyday conversations.

Remember when I told you about the short, catchy sound bites in which our most compelling public figures speak every time you see them? Sound bites are the indispensable tool for captivating an audience and accommodating the time constraints of interviews. Now contrast that with real life. Who among us speaks to family, friends, and colleagues in one-liners and bumper sticker slogans?

And don't all of us in real life go through bad moods and rough times that make us unlikeable more often than we care to admit? Public figures lose that right every time they speak to the media or to the public directly. While we're at it, haven't we all struggled for the right words to say in a stressful or delicate situation? We can get away with it among friends. But when public figures struggle in interviews, it seems like stonewalling.

When some public figures dare to be real in public, free of handlers and our mass expectations, they discover what it's like to be burned. In July 2015, Ariana Grande visited Wolfee Donuts in California with the man she was dating at the time, her backup dancer Ricky Alvarez. Inside the shop, Ariana and Ricky were acting goofy—with the vestiges of goofiness that might still linger in a twenty-two-year-old, which Ariana was at the time. In that spirit, Ariana decided to lick one of the donuts resting on a tray on the counter. Silly, but it wasn't the end of the world, right? It gets more complicated: When a donut shop worker brings out another tray of donuts, Ariana inexplicably states: "What the fuck is that? I hate Americans. I hate America."

That's where goofiness for a twenty-two-year-old should have made way for common sense. By twenty-two, a public figure should know never to hate on America publicly. The nation from which you make a living does not like to be dissed. Besides, didn't Ariana know that retail businesses usually have security cameras everywhere? Her conduct could have been caught on tape.

And so it was. The bakery handed its video to the tabloid television program TMZ. From there the tape went viral, inciting anger that spanned the United States. For a moment the story had the potential to wreck Ariana's career. But Ariana quickly released a videotaped apology in which she declared her love for America, and it was enough to reverse the damage.

Although Ariana was stunningly naive in making her comments at a public business, the store's tape lent credence to the alibi Ariana offered in her apology. She was, in fact, looking at the donuts with disgust when she opined on America. In her apology she said her comments referred to the excess of fattening foods in America and their resulting diseases.

The story never would have saturated the media had Ariana been an unknown. After one bad visit to a donut shop, the firestorm reinforced to Ariana and other public figures the dangers of being real-life authentic in public. That's why they view, and I view, the authenticity of public figures as a construct. Like the constructs behind our seven other traits of likeability, authenticity in the public sphere exists to convey the appearance of authenticity.

I understand how this is counterintuitive. To make things easier, whenever I teach undergraduates or law students about authenticity as a trait of public figures' likeability, I use the term "public authenticity" as a contrast to "real-life authenticity." That makes sense here as well.

When Donald Trump ran for president in 2016, he, more than any other major-party candidate for president in our lifetimes, seemed to bridge the gap between public authenticity and real-life authenticity. On the stump, he gave speeches off the cuff rather than from a teleprompter. Although he bragged about his intelligence at campaign rallies, his reliance on words that elementary school students could understand—and therefore all voters could understand—enhanced his authenticity and relatability to a sizeable number of Americans.

Every time he said something prejudiced or otherwise offensive to oppressed communities, Trump came across to his voters as unscripted rather than unacceptable. They were undeterred when, at a 2015 rally, Trump threw his entire upper body into his mockery of Serge Kovaleski, a *New York Times* reporter with physical disabilities.

For some voters it was one of many moments during the campaign in which Trump's public authenticity seemed like the real thing: He's not perfect, but he's real and he's ours.

Trump also engaged in fluorescent constructs for which his conservative base gave him a pass. Before he thought of running for president as a Republican, Trump's views on social issues were largely liberal. In 1999 he told an interviewer he was "very pro-choice." In 2000 he told the *Advocate*, an LGBTQ magazine, that he supported amending the Civil Rights Act of 1964 to include protections based on sexual orientation. In his 2000 book *The America We Deserve*, Trump wrote: "I support the ban on assault weapons and I support a slightly longer waiting period to purchase a gun."

And get a load of this: In 1999, Donald Trump proposed a one-time tax of 14.25 percent on Americans making $10 million or more, in addition to the annual taxes they were already paying. At the time, ABC News called Trump's idea the "biggest tax hike ever." Trump explained to the network how higher taxes on the mega-rich would help the middle class. Donald Trump, presenting himself as the paragon of authenticity when he ran for president in 2016, was hardly that. But to millions, the contradictions seemed to make him more human.

When constructs of likeability, including public authenticity, are radically removed from the truth, the public will figure them out. But the process can take years.

In 1973 and 1974, Watergate demolished the New Nixon construct that Richard Nixon and his team had developed in the 1960s—their narrative that Nixon had mellowed and was now more likeable—to help him win the 1968 presidential election. But Watergate proved that Nixon was, as ever, the Old Nixon.

Fast-forward to 2014. That's when dozens of women began to

make public statements that Bill Cosby had sexually assaulted them at various times since the 1960s. Cosby was convicted in one case in 2018. After *The Cosby Show* ended in 1992, many Americans would remember the series fondly. They continued, no doubt, to associate Cosby with the kind and ethical Dr. Heathcliff "Cliff" Huxtable, a man who knew how to respect women, including his wife, Clair, played by Phylicia Rashad.

Even though he was a sexual assaulter, Cosby benefited from his Dr. Huxtable construct for a whopping twenty-two years after the series ended—that is, until his accusers began to come forth in 2014. But when the real Bill Cosby turned out to be Dr. Huxtable's opposite, the construct waited no time to die.

When you think of celebrities who strike you as authentic, Kris Jenner, a star of reality television that all of us know is not reality, would never be among your top choices. But get her talking about her first ex-husband's death from cancer, or about her conversation with Caitlyn Jenner when Caitlyn revealed her decision to live as her authentic self. Suddenly, Kris demonstrates authenticity. Whether she was showing us public authenticity or real-life authenticity, no one could doubt it was based on real-life.

For that matter, we face the danger of going too far in our skeptical analysis of the authenticity that public figures present. To be sure, privacy decisions will always prevent public figures from presenting their authenticity in 100 percent alignment with their real selves. But that still leaves them plenty of room to maximize the truth in their public authenticity. In fact, a number of public figures insist on it.

Bruce Springsteen is among the public figures who maximize their true selves when they present their public authenticity. That doesn't mean Springsteen has shunned constructs all together. He has based his entire career on the construct of being a working-class rock 'n' roller. The construct has endured because it's rooted in the truth of Springsteen's early working-class life in Asbury Park, New Jersey. But once Springsteen made millions, he adopted a plushier lifestyle. Suddenly there was a jarring contrast between Springsteen's long-standing image and his new trappings of wealth. And it annoyed his inner circle.

But let's think about it. Hasn't Springsteen enhanced his public authenticity by holding on to his lifelong values and by not living below his means just to send a phony public message?

Perhaps no other star maximizes the truth in his or her public authenticity more than Daniel Day-Lewis. Frankly, it is tough to find a star more authentically odd. Day-Lewis seldom appears in public or releases public statements. He shuns constructs of likeability outside of his work on film. Like Springsteen but even more so, Day-Lewis just is.

Leonardo DiCaprio once described what it took to persuade Daniel Day-Lewis, at the request of director Martin Scorsese, to costar with him in *Gangs of New York*.

"We kind of walked in silence for about 10 minutes through Central Park," DiCaprio said. "It was incredibly surreal, and I just said to myself, 'I'm gonna wait until he's ready to speak.' Finally, in the middle of Central Park, he finds a bench and he goes, 'That looks good; would you like to sit?'"

But Leo couldn't seal the deal and wound up calling costar Tobey Maguire to give it a go. Maguire pulled it off, all right, but not because he found Day-Lewis to be in a more talkative mood on the day of their conversation. Maguire lucked out with his timing. Daniel Day-Lewis was still Daniel Day-Lewis, and he's never allowed handlers to make him who he isn't.

When a politician strives to come across as authentic, the goals are fundamentally different from those of a Hollywood entertainer. As Penn State political scientist Ben Jones explains in his article on "Authenticity in Political Discourse," an individual's authenticity carries more weight in the context of politics.

"Authenticity takes on heightened importance," Jones writes, "when the public seeks information on how representatives will act in contexts where the public is absent and unable to influence decisions." Jones distinguishes authenticity as "consistently upholding the values and commitments that define one's identity for reasons that one deems legitimate, and . . . a second-order commitment to accurately represent these values and commitments."

Of all the people I've known in public life, former New Jersey state senator Raymond Lesniak is among the most authentic. Whenever he presents himself in public, he embodies authenticity as we know it in real life. He is the opposite of phony. But he wasn't always.

I first met Raymond when I worked for Jon Corzine in 1999. Raymond and I took an instant dislike to each other, however much I love him as a brother today. But back then Raymond was the ultimate New Jersey political boss whose hands were firmly on the levers of power. He loved when others perceived him as such. He even *called himself* a political boss—which I've rarely heard other political bosses do—and seemed to relish the intimidation his self-description induced.

In my idealistic and unrealistic notion of political purity, I summoned all the disdain toward Raymond I could, and I showed it. I was holier-than-thou. I've since grown up, realizing one can be honorable without being a sanctimonious jerk.

In parallel over the years, Raymond also changed. A deeply reflective man open to self-examination and change, Raymond never was the one-dimensional boss he held himself out to be. He had perpetuated the image because he knew the perception of power leads to real power. Indeed, as his image of bossism grew, his power in the state legislature grew with it.

One day over lunch, Raymond and I talked about the endless twists and turns in our political lives. Then he paused. "Steven," he said, "I can't do this anymore." I was shocked. What was he talking about?

"I can't stake my career on wanting to be a boss," he said, "when I am a liberal at heart who entered politics just like you did: to make the world a better place. I have done that, but I want to do even more. That's what matters to me now. It's time for my boss days to end."

Raymond wasn't exaggerating about the good he'd done for New Jersey. He had successfully championed numerous laws to advance legal, social, and economic equality for every historically oppressed community that had a presence in our state. He had single-handedly spearheaded New Jersey's law to repeal the death penalty, making us the first state to do so in a generation. He had achieved that victory, as he achieved many others, when public opinion wasn't with him. He personified courage.

When Raymond relinquished his senate seat to run for governor of New Jersey in 2017, he lost in the Democratic primary because too many people knew him as the old Raymond, the inauthentic party boss, rather than the Raymond who has always been a progressive's progressive.

But Raymond won his inner battle. And he showed us how a public figure can insist on presenting the truth in public authenticity, even as he came to understand his true self through remarkable personal growth.

To understand public authenticity further, let's get to its three sub-traits: being true to your origins, coolness and self-possession, and self-disclosure.

AUTHENTICITY Subtrait: True to Origins

No one chooses the time or place or circumstances of birth. Yet everyone is shaped by environment: Our formative years mold who we are. Yes, if given the opportunity and resources, people are free to evolve and create their own identities. But no matter what they do, they can never fully escape their upbringings or backgrounds. In this sense, being authentic means acknowledging that our origins are always with us in one way or another.

Charles Lindholm, a professor of anthropology at Boston University, is an expert on what makes people authentic, especially on being true to your origins. Lindholm argues that "authentic objects, persons, and collectives are original, real, and pure; they are what they purport to be, their roots are known and verified, their essence and appearance are one."

From the moment Jennifer Lopez became a star, she has reminded us how fame has not gone to her head. In fact, she had the meme planned out even before she became the star she is today. In 1999 she released her first studio album, *On the 6*, referring to the 6 train on the New York City subway—the train Lopez took to travel back and forth between the Bronx and Manhattan. Her second album, 2001's *J.Lo*, includes the single "I'm Real." The song, which centers on a relationship, includes the line, "What you get is what you see." Could there be a more pithy summary of authenticity than that?

By the time her third album arrived, 2002's *This Is Me . . . Then*, Lopez was everywhere and people loved her. She had a high-profile romance with Ben Affleck, and the media referred to the power couple as "Bennifer." Her success, already through the stratosphere, catapulted into another universe when Lopez released the hit single

"Jenny from the Block," which includes the lyrics, "Don't be fooled by the rocks that I got / I'm still, I'm still Jenny from the block." The first verse documents her rise to fame while reminding listeners that, despite it all, she's remained true to her origins and to herself: "I'm real, I thought I told you / I really been on Oprah / That's just me / Nothin phony, don't hate on me."

Microsoft CEO Satya Nadella used a similar tactic with the title of his 2017 autobiography, *Hit Refresh: The Quest to Rediscover Microsoft's Soul and Imagine a Better Future for Everyone*. The idea of refocusing on a company's essence—the one that made it great to begin with—is a call to authenticity, a return to one's origins. It's about turning our eyes away from the leaves and fruit for a moment to concentrate on the roots.

When asked about rediscovering Microsoft's soul during an interview with *Harvard Business Review*, Nadella, going back to the beginning of the company, noted that its first product had been created "so that others can create more technology," and that that was what Microsoft was "at our core, in our soul." By refocusing the company as a tool provider, Nadella, who became the third CEO of Microsoft in 2014, following Bill Gates and then Steve Ballmer, has seen the company return to prominence. Microsoft finished 2018 as the most valuable public U.S. company by market capitalization.

AUTHENTICITY Subtrait: Coolness and Self-possession

To be cool is to have an instinctive ability not to give in to the norms of society or of whichever segment of society you find yourself in. Samuel L. Jackson is the epitome of coolness, thanks to his persona as a badass rebel—the persona that has made him one of the highest box office earners of all time. With the mention of his name, you can almost hear his voice slowly rising in righteous anger and intensity, as when he played a Bible-quoting criminal in 1994's *Pulp Fiction.*

Another Hollywood star who ignores the pressure of social norms is Jennifer Lawrence. A few years ago she was the best-liked celebrity on the Internet, largely because of her apparent rejection of likeability constructs. She does national interviews with a nonchalance that makes it seem she wouldn't mind if her stardom ended tomorrow. She often goes off script during live shows and doesn't care if she makes a mistake. She simply doesn't behave the way we usually see famous people behave.

When accepting the award for Best Actress for her role in *Silver Linings Playbook* at the eighty-fifth annual Academy Awards in 2013, Lawrence tripped and fell on the stage stairs in her Dior gown. But she played it off with her signature humor once at the microphone: "Thank you!" she said, trophy in hand, to a standing ovation. "You guys are just standing up 'cause you feel bad that I fell and that's really embarrassing, but thank you."

At the same event, Lawrence admitted she was hungry and ordered McDonald's while on the red carpet. After winning her Oscar, Lawrence gave frank and candid answers during the official press conference, admitting she had taken a shot of alcohol just prior to meeting with the reporters. Overall, her coolness and self-possession made the reporters and their questions seem pat and inauthentic by comparison. Her likeability has soared because of it.

But, given how the eight traits of likeability are all constructs, we have to ask: Is Jennifer Lawrence's authenticity an act? The best actors make it difficult to tell where performance begins and ends. As journalist Masha Tupitsyn points out, a number of people viewed Lawrence as "refreshingly 'authentic'" for speaking her mind during interviews and award shows. Still, Tupitsyn wonders whether Lawrence is expert at acting raw, spontaneous, and willing to go off script—in other words, cool.

Tupitsyn writes: "In addition to the acting we see an actor do on a movie screen, there is also the acting an actor does on all the screens that constitute celebrity culture in our post-digital world . . . In today's surround-sound media culture, the real question is: Where does acting happen, and is it ever not happening? If acting is a condition of life, it is hard for any of us to know not only what is real and what is fake, but also the relation between the two."

Rihanna, with her devil-may-care attitude, is also cool. Although Rihanna has never had a squeaky-clean, bubblegum pop image to begin with, since her 2007 album *Good Girl Gone Bad*, she's nearly claimed the enfant terrible corner of the music industry just for herself.

On her official Instagram account (@badgalriri; bio: "Throwing all the shade!"), Rihanna has a history of posting risqué images and content. In 2014, her account was temporarily suspended due to her breaking the social network's no-nudity policy. That same year she told the following to *Vogue* regarding her bad-girl persona: "I don't go out of my way to be a rebel or to have that perception, but a lot of the decisions I make, a lot of the direction I want to move, is against the grain, or against society's tight lane, and I'm aware of that sometimes. It might not be fitting with the norm, but that's OK for me."

You can almost hear T-Mobile CEO John Legere saying the same thing.

And can you imagine how difficult it must have been for journalist April Ryan to remain calm, cool, and collected when, in early 2017, after asking President Trump if he'd consider including the Congressional Black Caucus in shaping his agenda to tackle urban issues, he responded by asking if she'd like to set up the meeting, presumably because she's also black? And yet Ryan did.

"No, I'm just a reporter," Ryan replied.

In late 2018, after Trump had publicly called Ryan a "loser," Ryan responded during an interview on CNN, calmly stating: "Who I've been and who I am is who you know. I'm an open book. Anyone who knows me, knows me. What you see is what you get from me. The President called me a 'loser.' I'm not."

That's someone who's authentically cool and fortified by a robust sense of self-possession.

As much as Samuel L. Jackson, Jennifer Lawrence, Rihanna, and April Ryan have mastered the art of being cool, perhaps none of them is as cool as the the majority leader of the New Jersey Senate, Loretta Weinberg. I must disclose my bias: Not only is Loretta a state senator and my own state senator, I call her my second mother and she calls me her adopted son.

I met Loretta through politics. She has written more than one hundred civil and human rights laws in New Jersey, including several I helped to pass during my years running Garden State Equality.

At eighty-four, she is the oldest member of the New Jersey legislature, as well as the most progressive member. She confounds statistics that show seniors are more conservative on social issues than are other voters. But Loretta has always defied society's norms as the Samuel L. Jackson of her own life and career. She is the ultimate badass.

She's used that perception, which coincides with the reality of who she is, to leverage her way to the top of the power structure in New Jersey politics. As senate majority leader, she's the consummate political insider. But she never joined the dark side, keeping all her outsider's perspectives that New Jerseyans have come to love. She remains the fiery reformer who pulls no punches when others in politics, regardless of party, cut corners on the transparency and accountability the public deserves. And she is still the grassroots organizer who inspires the love of thousands of progressive activists across the state. Never have I come across another public official who so effectively combines the perspectives of a political insider and political outsider, buttressed by the understanding that both approaches are necessary to change the world.

As if that weren't cool enough, further proof rests in Loretta's life-long fight to protect the LGBTQ community. Until she and I met in 1999, she hadn't had an openly gay relative. She became my community's hero simply because it was the right thing to do.

At the same time, you have to wonder which event or person in Loretta's life prompted her to embrace LGBTQ people as early as 1950, when she attended Beverly Hills High School in California. There she sensed one of her favorite teachers was gay. She had the same hunch about a classmate named Richard Chamberlain. She adored them both, and from there her love of the LGBTQ community became as natural to her as breathing.

Had she ever thought of toning down her support for LGBTQ equality in the decades before America would finally come around?

"You've got to be kidding me," she said. "I've been waiting for the world to catch up to me."

AUTHENTICITY Subtrait: Self-disclosure

Warren Buffett's approach to authenticity couldn't be more different from Daniel Day-Lewis's. Buffett engages in self-disclosure—or, rather, careful self-disclosure—to come across as real to the rest of us. Self-disclosure is the third subtrait of authenticity.

Buffett has told reporters he eats like a six-year-old, guzzling down five cans of Coke each day. Mind you, he happens to own several shares in Coca-Cola. One time he ordered Dairy Queen for dessert while dining at the fancy Four Seasons restaurant in New York. You guessed it: He also owns several shares of Dairy Queen.

"I have everything I want," Buffett has said. "I'm happy." He's even admitted he tap dances into his office each morning.

None of Buffett's self-disclosure in those details is particularly revealing, and that's why I often call the subtrait "careful self-disclosure." The public figure appears to be self-revealing. Here's about as far as Buffett will go: He's happy to tell reporters about the time he got rejected from Harvard Business School, but also that it turned out to be the best thing that ever happened to him.

Tiffany Haddish, like many other comedic talents, has boosted her likeability by inserting self-disclosures into her humor. During her stand-up routines, Haddish has joked about everything from her time in foster care to living in her car when she couldn't afford rent. One running gag she has about her sincere love for the deals website Groupon—and the time she took Will and Jada Pinkett Smith on a discounted New Orleans swamp tour—ended up landing her a gig as the company's spokesperson. She appeared in Groupon's 2018 Super Bowl ad.

In 2017, Haddish published a memoir titled *The Last Black Unicorn*. In it, she revealed that she was basically illiterate up until high school and that she married and divorced the very same man two times, among other things.

When Haddish reportedly bombed at a 2018 New Year's Eve gig in Miami, she admitted it. "Yes this happened," she wrote on Twitter. "I wish it was better Miami. I prayed on it and I have a strong feeling this will never happened [*sic*] again."

Her openness and honesty with her ups and downs have made Haddish come across as a genuine person.

In a similar manner, Academy Award–winning actor Lupita Nyong'o has talked openly about her struggles with identity and the influence images can have on a person's self-esteem and sense of worth.

In February 2014, Nyong'o received the Best Breakthrough Performance Award at an event organized by *Essence*. During her acceptance speech, Nyong'o said the following: "I want to take this opportunity to talk about beauty. Black beauty. Dark beauty. I received a letter from a girl and I'd like to share just a small part of it with you: 'Dear Lupita,' it reads, 'I think you're really lucky to be this Black yet this successful in Hollywood overnight. I was just about to buy Dencia's Whitenicious cream to lighten my skin when you appeared on the world map and saved me.'"

Nyong'o continued, talking about her own personal experience: "I remember a time when I too felt unbeautiful. I put on the TV and only saw pale skin. I got teased and taunted about my night-shaded skin. And my one prayer to God, the miracle worker, was that I would wake up lighter-skinned."

After telling the crowd that she had begun to accept her dark skin after being exposed to prominent, successful dark-skinned women, Nyong'o concluded her speech by addressing the girl who had sent her the letter: "And so I hope that my presence on your screens and in the magazines may lead you, young girl, on a similar journey. That you will feel the validation of your external beauty but also get to the deeper business of being beautiful inside. There is no shade in that beauty."

It's impossible to see the inspiration behind this moment as coming from anywhere other than a place of authenticity. Nyong'o's act of self-disclosure is sincere, and it's hard not to smile when thinking about what her words must have meant to both that young girl and young girls everywhere.

RELATABILITY:
Similarity + Physical Proximity
+ Vulnerability

If I were to ask you which actor is seen by Americans as the epitome of relatability, I'd bet 90 percent of you who are thirty-five or older would come up with the correct name within three guesses. I'm talking about Tom Hanks, of course.

His films have grossed more than $9 billion worldwide—yes, that's "billion" with a *B*. His Celebrity DBI scores have placed him within the top five most likeable celebrities for years.

How does Hanks manage to be so likeable? He is gifted at appearing as human as the rest of us—aging, occasionally a little paunchy, and always challenged by life as are the rest of us. When he takes on a role, he invariably rewrites his parts in the script to eliminate grandiosity he believes doesn't ring true to how the rest of us mere mortals behave in real life. He'll even add elements of normalcy if he has to.

When he was interviewed in *Vanity Fair*, he reflected on his early career and said he finally reached a "modern era of moviemaking. My work has become less pretentiously fake and over the top." Not a lot of actors would look back on their career and characterize it like that. He's just like one of us, or so his construct has it.

Offscreen, Hanks also projects the same down-to-earth personality. The bio for his official Twitter account, for example, reads: "I'm that actor in some of the movies you liked and some you didn't. Sometimes I'm in pretty good shape, other times I'm not. Hey, you gotta live, you know?"

Indeed, it's hard to picture Hanks being an annoying jerk or even playing one in a film. As director Paul Greengrass said about Hanks in a September 2013 issue of *Parade*: "He can also embody the Everyman like no one else. You don't feel he has superpowers; he's just like any-one would be, going, 'How [can I] cope with this?'"

That's why so many insiders, not to mention his fans, describe Hanks as the Nicest Guy in Hollywood. A 2012 *Rolling Stone* pro-file, for example, phrases Hanks's likeability as follows: "This is Tom Hanks. The Nicest Guy in Showbiz. America's Sweetheart. You could probably put him in the Staples Center men's room and he'd spend the next three hours passing out paper towels."

That's not too far from the truth. Accompanying a 2013 *Huffing-ton Post* article titled "As if You Needed Any More Proof That Tom Hanks Is the Nicest Guy," video clips showed Hanks backstage at his Broadway show *Lucky Guy* being an Everyman who was playfully interacting with an autistic fan.

Relatability often occurs, and likeability often skyrockets, after a public figure commits a blunder. In a paper titled "The Effect of a Pratfall on Increasing Interpersonal Attractiveness," published in the journal *Psychonomic Science* way back in 1966, researchers found evi-dence that when a public figure with power or fame makes a clumsy blunder, the masses like that person more. The mishap humanizes the public figure, therefore making him or her more relatable. In es-sence, the so-called pratfall effect boils down to the fact that compe-tent people appear more approachable and less threatening after they commit an incompetent act. Jennifer Lawrence or her team may be onto something.

But the blunders have to be within reason. New York City Con-gressman Anthony Weiner's blunders were not within reason and occurred after his acts of public contrition. So did Robert Downey Jr.'s, but Downey never wore his contrition so brazenly on his sleeve. He was authentic and relatable because he practically clued us into his treatment in real time. And let's face it: Downey never sexted photos, as Weiner did, including the time Weiner sexted a photo that included his four-year-old son.

To understand a public figure, we have the person's family as our most available point of reference. We all have families. Public figures' families are ready-made tools to validate the star's warmth and to prove the star is relatable because he or she gets along so well with those who know the star best.

That's why Barack Obama not only featured Michelle as the You-Tube star of his presidential campaigns but also ran several contests that offered everyday voters the chance to have dinner with Barack and Michelle. Once the campaign chose the winning voters, the Obama campaign would create YouTube videos that showed Barack, Michelle, and the voters dining together and laughing together at a table in some brick-walled casual restaurant. You couldn't help but think of the Olive Garden commercials that told us, "When you're here, you're family."

So ingrained is family as a construct of relatability that Donald Trump's handlers couldn't stop themselves from highlighting his family at the 2016 Republican National Convention in Cleveland. Inside a convention hall at which most delegates would have described themselves, no doubt, as family-first social conservatives, all of Trump's children from three marriages spoke at the podium—except for Barron, age ten, who appeared at the end when the confetti dropped.

The Trump campaign could have done something unprecedented for a national convention: deemphasize the candidate's family. Instead, the solution was to deemphasize the candidate as a spouse and have all Trump's adult children talk about what a great father he was, hoping all parents could relate. Melania did not speak much about Trump as a spouse but, rather, delivered a boilerplate speech about the universally cherished values of love and hard work that had suspicious similarities to the speech Michelle Obama delivered in 2008, minus the love for Barack.

RELATABILITY Subtrait: Similarity

Ursula Burns, former Xerox CEO and current CEO and chairperson of Amsterdam-based telecommunications company Veon, is the first African-American woman to head a Fortune 500 corporation. Burns's mother, a Panamanian immigrant and single mom, raised her children in the Baruch Houses, a public housing project on Manhattan's Lower East Side. She supported Ursula and her two siblings with income from doing laundry and providing day care for other parents.

Ursula Burns started her career at Xerox as a summer intern in 1980, in between her studies for bachelor's and master's degrees in mechanical engineering. Twenty-eight years later, she became CEO. To come across as likeable, Burns simply needed to let her authentic story do the talking, stressing the concept of family in which everyone could find similarity. Our families may be different, but we all have one and can recognize universal patterns. In her first company-wide meeting as Xerox CEO, according to the *New York Times*, Burns told the Xerox family to start acting like a *real* family.

"When we're in the family, you don't have to be as nice as when you're outside of the family," said Burns. "I want us to stay civil and kind, but we have to be frank—and the reason we can be frank is because we are all in the same family." Burns was intending to encourage Xerox's 130,000 employees to work with less fear, take more risks, and strive for honest communication with one another when things just weren't working, knowing that at the end of the day everyone is on the same side.

In the business world, LinkedIn CEO Jeff Weiner puts the concept of family front and center in his leadership. Has it worked? He has topped Glassdoor's rankings of the CEOs most popular with their own employees.

Weiner has organized a "Bring Your Parents to Work Day" at LinkedIn. He brought his own parents into the office, and employees brought theirs, in an effort to help bridge the generation gap that pervades the tech industry. In 2016, Microsoft bought LinkedIn for $26.2 billion.

The authenticity and relatability of CEOs can produce palpable results. *Harvard Business Review* reports that companies are now pushing business leaders to become more authentic and relatable for two reasons. First, trust in business leaders declined to a record-breaking low in 2012, according to data from the Edelman Trust Barometer. Second, a 2013 Gallup poll found that only 13 percent of employees worldwide report feeling engaged with the work they do. It is not a huge leap, then, to posit that likeable CEOs can change a company's culture and therefore its productivity and profits.

In the world of film, Sandra Bullock, often dubbed "America's sweetheart," comes across as pretty similar to the rest of us. Several of her movie roles involve playing an ordinary person dealing with extraordinary circumstances.

In 1994's *Speed*, for example, she plays a passenger on a runaway bus. In 2009's *The Blind Side*, for which she won an Academy Award for Best Actress, Bullock plays a mother who adopts a troubled teenager who, with some help and encouragement, goes on to become a football star, eventually getting drafted into the NFL. In 2011's *Extremely Loud & Incredibly Close*, Bullock plays a mother whose husband dies during the 9/11 attacks. In 2018's *Bird Box*, Bullock plays a mother struggling to survive an evil supernatural force that is causing most of humanity to commit suicide. You get the idea. A large part of

Bullock's relatability stems from the struggling, family-oriented characters she so often portrays on screen.

For the past few years Bill Gates has sneakily participated in a massive Secret Santa exchange that takes place on Reddit, one of the world's most visited websites. Each year one lucky participant gets a boatload of goodies ranging from an Xbox and various video game paraphernalia to donations to charities under the recipient's name to a signed letter and photograph of Gates himself.

Gates's decision to participate in the annual online gift exchange always results in great PR for him, but it also sends a signal that he's not different than the average anonymous person on the Internet who wants to celebrate the joys of the holidays in a very modern way.

RELATABILITY Subtrait: Physical Proximity

Jeff Weiner's relatability at LinkedIn runs deeper. One employee in the Glassdoor survey noted Weiner's biweekly "all-hands-on-deck" meetings as one of the most visible ways in which Weiner is more accessible than other Silicon Valley CEOs. Another employee described how Weiner still interviews candidates face-to-face and takes new employees around all by himself. He exudes the second subtrait of reliability: physical proximity to others. Has it worked? In 2014, a startling 100 percent of LinkedIn employees who filled out the Glassdoor survey said they liked Weiner's leadership.

Physical proximity as a subtrait of relatability has its tricky limitations. In the 1992 presidential campaign that led to his election, Bill Clinton demonstrated how to pull off the balance. Some of you will remember the second debate in the general election that year: the town hall debate featuring Clinton, the first President Bush, and Ross Perot. A voter in the audience asked President Bush how the national debt and recession affected him personally. He couldn't answer. The voter and moderator Carole Simpson kept giving Bush a chance. The voter even explained why she was asking the question. If the faltering economy wasn't affecting Bush personally, how could he have the instincts to fix it?

Again he couldn't answer. Then again.

Next it was Bill Clinton's turn to answer. He started walking toward the voter in the audience. As he walked, he said to her: "You know people who lost their jobs and their homes?"

She nodded. Clinton kept walking toward her, farther away from his seat onstage than any previous presidential candidate in history. "I've been governor of a small state for twelve years," he said. "In my state, when people lose their jobs there's a good chance I'll know them by their names. When a factory closes, I know the people who ran it. When businesses go bankrupt, I know them."

The camera caught the voter nodding approvingly. Clinton went right to the edge of the stage, almost into the audience, but he did not step off the stage to get closer. He did not want to invade the voter's personal space. He knew his unprecedented walk was enough. He let his eye contact and casual body language—signifying his appreciation for the question—take him the rest of the way to the voter, to his coming across as relatable, and to his making that moment the key to his winning the election.

Al Gore, in contrast, didn't understand the tricky limitations of physical proximity in coming across as relatable. In the 2000 town hall debate, Gore strode obnoxiously into George W. Bush's personal space as Bush was speaking to the audience. Gore looked as if he might slap Bush out of exasperation from Bush's alleged stupidity. When Bush noticed, he did a double take with good-ol'-boy Texas charm that seemed to say, "Dude, relax. We're only running for president." Courtesy of Gore, Bush had his most likeable moment of the three debates between them.

Surely you remember the town hall debate between Donald Trump and Hillary Clinton in 2016. Trump paced behind her so closely, and with such increasing hostility, he inspired an uproarious parody on *Saturday Night Live* in which Alec Baldwin portrayed Trump as a human-eating land shark. In *What Happened*, her post-campaign assessment, Clinton revealed her inner thoughts. "Back up, you creep, get away from me," she wrote. "I know you love to intimidate women but you can't intimidate me, so *back up*." Had she revealed those thoughts at the debate, her authenticity and relatability would have skyrocketed.

In recent years we've seen the likeable power of physical proximity as we've watched the friendship between George W. Bush and Michelle Obama. We see their chemistry every time they are next to one another at public events. They show mutual adoration through frequent hugs and hearty laughter at the other's jokes. It would be hard to forge the photo of them in September 2016 at the opening of the National Museum of African American History and Culture in Washington, D.C. Bush is seen closing his eyes and leaning into Obama as she wraps her arms around him with a beatific glow that one reserves for family and the closest of friends.

Another heartwarming public moment between George and Michelle came in September 2018, at the funeral of Senator John McCain. Cameras caught Bush taking a cough drop from his wife, former first lady Laura Bush. He handed it over to Michelle, who sat beside him once again. The moment went viral for its simple humanity and relatability. A few months later, at the December 2018 funeral of Bush's father, George H. W. Bush, video emerged of Bush handing

Michelle yet another candy or mint or cough drop as he shook her hand with a warm embrace. Her face broke out into an unrestrained smile.

How did Bush and Obama become almost like family? "President Bush and I are forever seatmates because of protocol—that's how we sit at all the official functions," Michelle Obama explained on NBC's *Today* show in late 2018. "So he is my partner in crime at every major thing where all the formers gather."

There you have it: Likeability by mandated physical proximity.

In January 2017, Facebook CEO Mark Zuckerberg announced on Facebook that he planned to tour the United States, traveling to around thirty states he hadn't spent much time in before to visit with the people who live there. "After a tumultuous last year, my hope for this challenge is to get out and talk to more people about how they're living, working and thinking about the future," he wrote.

Even the precocious whiz kid who prides himself on connecting the world through his social media platform—and probably knows more about the average American's daily habits than any person in history—believed contact through the Web isn't a replacement for the real thing. He understood that some physical proximity is necessary to understand and relate to another human being.

RELATABILITY Subtrait: Vulnerability

When public figures admit that sometimes they feel vulnerable, they become more relatable. When they become more relatable, they become more likeable. The math isn't too difficult.

Consider Carrie Underwood. After winning the fourth season of *American Idol* back in 2005, she become a country star. Her career was off and running.

Then, in late 2017, days after cohosting the 51st Annual Country

Music Association Awards show in Tennessee; various media outlets reported that Underwood had fallen on some steps outside her
home and sustained injuries to her wrist and face. She was taken to
a hospital for treatment. "Thanks so much for all the well wishes
everybody," she wrote on Twitter. "I'll be alright . . . might just take
some time . . . glad I've got the best hubby in the world to take care
of me."

And then things went silent for a while as Underwood disappeared
from the public eye.

In January 2018, Underwood wrote a letter to her fan club, stating, "It's crazy how a freak random accident can change your life." She
went on to explain that she required more than forty stitches to repair
her face, and "even though I've had the best people helping me, I'm
still healing and not looking quite the same." In other words Underwood was vulnerable. "When I am ready to get in front of a camera, I
want you all to understand why I might look a bit different," the letter
continued. "I'm hoping that, by then, the differences are minimal,
but, again, I just don't know how it's all going to end up."

When Underwood did finally return to the limelight, with a performance of her new single "Cry Pretty" at the Academy of Country
Music Awards show in Las Vegas in April 2018, she looked totally
fine. As the *Washington Post* put it, "She looked her usual glamorous
self." The scar, it turns out, runs from her upper lip to nose, and is
not easy to spot.

Though some blamed the singer for over-hyping her injuries—the
fall broke her wrist, too—Underwood later revealed that, for a period
of time, she couldn't sing at all. The stitches got in the way and the
whole ordeal got to her head. "Do I sound the same? Is my diction
the same? Does my mouth move the same as it did before?" she told
a reporter that she recalled thinking to herself at the time. Everyone

assured her she was fine, but by revealing her doubts and fears to her fans she likely made herself more endearing, more relatable.

Like Carrie Underwood, comedian Dave Chappelle suddenly disappeared for a while in the spring of 2005. Comedy Central, which was planning to launch the third season of his show, brought everything to a halt. In a statement, the network said production of Chappelle's show had been suspended "until further notice" and that "all parties are optimistic that production will resume in the near future."

Rumors began to surface that Chappelle had either gone crazy or fallen deep into crack addiction. Why else, the thinking went, would someone abruptly walk away from critical success, far-reaching fame, and a reported two-year contract worth $50 million?

A couple weeks later, however, *Time* found Chappelle and reported that he was staying at a friend's house in South Africa. He hadn't gone crazy or fallen into drug addiction. "Let me tell you the things I can do here which I can't at home," said Chappelle in an exclusive interview with *Time*. "Think, eat, sleep, laugh. I'm an introspective dude. I enjoy my own thoughts sometimes. And I've been doing a lot of thinking here."

As it turned out, Chappelle simply didn't want to surrender his soul for all the ugliness that tends to come with fame, such as the loss of privacy, the battle for creative control, and the suspicion that people only want to be your friend for your money. "During my ascent, I've seen other people go through that wall to become really big," he told *Time*. "They always said that fame didn't change them but that it changes the people around them. You always hear that but you never really understand it. But now that I'm there that makes a lot of sense and I'm learning what that means. You have to have people around you that you can trust and aren't just out for a meal ticket."

About a year later, Chappelle appeared on *Oprah* to share his story.

"I wasn't crazy, but it's incredibly stressful," he said of walking away from his show. "And I felt like in a lot of instances I was deliberately being put through stress because, when you're a guy that generates money, people have a vested interest in controlling you. And I feel like the people that were trying to control me were putting me through stressful situations. The way the people around you position themselves around you to get in your pockets and in your mind is infuriating to me."

In short, Chappelle felt vulnerable in a toxic environment and decided to walk away. Many people respected and understood his decision to do so. They admired him for wanting more in life than money and fame, and that made him more relatable.

Gwyneth Paltrow: When Authenticity Is the Enemy of Relatability

Has anyone else in public life had his or her likeability questioned as much as Gwyneth Paltrow?

Even the most scandalously unlikeable men have escaped the enduring cynicism that has dissected—and distorted—the likeability of female celebrities such as Paltrow. Later in the book, we'll explore the double standards with which the public views the likeability of women, as well as that of people of color and my own LGBTQ community.

But make no mistake: The portrayal of Gwyneth Paltrow as unlikeable is an industry unto itself. In 2011, *Time* described Paltrow as the opposite of "America's sweetheart." In 2013, *Star* magazine named her the most hated celebrity in America.

What gives? She has never been involved in a scandal. She has never said anything sexist, racist, or homophobic. And she hasn't run for office, so she has no political enemies out to get her. But she's become a time bomb when it comes to combining authenticity with relatability, and she makes things worse every time she engages in constructs to achieve these traits in a public setting.

Let's put the life of Gwyneth Paltrow in context. She is privileged and always has been. She was born in Los Angeles to two show-business parents, actress Blythe Danner and the late film and television director Bruce Paltrow. In high school, Gwyneth attended an elite private school on Manhattan's Upper East Side. Before the age of twenty, she secured the role of Wendy in Steven Spielberg's 1991 hit adventure film *Hook*, starring Robin Williams as Peter Pan, Dustin Hoffman as Captain Hook, and Julia Roberts as Tinker Bell. It's worth noting that as talented an actor as Paltrow might be, Steven Spielberg is her godfather. See where I'm going? Right from the start, Paltrow's *authentic* life was one of fame and power and having early opportunities most of the rest of us didn't have.

Things tend to go wrong for Paltrow when she tries to relate her genuine thoughts and experiences with us common folks. She may be the one celebrity who should strive for less authenticity—and I mean the real kind.

In an interview with E! News in 2014, for example, Paltrow discussed taking time off from acting so she could focus on her kids after she and husband Chris Martin of Coldplay had split up. It was a moment to show similarity through family, and her vulnerability following divorce. The end of their marriage, however, was a "conscious uncoupling," as Paltrow called it, which set off thousands of derisive laughs.

Her underlying decision to focus on parenthood was one to which millions of Americans could have related. But listen to how she managed, instead, to insult parents, including those who work in an office and those who raise kids at home.

"When you have an office job," she told E! News, "it's routine and, you know, you can do all the stuff in the morning and then you come home in the evening. When you're shooting a movie, they're like, 'We need you to go to Wisconsin for two weeks,' and then you work 14 hours a day and that part of it is very difficult. I think to have a regular job and be a mom is not as—of course there are challenges— but it's not like being on set."

That's right. According to Paltrow, being a movie star is the hardest work of all. She portrayed her life as if somehow she were a victim. Her vulnerability was that she was rich and famous.

When she wrote a cookbook, *It's All Good*—no doubt understanding that Martha Stewart, Rachael Ray, and Ina Garten had hit the relatability jackpot with their skills—Paltrow might have put a sign on her back saying, MOCK ME. I'M OUT OF TOUCH.

She provided a recipe for an effete egg-white omelet inspired by her friend Jean-Georges Vongerichten, restaurateur to the stars. She went on about proper duck bacon for a "cassoulet." And she warned readers to eat only birds from the wild, "the way it was meant to be."

Some news outlets took the bait and indeed mocked her. For three meals a day from Paltrow's cookbook, the cost of ingredients averaged $300—totaling $2,100 a week.

Making matters worse, her lifestyle website, Goop, which initially launched as a weekly email newsletter back in 2008, showcased a specific "chateau for eight in the French countryside with tennis courts and a pool" that "makes for a nice family getaway."

In November 2014, *Entertainment Tonight* published an article titled "This Is How Much It Costs to Buy Everything on Gwyneth Paltrow's 2014 Goop Gift Guide." The article highlights such egregiously priced items as a travel backgammon set for $550 and a juicer for $4,739. Happy holidays, y'all! The total cost to purchase one of each item on the list: $107,309.49.

For someone so conscious of her image, Paltrow is not perceptive in how she treats the press corps. As she emailed a gaggle of her celebrity friends: "*Vanity Fair* is threatening to put me on the cover of their magazine without my participation. I recommend you all never do this magazine again."

Wait a second. Paltrow not only asked her friends not to speak to *Vanity Fair* about her, but she also asked that they try to marginalize *Vanity Fair*? That would be like a politician asking other politicians to try to marginalize the *New York Times*. Even Vladimir Putin would know better. At least he'd know better than to put his edict in writing.

Apparently one or more of Paltrow's friends found her request unlikeable enough to leak it.

As *Atlantic* editor Eleanor Barkhorn described Paltrow: "She's trying to maintain the trappings of the A-list lifestyle while at the same time seem relatable, and it's not working."

If Gwyneth Paltrow wants to boost her likeability, she should stop trying to portray the way she lives as a modest way we all can relate to. Because we can't.

In July 2018, the *New York Times Magazine* published a profile on Paltrow reporting that Goop was worth an estimated $250 million and that Paltrow's many haters had helped contribute to that valuation. In the article, when asked how Goop planned to attract "people of lesser incomes," Paltrow responded: "It's crucial to me that we remain aspirational."

That might explain how Paltrow is both unlikeable yet financially successful: People want to live like her, and Goop's business model depends on promising that. But it keeps Paltrow's followers in a permanent state of ambitiously seeking, where one door just leads to another room with more doors. Oddly, being "aspirational" turns Paltrow's negative relatability into a positive for enough Americans. Still, you have to wonder whether Gwyneth would be more likeable to more Americans were she to substitute her authenticity with public authenticity.

Summary: Authenticity and Relatability

Although public figures never show us their entire private lives, warts and all, some public figures present themselves with more authenticity than others. Depending on the CEO, politician, or celebrity, different degrees of revelation work better to build likeability.

But authenticity alone, in one form or another, is not enough. The public figure must also come across as relatable to complete the foundation traits. It's true that famous people are, by definition, not everyday people like the rest of us. They receive certain privileges and face particular pressures the rest of us don't, making their lived experiences removed from ours. That said, once public figures successfully combine authenticity with relatability, they have reached the halfway point in the journey toward likeability. The game is now theirs to lose.

Authenticity requires you to be true to your origins. Perhaps you don't think fondly of your upbringing, but you can't escape it, either. As much as you might strive to forge a new identity, there are limits to what you can achieve. To boost your likeability through authenticity, you embrace those limits rather than sweep them under the rug.

Coolness and self-possession, along with the ability to engage in self-disclosure, come from taking a hard look at yourself and liking the imperfect but wonderful person you are. It will make you less afraid to let others enter your world.

To hone your relatability, reach out more frequently to others. How can two people possibly find common interests if they don't have any depth of knowledge about each other? Similarity isn't likely to occur between virtual strangers.

And that's where physical proximity comes into play. You have to spend time with others to get to know them. When you do, it will become obvious that everybody hurts. None of us is without struggle or worry. When you are willing to share your own vulnerabilities, others will share theirs, and you will have strengthened the foundation of your likeability.

CHAPTER 7

The Clincher Traits: Protectiveness and Reliability

P rotectiveness and reliability have the potential to make or break the entire likeability package. That's why I call them the clincher traits.

Someone who has both traits banishes our anxiety. A protector shelters others from harm, physical and mental. Protectors can be strong and brave, bold and ferocious, or instinctive and empathic. They are vigilant and always ready to confront enemies on the horizon. They have the power to bring about change on either a macro level or an intimate and personal level.

A reliable person follows through on promises and pronouncements, remains steadfast in times of chaos, and stays on message, the shifting winds notwithstanding.

Protectiveness and reliability have a symbiotic relationship. No one can make us feel safe if we don't perceive him or her to be reliable. That's one of the reasons it is so difficult for public figures to recover once they have fallen from grace, a subject I'll cover later on. Conversely, no one can make you feel he or she is consistent—someone you can rely on—if that person doesn't make you feel safe in the first place.

PROTECTIVENESS:
Toughness + Courage + Self-confidence

Given that we Americans view politicians as patently untrustworthy, we long to believe they're capable of protecting their constituents. In an annual Gallup poll, politicians and lobbyists consistently rank as the least trustworthy, behind even car salespeople and telemarketers.

We weren't always so cynical about politicians. Once the Cold War between the U.S. and the former Soviet Union became full-blown in the 1950s, voters looked to Republicans to keep the country safe. Whereas Democrats since Franklin Roosevelt and his New Deal became the party of compassion, the Republicans succeeded at being perceived as the party tough abroad and tough at home—the party most likely to prevent the harms of communism, terrorism, and violent crime from wounding America. President Nixon took on the mantle of law and order. President Reagan dared Mikhail Gorbachev to tear down the Berlin Wall and end communism, and the first President Bush followed through until both happened.

Whatever else can be said about his presidency, the second President Bush had an instinctive feel for projecting protectiveness. Three days after the September 11, 2001, attack on the World Trade Center, he visited Ground Zero. What followed was his completely impromptu and memorable speech to Ground Zero workers, delivered through a bullhorn. Standing on top of a pile of rubble, he exclaimed, "I can hear you! I can hear you! The rest of the world hears you! And the people—and the people who knocked these buildings down will hear all of us soon!"

President Bush's words were met with patriotic chants of "USA! USA! USA!" His protective rhetoric sent his likeability ratings through the roof. In the months immediately following 9/11, his popularity hovered around 87 percent. No longer was he the president who had won the 2000 election on questionable grounds. He was now a heroic wartime president.

In the 2004 presidential election, the Democratic Party strategically nominated John Kerry, a war hero the party believed could trim the protectiveness deficit in a post-9/11 America. Notwithstanding Kerry's credentials, Republican supporters attacked his protectiveness with shock-and-awe dispatch.

Ads featuring fellow Vietnam veterans branded Kerry a liar when it came to serving America. Attacking his silver star, bronze star, and three purple hearts, they alleged he lied about the extent of his service and injuries that he received when he was in charge of a type of navy boat known as a Swift Boat. The problem is, the discreditors didn't serve alongside Kerry directly, and Kerry's own crew corroborated the Democrat's heroism. The ads, made by a group called Swift Boat Veterans for Truth, were a political fabrication. To this day, "swift boating" in politics means to attack an opponent with a total lie. In Kerry's case, the ads against him worked, demolishing his protectiveness—the heart of why Democrats nominated him to face George W. Bush in the aftermath of 9/11. The ads came to symbolize the strategy of Republican Karl Rove: Don't kill your political opponents on their weaknesses. Kill them on their strengths so they can't survive.

PROTECTIVENESS Subtrait: Toughness

Let's turn to protectiveness and its first subtrait, toughness—the kind that can take care of others.

Since the premiere of her show in 1996, Judge Judy Sheindlin has been a fixture of American culture. During the show's 2009–2010 season, *Judge Judy* became the first daytime program in about a decade to surpass *The Oprah Winfrey Show* in viewership.

Judge Judy is ferocious in the courtroom and in fulfilling our fantasy. Who among us doesn't want the instant justice she delivers when we are wronged? Even better, her verdicts are final.

Though she was a judge for fourteen years before she landed her show, never forget that she became a character—or, more aptly, a bigger character—once she became a star. She had a reputation in the courts for being smart, tough, and quick, and television editing can make her look even smarter, tougher, and quicker. Remember, likeability in the public eye is a take on reality.

She also has a staff of dozens who find her the best legal disputes and the most aggravating defendants from whom she protects the plaintiffs and, by extension, the rest of us. According to Randy Douthit, the show's executive producer and director, "Probably the return on the cases we actually can use out of everything coming in is only about three percent." He adds that the best kinds of cases involve people with some kind of prior relationship, including spouses, former lovers, and parents and their children. "That way it pulls in the audience a little bit more, there's an emotional tie that's been broken, and you end up with a bit of a mini soap opera," said Douthit.

The formula works. According to one survey published in early 2016, nearly 10 percent of recent college graduates polled thought Judith Sheindlin was on the Supreme Court.

In the tech world, Google CEO Sundar Pichai demonstrated toughness when, in August 2017, news broke that he had fired a software engineer for writing a memo titled "Google's Ideological Echo Chamber," which argued, among other things, that the low number of women working in the tech industry was more a result of biological and inherent personality differences than discrimination. The document asserted several sexist ideas, such as the notion that women aren't wired to deal with high-stress jobs.

Pichai sent a company-wide email stating that some sections of the memo had violated the company's code of conduct and done damage by "advancing harmful gender stereotypes in our workplace." In his letter, he wrote that "much of what was in that memo is fair to debate, regardless of whether a vast majority of Googlers disagree with it" but that, ultimately, he felt his role was to help "create a more inclusive environment for all." And so he made the tough decision and fired that employee. He ended his family vacation early, too, to return to work and deal with the matter.

PROTECTIVENESS Subtrait: Courage

Courage, the second subtrait of protectiveness, is the ability to act when others won't or can't. It's the ability to stand up when your peers tell you to sit down. It's not the absence of fear or doubt but rather the willingness to speak out despite them.

Jeffrey Sonnenfeld is a senior associate dean of leadership programs at the Yale School of Management. He's also the founder and president of the Chief Executive Leadership Institute, and he taught at Harvard Business School for a decade. Sonnenfeld knows what good leadership looks like, especially in the business community.

In August 2017, Sonnenfeld wrote an opinion piece for *Fortune* titled "Ken Frazier: The Strongest Man in the World," which praised Frazier, CEO of the pharmaceutical giant Merck, for his bold resignation from President Donald Trump's American Manufacturing Council. "Crises are tests of character," wrote Sonnenfeld. "Coming off this weekend . . . Frazier passed heroically."

Frazier had quit in protest over Trump's response to the violence that occurred between white supremacists and neo-Nazis and those who had gathered to oppose them at a rally in Charlottesville, Virginia. During a press conference, Trump condemned the hatred and violence that, as he saw it, originated "on many sides."

On Twitter, Frazier released a statement declaring that "America's leaders must honor our fundamental values by clearly rejecting expressions of hatred, bigotry and group supremacy, which run counter to the American ideal that all people are created equal." Frazier closed his statement with the following: "As CEO of Merck and as a matter of personal conscience, I feel a responsibility to take a stand against intolerance and extremism." And so he did.

Trump lashed out at Frazier with his own tweet, accusing Merck of both gouging consumers with high drug prices and taking jobs away from American workers.

Soon after Frazier's resignation, more CEOs on the manufacturing council followed his lead and withdrew from the council. Within days the remaining members decided to disband the council outright. Frazier's stream of courage had led to a river of consequence.

Frazier, among a handful of African-American CEOs of Fortune 500 companies, stood up to the president of the United States of America over race. That was beyond the right thing to do. It was courage because of the potential consequences. In an article entitled "Outraged in Private, many C.E.O.s Fear the Wrath of the President," the *New York Times* added that because Merck depends on the government to buy many of its drugs, Frazier's decision to defy Trump involves a potential economic risk for his company, which "demonstrates just how brave Mr. Frazier was in taking a stand."

But there is justice. After Frazier's resignation from the manufacturing council, Merck experienced a notable bump up in consumer perception.

If you want to see change, sometimes you have to *be* the change. In another example of courage, the world's youngest female leader, New Zealand's prime minister, Jacinda Ardern, did just that.

In September 2018, Ardern became the first world leader to bring a baby—her infant daughter, Neve Te Aroha Ardern Gayford—to the United Nations General Assembly in New York City. The *New York Times* reported that images of Ms. Ardern holding her three-month-old child "were published in newspapers and shared on social media around the world." Ardern's partner, television host Clarke Gayford, who was also in attendance, held baby Neve on his lap while Ardern delivered her speech. "If I can do one thing, and that is change the way we think about these things, then I will be pleased we have achieved something," said Ardern about her situation and women seeking to balance a career with parenting. Gayford tweeted an image of Neve's makeshift UN identification card. The description reads: "New Zealand First Baby."

PROTECTIVENESS Subtrait: Self-confidence

Although her humor is often self-deprecating, or maybe because of it, Tina Fey displays self-confidence, our third subtrait.

After a successful stint on *Saturday Night Live* as a head writer and performer, where she also coanchored the "Weekend Update" segment, Fey went on to create the hit NBC sitcom *30 Rock*. Throughout her career Fey has received numerous awards, including several Emmys and three Golden Globes. In 2008, the Associated Press named her Entertainer of the Year. In 2009, *Time* put her on its list of the World's Most Influential People. In 2010, Fey was selected to receive a star on the Hollywood Walk of Fame.

No one needs to convince you of Tina Fey's talent, but it's time to discuss her self-confidence. Often it comes through in her advice to young women. In 2010, for example, during an interview with *Esquire*, Fey directed the following words to women looking to get into comedy: "One, you don't have to be weird or be quirky to get your job done. And two, comedy skill is not sexually transmittable. You do not have to sleep with a comedian to learn what you're doing. Male comedians will not like that advice, but it is the truth."

Also, as noted in *Time*, Fey was taking shots at Bill Cosby's history of rape allegations on both *SNL* and *30 Rock* for years before it became acceptable to do so in the industry. In 2005, for instance, during *SNL*'s "Weekend Update," Fey and coanchor Amy Poehler joked about the general silence around the accusations due to Cosby's clout in the entertainment business. Both her self-awareness of the situation and willingness to speak out by joking about not being able to speak out are sure signs of self-confidence.

Sometimes self-confidence is evident in bold decisions. Consider Mary Barra, chairperson and CEO of General Motors, and the first woman to lead a global automaker. Given her pioneering role, Barra often comes across as someone ready to shake up the corporate culture. But when she does, it's not always as we might expect.

For instance, when Barra became GM's chief of human resources in 2009, prior to becoming the company's CEO, she distilled the company's ten-page dress code into two words: "dress appropriately." Some fellow managers apparently got upset over this simple yet bold change. Later, in 2015, during an awards show that promotes progressive changes in the workplace, Barra called her dress-code policy the "smallest biggest change" she's ever made at GM. She explained that her dramatic shift to GM's dress code underlined her philosophical approach to managing the company. She wanted to give individual managers more power and responsibility while also keeping the organization's bureaucratic nature as lean as possible.

According to reports, Barra has a history of this behavior. She reduced the number of required HR reports by 90 percent and cut the employee policy manual down by 80 percent. You can't get away with moves like that unless you're one self-confident leader.

RELIABILITY:
Trust + Stability + Accountability

During the 2004 presidential campaign, Democratic candidate John Kerry got demolished on reliability. His political opponents ran ads highlighting his votes for an $87 billion appropriation for combat in Iraq and Afghanistan.

Kerry had said: "I actually did vote for the $87 billion, before I voted against it." In a stroke of advertising genius, the Bush campaign showed a video of Democrat Kerry windsurfing in Nantucket in opposite directions, back and forth, back and forth. As the video played, the narrator spoke about Kerry's $87 billion flip-flop. The tag line read, "John Kerry. Whichever way the wind blows." Game, set, and match for George W. Bush. His campaign killed Kerry's reliability in thirty seconds flat and gave credibility to the Swift Boat Veterans for Truth ads that hadn't proven to be true.

To be reliable is to be consistent in the face of inconsistency and dependable through times of change and uncertainty. Reliability is not stubborn rigidness or the opposite of flexibility; rather, it means someone is going to remain responsible despite the circumstances. You can count on the person to stay true.

As moderator of ABC's *The View*, Whoopi Goldberg is the personification of reliability. She's progressive, yes, and opinionated, definitely, but she avoids the extremes that have polarized the nation in recent years. When debates on the show get heated, directors switch the camera to Goldberg, who often calms the situation and sends us all on a commercial break to cool down and potentially buy some homeowner's insurance. Then she's there to greet us and reset the tone when the show returns.

In 2007, when Goldberg replaced Rosie O'Donnell as moderator of *The View*, the idea was that Goldberg would bring a more tempered energy to the set. As the *New York Times* had reported, "Goldberg pledged to avoid stoking the drawn-out feuds—whether with the likes of Donald Trump, or Elisabeth Hasselbeck, a fellow panelist—that fueled Ms. O'Donnell's on-camera persona like cans of gasoline. And while she expects that she and her new colleagues will sometimes disagree—about whom to support for president next year or the wisdom of the Iraq war, which Ms. Goldberg has vehemently opposed—she offered assurance that those arguments would never become personal and that there was no place for grudges."

As Goldberg herself said upon taking the job: "Sometimes you get excited, but you move on. You move it forward. You go on to the next thing. You don't harbor any ill will. If you do, you deal with it—afterward."

But Goldberg is human, and she doesn't always deal with things afterward. In July 2018, right on the air, Goldberg got heated with guest Jeanine Pirro, former judge, a conservative news pundit, and current friend of Donald Trump's. Pirro came on *The View* to discuss her new book, *Liars, Leakers, and Liberals: The Case Against the Anti-Trump Conspiracy*. She and Goldberg got into a shouting match. The yelling reportedly continued off-air.

After Goldberg cut to a commercial break during the heated exchange and the show returned, she offered an apology to viewers: "I very rarely lose my cool and I'm not proud of it; I don't like it," she said. "But I also don't like being accused of being hysterical, because that's one of the things I try not to be on this show."

That's why the *Washington Post* has called Goldberg the show's "designated adult." That's reliability.

RELIABILITY Subtrait: Trust

The first subtrait of reliability is to convey trust—to make others trust you will be there for them every time. Consistently getting top grades for trust is Morgan Freeman, the actor we can always trust as our reliable protector.

In 2016, *Time* examined Freeman's voice and its capacity to evoke a sense of competence and authority—qualities we long to trust. Interestingly, the depth and vibrato of his voice is not just a great actor's tool but also resonates with our brains. As *Time* noted: "In scientific experiments, people consistently perceive low-pitched voices in men as stronger and more physically attractive than male voices with a higher pitch." That may be one reason that women in public life face a grueling double standard in coming across as likeable. More on that to come.

In 2010, Morgan Freeman replaced Walter Cronkite as the announcer for the nightly introduction of the *CBS Evening News*. Cronkite himself had anchored the program until 1981 and was so popular based on viewers' trust that he became known as the most trusted man in America. That's the stratospheric standard of trust Freeman had to meet. No doubt CBS considered the data. Freeman came in third in *Forbes*'s 2014 list, behind only Tom Hanks and Carol Burnett.

Like Walter Cronkite, whose assessment helped to sour public opinion against the Vietnam War, Freeman's authoritative yet soothing pitch conjures the image of a man with gravitas who will speak out for what is in the best interest of the public, even if it challenges conventional opinion. And Freeman delivers on this expectation.

Born in 1937 in Tennessee, Freeman has an underdog story everyone loves. He struggled for decades as an actor until becoming a movie star at the ripe age of fifty—an age at which some in Hollywood call it quits.

Freeman has garnered a reputation as a wise elder, a perception based on his having become a public figure only in middle age. By bypassing public scrutiny at the stage when many younger celebrities make career-ending public gaffes, Freeman rose to prominence after having lived a more normal life than most A-list stars. Though we have no reason to question his persona, Freeman emphasizes it by meticulously selecting on-screen roles that present him as our benevolent, moral protector and wise elder statesman.

For example, Freeman played Nelson Mandela in *Invictus* and God in the films *Bruce Almighty* and *Evan Almighty*. In 2016 he asked the big questions in a *National Geographic* television network series, *The Story of God with Morgan Freeman*. A less revered actor would be critically panned for such hubris. Not Freeman. For the three decades he has graced the silver screen, each of the characters he has played offers profound insights to a public seeking reliable counsel. The vessel with which they are brought to life, Morgan Freeman, could sell even the most baseless ideas to an entranced audience.

As director Jon Turteltaub once described it: "Morgan is kind of like a statue you just know is going to be there and know it's going to be solid and know it's going to be beautiful. You don't question if it's going to be beautiful tomorrow or the next day. It's something you can trust. When Morgan Freeman is on screen, you feel safe . . . He's that actor that was a lock that everyone could rely on."

All that said, in May 2018 multiple women came forward accusing Freeman of sexual harassment, inappropriate touching, and generally making them feel on edge, whether on set, at his production company, or while promoting his films. Did Freeman's #MeToo moment affect the perception of his reliability? We'll get to that when we examine the impact of scandals on likeability later in the book.

Suffice it to say, it is possible to endure scandal and emerge as reliable nonetheless. Let's look at an example from the business world. By late 2015, Chipotle Mexican Grill was in trouble. Due to multiple foodborne illness outbreaks—E. coli, norovirus, salmonella—at several store locations, the public simply did not trust the restaurant chain. Sales sank. Share prices dropped.

In early 2018, the company announced that Taco Bell CEO Brian Niccol would replace founder Steve Ells as Chipotle's new leader. Stakeholders hoped, and possibly prayed, that Niccol could revive the brand's likeability.

Almost immediately Niccol began turning things around. In a conference call with investors, he stressed the need to make the Chipotle brand more visible—meaning more advertising. In an interview with CNBC, he said, "Job number one is to remind people why they love Chipotle." As a *Bloomberg* headline put it, "Chipotle's New CEO Is Saying the Right Things."

Sure enough, in September 2018, the burrito chain launched a new ad campaign called "For Real," which highlighted the brand's commitment to using "real food made with real ingredients" by featuring each of Chipotle's fifty-one ingredients, from avocado to oregano to yellow onion. The campaign appeared on television, on billboards, in print, and on social media. The marketing effort went right to the heart of the question potential customers faced when deciding to enter a Chipotle: Am I going to get sick after eating here? The TV spots involved a lot of close-up shots of fresh-looking food being prepared for consumption, and it seemed to work.

About a month after launching its "For Real" campaign, Niccol said the chain had experienced a "noticeable" jump in sales. "Our 'For Real' campaign celebrates what is uniquely Chipotle," Niccol told investors. "Real flavors, real ingredients, and real cooking techniques result in food that simply tastes better."

As 2018 turned into 2019, Chipotle Mexican Grill was one of the best annual performers on the S&P 500. CNN named Niccol CEO of the year. He had rebuilt trust.

RELIABILITY Subtrait: Stability

Dwayne "the Rock" Johnson is stable. Rocks usually are. Notwithstanding being in the public spotlight for over two decades—first as a professional wrestler, then as a movie star—Johnson has lived scandal-free in the public eye.

That's why it seemed odd when, in January 2019, the UK tabloid *Daily Star* quoted Johnson as insulting his fans. According to the publication, Johnson had called today's young people "generation snowflake" and argued they're simply "looking for a reason to be offended."

It turned out the whole thing was fake.

As soon as news began to spread that Johnson thought millennials were a fragile bunch, he jumped on Instagram to set the record straight. "The interview never took place, never happened, never said any of those words, completely untrue, 100 percent fabricated," Johnson said firmly.

Johnson went on: "I've gained such a great trust and equity with all you guys, all around the world over the years, and you know it's not a real D.J. interview if I'm ever insulting a group, a generation, or anyone, because that's not me and that's not who I am and that's not what we do."

The *Daily Star* quickly removed the article from its website without comment.

Clint Eastwood is another icon of stability who temporarily lost this trait during a rambling speech to an empty chair at the 2012 Republican National Convention.

As you might guess, the source of Clint Eastwood's public likeability is the same as that for Morgan Freeman: It's in his voice.

But in Eastwood's case the voice is a fabrication—one he expertly presents to reinforce the perception of steady masculinity and constant strength. As Morgan Freeman himself told *Esquire* magazine back in 2012, "The voice [Eastwood] uses when he's acting is not the voice he uses when he's not . . . He established that voice when he was doing spaghetti westerns with Sergio Leone, and he's used it ever since. People use it when they imitate him because it's the only voice they know. But it only comes out when you mic him up and he's on the set and acting. And then he uses *this* voice and I don't know why . . ." The two men, by the way, are good friends. They've worked together on three films: *Unforgiven* (1992), *Million Dollar Baby* (2004), and *Invictus* (2009).

For many years Eastwood has used his vocal construct to help him play the role of America's perennial tough guy. Whether an outlaw cowboy in *The Good, the Bad, and the Ugly* or the antihero cop in the Dirty Harry series, Eastwood usually embodies a rugged, masculine ideal on screen. But remember: Likeability is a construct rooted in reality.

As a twenty-one-year-old soldier during the Korean War, Eastwood was on a bomber plane that crashed into the ocean just off the coast of Northern California. As the story goes, Eastwood and the pilot were forced to swim through shark-infested waters to safety—undoubtedly requiring high physical skill and grit. He obviously had the gift of stability after his speech at the 2012 Republican Convention that made him a pop-cultural laughingstock. He rode it out by refusing to second-guess himself and continued seamlessly on track with his career.

RELIABILITY Subtrait: Accountability

Far from the silver screen and firmly anchored inside the Beltway, the late Katharine "Kay" Graham, the iconic *Washington Post* publisher, was nothing but accountable to her reporters. Indeed, she not only shielded them from attack but also served as the unbreakable backbone of support for a who's who of Washington leaders.

Graham presided over the *Post* during its most critical and influential time in history. She took the reins of the newspaper in 1963 after the suicide of the publisher, her husband, Philip Graham, and officially served as publisher from 1969 to 1979 and as chairwoman of its board of directors from 1973 to 1991. In 1972 she became the first female CEO of a Fortune 500 company.

As the late Nora Ephron, a popular filmmaker and author, gushed, "The story of her journey from daughter to wife to widow to woman parallels to a surprising degree the history of women in this century."

When Philip was alive, he and Kay lived a charmed life among Washington, D.C.'s upper crust. Their high-powered dinner parties of Washington insiders, which Kay continued after Philip died, never interfered with her journalistic integrity.

As Sally Quinn, a *Post* journalist who was married to the newspaper's legendary executive editor, the late Ben Bradlee, noted, Kay "had all these incredibly powerful and famous friends and people who would put enormous pressure on her, particularly if they had done something wrong, and the Post was relentless about reporting it . . . She would always protect people and stick by the reporters, no matter what."

Throughout her tenure at the *Post*, Graham maintained a fierce loyalty to her reporters, trusting their journalistic impulses and allowing them to report early on some of the most controversial stories of the 1970s. As Walter Cronkite raved, "The publisher has to be the moral force of the newspaper . . . [Graham] carried herself as a queen . . . and she was a queen in her own field."

Graham's accountability impulses were put to the test in 1972 when two young reporters named Bob Woodward and Carl Bernstein brought the Watergate story to then executive editor Ben Bradlee for further investigation. As publisher, Graham could have dismissed the story outright as many others had. Instead, she supported their efforts, and the *Post* began to cover Watergate when hardly any other paper would touch it due to its potential for controversy.

In Pulitzer Prize–winning reporting, Woodward and Bernstein, with Graham's blessing, began to piece together the highest corruption scandal and attempted cover-up in recent U.S. history—one that directly implicated the president of the United States, Richard Nixon, and led to his resignation.

The threats began slowly, and the denials were swift. John N. Mitchell, the attorney general of the United States under President Nixon, reacted to an early story on the scandal with a threat that will live in infamy: "All that crap, you're putting it in the paper? It's all been denied. Katie Graham's gonna get her tit caught in a big fat wringer if that's published. Good Christ! That's the most sickening thing I ever heard."

The sexism continued, and Nixon and his team continued their assault on the *Post* and its reporters. The Committee for the Re-Election of the President, mockingly referred to by the acronym CREEP, got a court to issue five subpoenas to three journalists and two non-journalists.

The subpoena ordered them to testify in CREEP's civil suit and bring with them any evidence related to their reporting on Watergate. The subpoena arrived at the *Post*'s headquarters with Carl Bernstein's name on it. But before CREEP could officially serve Bernstein, his notes were swiftly transferred into Graham's custody.

In recounting the story of their Watergate investigation in their book, *All the President's Men*, Woodward and Bernstein wrote: "Can't you see the pictures of her limousine pulling up to the Women's Detention Center and out gets our gal, going to jail to uphold the First Amendment? That's a picture that would run in every newspaper in the world. There might be a revolution."

During her tenure as publisher of the *Washington Post*, Graham offered her reporters accountability unparalleled among public figures, perhaps unexpected of a woman at the time. She was unyielding about doing what was morally right, even when others disagreed or were too afraid to act. She was the embodiment of the third trait of reliability, accountability, which she achieved time and again with integrity. As Carl Bernstein has said, "I would hope that the head of the institution where I worked would maintain the principles Katharine Graham did even today."

No wonder people of all political stripes in Washington, other than the wrongdoers, could agree on one thing: They liked Katharine Graham.

Beyoncé is similarly reliable. After rising to fame as a member of the R&B girl-group Destiny's Child in the late '90s, she went on to become one of the most successful solo artists of all time. She's won nearly too many awards to count, and appeared on every list of the best, top, most influential people in existence, or so it seems. Whether it's her powerful voice, dancing, fashion, or spirited live performances, Beyoncé sets the pace.

In 2007 she became the first ever non-model and non-athlete to appear on the cover of *Sports Illustrated*'s swimsuit edition. "It takes a lot of guts," Beyoncé told *People* about the photo shoot. "I'm really a shy person. But in my everyday world, as a musical performer, I'm playing a character. I had to tap that same character."

If anything, her confession not only highlighted the construct of likeability at play in her career but also her amazing ability to transform into the Beyoncé character.

In January 2013, however, she found herself in trouble. After singing the national anthem during President Obama's second inauguration, she faced some heavy criticism: People accused her of lip-synching. She later admitted singing over a prerecorded track for reasons related to the venue and the lack of a proper sound check—all too common in the music business.

A few days later, at a news conference for her upcoming performance during the Super Bowl XLVII halftime show, Beyoncé took to the stage and immediately asked all the reporters in attendance to stand. They did, because, as one YouTube commenter put it, "When Beyoncé tells you to stand, YOU STAND."

Suddenly, without any notice or explanation, Beyoncé launched into an a cappella rendition of "The Star-Spangled Banner." And not a single note was out of place. Once the applause died down, Beyoncé asked everyone in the room and any doubters at home: "Any questions?"

That's accountability, Beyoncé-style.

The Defense Industry CEOs
Who Reliably Protect America

When you think of the military-industrial complex, you probably think of men in military uniforms who receive tanks, jets, bombs, and submarines from defense contractors led by businessmen who got the orders done right and on time. And they do it time and again, reliably. If they didn't, we might not know, because we might not be alive to know.

From government and industry, they are powerful men who come together to keep the country safe. In the defense industry, the CEOs of the top five companies are surely worth naming. They are Marillyn Hewson, CEO of Lockheed Martin; Kathy Warden, CEO of Northrop Grumman; Phebe Novakovic, CEO of General Dynamics; and Leanne Caret, CEO of Boeing Defense, Space & Security. The fifth major defense company, Raytheon, is run by Thomas Kennedy. Some bankers on Wall Street reportedly refer to him as "the last man standing."

That's right. The industry responsible for protecting America is led by women. It's a remarkable contrast to the rest of the business world, where just twenty-four companies on the Fortune 500, or 4.8 percent, have women CEOs.

At Lockheed Martin, the world's largest defense contractor, Marillyn Hewson is leading the charge. From the time she became CEO on January 1, 2013, the company's shareholder return has been 309 percent, compared to 107 percent for the S&P 500. And in protecting investors she has also protected the nation. She made sure Lockheed's F-35 fighter jet program, years in development at a cost of $400 billion, saw the light of day. *Chief Executive* magazine named Hewson its 2018 CEO of the Year. Also in 2018, *Harvard Business Review* placed Hewson at #29 on its annual list of Best-Performing CEOs in the World.

The other three women CEOs share Hewson's self-confidence. Northrop Grumman's Kathy Warden said this to the alumni magazine at her alma mater, James Madison University: "One of the most important things for women to remember is to be resilient. There are going to be times when it's tough. Be confident in your ability to contribute. It's what got you there. It's what will make you successful."

The payoff? "For the rest of your life you're willing to take on the things that other people might shy away from," said Warden. "You really build confidence that sustains you in making tough decisions."

In 2015 a defense industry consultant told *Fortune* that General Dynamics had a tougher environment than its rivals, and that under Phebe Novakovic, a former CIA officer who became CEO of the company in January 2013, "consequences for failing to perform are even more immediate than they were in the past."

Indeed, not even a month into her new executive position, Novakovic admitted to investors that in some respects General Dynamics had taken its eye off the ball. But she reassured shareholders that she would be as focused as a "laser beam" when it came to returning value to the company.

Novakovic's pledge to be accountable is working. In 2018, *Barron's* named Novakovic one of its CEO turnaround experts. "She battled to right-size the aerospace and defense contractor and won, sending its financials and stock price skyward," the publication wrote. In other words, she increased efficiency and reduced costs, leaving the company with a better profit margin. General Dynamics' stock, as a result, has vastly improved, outperforming the S&P 500.

At Boeing Defense, Space & Security, Leanne Caret recently beat the competition to win a lucrative $805 million contract with the U.S. Navy to build four drones capable of refueling fighter jets in mid-flight by 2024. And make no mistake about it: Caret is competitive. "At the end of the day I want to be known as a good leader, not only as a good female leader," she wrote in an email to the *Washington Post*. "My goal is to be a role model for men as well as women."

There's no telling how many hurdles these four female CEOs have had to overcome to get to where they are today. "Every one of these incredible women all have experience working in STEM fields [science, technology, engineering, and math] in some facet or another," Karen Panetta, dean of graduate education at Tufts University's School of Engineering, told *Politico* in early 2019. "It trains you to learn how to fail. People don't think about the failure or the disappointment that they've had along the way. It's the distinguishing factor between women that make it versus those that don't."

In other words, to make it as far as they have in their specific field of work, Kathy Warden, Marillyn Hewson, Phebe Novakovic, and Leanne Caret have had to show the utmost traits of protectiveness and reliability. As Yale's Jeffrey Sonnenfeld put it, "Their roles are not ornamental or driven by political correctness, but the culmination of a terrific performance in challenging mainstream career track postings."

But it raises the question: If, through the 2016 election, America could not yet bring itself to elect a woman president—at least in the electoral college—how did these four women rise to the top of a profession vital to America's survival? The answer lies in what Hillary Clinton told the 2016 Democratic National Convention: "The truth is, through all these years of public service, the service part has always come easier to me than the public part."

Indeed, Americans have long embraced women for their service, especially as siblings, moms, and wives, roles for which protectiveness and reliability are vital. In 2013, shortly after taking the reins of Lockheed, Marillyn Hewson wrote in *Politico* how she developed those likeability traits growing up. "I was 9 years old when my father—a strong, vibrant man in his early 40s—died of a heart attack. Suddenly and unexpectedly, [my mother] found herself a single parent of five children, ages 5 through 15, the love of her life gone and the world turned upside down.

"Each of us looked after our younger siblings," Hewson continued. "We cleaned, painted and did odd jobs in the apartment building. Taking on those responsibilities made us stronger, wiser and more self-reliant."

The protectiveness and reliability Hewson was forced to adopt in childhood has carried over to her current job. But as extraordinary as her service to Lockheed and the nation have been, few Americans outside the business world have heard of her or the other three women CEOs. In contrast, practically all of us have heard of Bill Gates, Warren Buffett, and Tim Cook. And therein lies the rub. The sexism in our society rests not in the service part of "public service" but in the public part, and that, no doubt, is what made Hillary Clinton uncomfortable throughout her career.

Americans are fine with giving women the power to protect them, and trust that women can do it reliably. But once women try to step into the spotlight, the sexism rooted in gendered roles in many American homes—less common but surviving nonetheless—takes over. Suddenly protectiveness and reliability in women don't count as much. In the pages ahead, we'll examine the public's double standards of likeability further.

Summary: Protectiveness and Reliability

Perhaps more than any other pair of likeability traits, protectiveness and reliability are interconnected. It's hard to believe someone has your back if he or she is inconsistent. Without consistency, that person can't possibly be vigilant about defending those in danger. Public figures who believe otherwise risk that we'll run away from them forever.

When looking to improve your own protectiveness, don't consider reliability to be an isolated trait that you can work on later.

If you want to present yourself as tough, confront tough people and problems for the sake of those who can't or won't. Don't shy away from the difficult or the dirty, because anyone can do that. And when you take on the challenge, do it with integrity and honesty, because toughness without trust is not a good combination.

As admirable a subtrait as courage is, it rings hollow without stability. If your courage is just as likely to appear as it is to disappear, do you really possess it? Remaining steadfast in the face of uncertainty is a cornerstone of bravery.

If you're willing to be held accountable—that is, ready to explain how you made your decisions and then how you implemented them—you need to show self-confidence. If you have belief in your convictions, stand tall and take it on the chin when things go wrong. Then make amends, clean up the mess, and move on to the next project. Being likeable doesn't mean being perfect. That's impossible. But being confident enough to receive criticism and admit fault is an unmistakable sign of likeability.

CHAPTER 8

The Conscience Traits: Perceptiveness and Compassion

This is it: our final pair of likeability traits. Perceptiveness and compassion are the conscience traits because they get to a public figure's moral core.

Perceptiveness is the ability to detect nuance. It could be a shift in the room, a change in tone in a conversation, or the sudden guardedness when someone else tries to hide a secret hurt. It's about intuition and emotional sensitivity.

Compassion is the willingness to act on perceptiveness through love, kindness, and active care. Together, perceptiveness and compassion shed light on a public figure's feelings for other human beings.

PERCEPTIVENESS:
Fluidity + Curiosity + Humility

Perceptiveness isn't the same as intellect. Perceptiveness is about being able to accurately assess the mood of another person, a room, or a nation and act accordingly. Someone who is perceptive has sensitivity to both his or her own feelings and the feelings of others.

When President Barack Obama sang "Amazing Grace" during the memorial service for those who had died during the tragic shooting in Charleston, his extraordinary powers of perception were on full display. He did exactly the right thing to bring healing to those who were suffering because of yet another catastrophic incident of gun violence.

Perceptiveness is the ability to read between the lines of what people are saying and doing and to understand the intentions behind those words and deeds.

That said, a person who is perceptive doesn't have to agree with the opinions of others or even like them. Perceptive people are far from being sycophantic people pleasers. Rather, they are simply able to recognize others' emotions and factor those in the decision-making process.

At the root of perceptiveness is emotional intelligence (EQ), an idea developed by Peter Salovey, now president of Yale University, and John D. Mayer of the University of New Hampshire (and popularized by *New York Times* science journalist Daniel Goleman in his 1995 book, *Emotional Intelligence: Why It Can Matter More Than IQ*). The concept became part of the national conversation with stunning speed. In a country preoccupied with test taking and aptitude measuring, here was a talent or gift that occupied a central role in human interaction but was virgin territory in terms of exploration, much less quantification. Eventually EQ claimed its rightful position as a coequal to IQ.

In 1990, Salovey and Mayer sought to define "EQ" as a set of skills that allow an individual to identify and regulate feelings in both herself and others while also using those feelings for motivation toward success. Emotional intelligence is about making an accurate appraisal of the situation, then expressing the right emotions at the right time in the right way. In short, EQ allows individuals to be perceptive.

Hollywood's archetype of perceptiveness is Steven Spielberg, an Academy Award–winning director who understands the American audience better than any other filmmaker, past, present, or likely even future. It's as if he has a magic map that tells him which buttons to push to make his audience smile, laugh, cry, gasp, or scream.

Spielberg began his directing career in the early 1970s but garnered significant critical praise following the release of *Jaws* in 1975. Spielberg has directed more than thirty films, many of which are both critically well received and commercially successful—a dream combination for any Hollywood studio. Nine of his films have been nominated for Best Picture at the Academy Awards. On the review aggregation website Rotten Tomatoes, thirty of the thirty-four films he has directed have received overwhelmingly more positive reviews than negative ones.

Spielberg's films range from socially conscious features about American history such as *The Color Purple* and *Lincoln*, to sobering war films such as *Schindler's List* and *Saving Private Ryan*, to thrillers such as *Jaws* and *Raiders of the Lost Ark*, to touching children's classics such as *E.T.* and *War Horse*. Whatever the kind of film he makes, Spielberg excels like no other in his field at drawing in moviegoers of all kinds.

According to the Numbers, a website run by Nash Information

Services to track the business side of Hollywood, Spielberg is the top-grossing director of all time. His movies have brought in more than $4.5 billion dollars, nearly double his closest challengers.

The "Spielberg effect" extends to his close collaborators as well. Harrison Ford and Tom Hanks—two frequent Spielberg film stars—come in first and third for all-time-grossing stars in a leading role. John Williams, a longtime collaborator in scoring Spielberg films, ranks third for individuals in technical roles, a category that also includes producers and casting directors. According to Hanks, Spielberg succeeds, and helps others to do so as well, because he challenges everyone around him to think outside of the box.

Hanks notes: "Steven does this incredible thing when he casts you. He empowers you with the scene. He wants you to come in with ideas that are beyond the page, beyond the text, and even, I think, beyond the purview of your own character . . . And when you do that, Steven becomes giddy . . . Steven [gets] us to say things in so many different permutations and so many different ways . . . [and] even though the camera's out doing a bunch of stuff that's fantastic, he's getting great stuff out of you."

PERCEPTIVENESS Subtrait: Fluidity

By encouraging his actors to participate in the creative process, Spielberg is able to draw out soul-baring performances. He has the first subtrait of perceptiveness I call fluidity, that in which someone is flexible enough to perceive the differentiation among others, or at least the evolution of others, and to go with the flow. Spielberg's fluidity in allowing actors to be their best, on their own terms as well as his, is the key to his perceptiveness. Fluidity, Spielberg proves, is the opposite of rigidity.

Some critics grant his ability to touch our hearts and elicit an emotional response as if on cue, as if he was a master manipulator of human emotions. That's too cynical. Spielberg is a master of perceptiveness, and it stems from his own personal philosophy. He is often quoted saying, "I always like to think of the audience when I am directing, because I am the audience."

Spielberg prefers to make films that will delight his audience rather than satisfy some self-involved, rigid artistic vision. His unsurpassed talent for connecting with the audience also stems from the subjects he chooses to focus on.

Let's look deeper at Tom Hanks, a close confidant of Spielberg's. Ranked the "Most Trustworthy Celebrity" by *Forbes* in 2014, Hanks possesses an unsurpassed knowledge of what the audience wants to see from its stars on the silver screen.

As the ever-dependable everyman in numerous films, Hanks carefully curates his roles to match the kind of person that most men identify with and most women expect to date at some point down the road. In one famous anecdote, while reading the script for the classic film *Sleepless in Seattle*, Hanks challenged director and cowriter Nora Ephron's take on the dynamic between Hanks's character and his son.

The script had originally called for widower Sam—Hanks's role—to take off for a weekend with a woman but had Sam backing out because his son couldn't deal with his dad dating. "This is horseshit," Hanks said he told Ephron. "A man who has not gotten laid in four years and he's got a shot and he's not gonna go because his son doesn't like the girl? I got news for you, that kid's going to the sitter and I'm going off to get laid." Ephron wound up changing the plot device. But, as Hanks noted, "the logic of drama has to be shaped as true human behavior. It has to be logically irrefutable."

Talk about a perceptive insight.

In a post-9/11 America with Donald Trump in the White House, comedian Kumail Nanjiani, who was born and raised in Pakistan, is perceptive enough to know that a number of people, sadly, won't like him because of his accent and skin color. But he's played this to his advantage, working the material into both his stand-up comedy routine and character Dinesh Chugtai on the hit HBO show *Silicon Valley*. In October 2017, during his opening monologue as host of *Saturday Night Live*, Nanjiani cracked several jokes about race, religion, and how spiteful people on the Internet often tell him to go back to India. One example: "Islamophobia is kind of like *Will & Grace*: It was huge a while ago, and then we thought it was gone and done, but now it's back and bigger than ever."

His 2017 semiautobiographical film *The Big Sick*, which Nanjiani stars in and cowrote with his wife, Emily V. Gordon, deals with the ups and downs of intercultural romance. Many critics appreciated its fresh take on the romantic comedy genre, as it received an Academy Award nomination for Best Original Screenplay.

Or how about Martha Stewart? She's perceptive enough to know her clean-cut image has been forever altered due to her five-month stint in prison back in 2004 for charges related to insider trading. Instead of trying to deny or hide that period of her life, Stewart has shown her fluidity by embracing it and using it to her advantage.

In March 2015, for instance, Stewart participated in a comedy roast of pop star Justin Bieber for Comedy Central. Her racy jokes, often at her own expense, blew her uptight image to smithereens.

"Let's get to the reason I'm here tonight," she said, "which is to give Justin Bieber some tips to use when he inevitably ends up in prison. I've been in lockup and you wouldn't last a week, so pay attention. The first thing you'll need is a shank. I made mine out of a pin tail comb and a pack of gum."

Critics loved it. *Time* said "Martha Stewart's Performance at the Justin Bieber Roast Was Worth Celebrating." Stewart's self-perceptiveness, rooted in her willingness to keep her image fluid, promises to add a whole new dimension to her career.

PERCEPTIVENESS Subtrait: Curiosity

If the business world had a Steven Spielberg or a Tom Hanks, unsurpassed in their ability to deliver on what their audiences want to see, it would be Amazon CEO and *Washington Post* owner Jeff Bezos.

Bezos is known to leave an open seat at the conference table during meetings. He assigns this seat to "the most important person in the room," the customer. In his quest to make Amazon the "earth's most customer-centric company," Bezos has brought "The customer is always right" into the digital age.

Former executives brim with stories of Bezos's crusades on behalf of Amazon shoppers, ranging from an extended ordering window for next-day delivery to sturdier boxes to allow for reuse. He is vigilant to avoid web page glitches and out-of-stock products, knowing that customers, too, harbor disdain for these inconveniences. The company now hires specially trained employees, known as "Customer Experience Bar Raisers," whose main role is to deliver on this vision.

According to a customer satisfaction index produced at the University of Michigan, Amazon consistently ranks among the top companies for best customer experience.

Bezos's intense focus on Amazon's more than 100 million Prime members and other customers has led some to criticize his attention to the company's more than 50,000 employees. In 2015 the *New York Times* published an exposé on poor working conditions in Amazon's Seattle headquarters.

As one former Amazon employee recalled in the article, "You walk out of a conference room and you'll see a grown man covering his face . . . Nearly every person I worked with, I saw cry at their desk."

Although Amazon denied the claims, it would soon address them, including by creating a new six-week-paid-leave policy for new parents.

In 2016, *Fortune* ranked Bezos as the World's Greatest Leader—ahead of both Angela Merkel, the chancellor of Germany, and Pope Francis—for his vision at the helm of Amazon, as well as his reimagination of the customer experience at the *Washington Post*, the seminal publication he purchased in 2013.

Under Bezos's leadership, Amazon has also pioneered the use of big data to boost customer satisfaction. For instance, Amazon's recommendation engine, which looks at past customer purchases and searches to determine possible consumer preferences, set the industry standard.

According to Brian Kardon, chief marketing officer for Lattice Engines, Amazon "knows what you put in your shopping cart—what you covet but didn't buy. It knows your product ratings, where you live, what your neighbors buy. If you live in Chicago, Amazon doesn't have to know it's snowing, but they know that your neighbor bought a shovel and eight pounds of salt." Amazon's big-data approach is so successful that it effectively allows the company to read consumers' minds and anticipate prospective future purchases based on just a few clicks of a button.

As mechanical as Bezos's methods may seem, they are rooted in one of the most human qualities among us: curiosity. Bezos's use of data is a manifestation of his curiosity to measure what consumers think and how they act. Curiosity is the second subtrait of perceptiveness.

Bezos's data-driven consumer rapport parallels that which Barack Obama used in his successful presidential campaigns. In politics, perceptiveness by the numbers is known as "microtargeting." Microtargeting allows campaigns to target individual voters, one by one among hundreds of millions of them, based on data showing each voter's consumer preferences. For example, magazine subscriptions tell us a lot about where a voter stands politically. *National Geographic* subscribers have a special interest in the environment. *Guns and Ammo* subscribers, obviously, are likely to oppose gun regulations.

Microtargeting not only demonstrates which candidate a voter leans toward but also which political arguments might get that voter to change his or her mind. In politics as in business, that's how scientific the trait of perceptiveness has become. And it got that way by people being curious.

Healthy curiosity usually leads to creativity, and people often find creative people likeable.

Lin-Manuel Miranda is a case in point. His all-time hit musical *Hamilton*, about Alexander Hamilton, has almost nothing that makes it a formulaic success. Think about the enormous risk Miranda took: The first secretary of the treasury meets hip-hop meets Broadway meets a gloriously diverse cast. You can't dream this stuff up unless you're someone who's open to letting ideas collide no matter how incongruent and unorthodox they may seem at first.

If that wasn't genius, it was going to be one of the most colossal flops in the history of stage or screen. But, yes, it was genius. *Hamilton* received a record-breaking sixteen Tony Award nominations across thirteen categories, resulting in eleven wins, including Best Musical and Best Original Score. And the show is still going strong. During a seven-day period of the 2018 winter holiday season, *Hamilton* grossed more than $4 million—"The first Broadway show ever to make that much money in a single week," according to the *New York Times*.

Sean Bailey, president of production at Walt Disney Studios, which has worked with Miranda on films such as 2016's *Moana* and 2018's *Mary Poppins Returns*, has described Miranda as "intensely curious." Likewise, theater producer Jeffrey Seller, who's worked on *Rent* and *Avenue Q*, and with Miranda on *Hamilton* and *In the Heights*, has said, "[Miranda's] curious mind is something I'm always attracted to."

PERCEPTIVENESS Subtrait: Humility

In the 1992 presidential town hall debate, Bill Clinton didn't just show relatability as he walked toward the woman who asked the candidates whether they understood American suffering. He showed perceptiveness and specifically humility. He listened.

David Mercer, the former deputy finance chair of the Democratic National Committee who worked on the 1992 campaign, said in that one moment Clinton revealed he had a clear "finger on the pulse of the American mood."

Tim Cook is the business world's Bill Clinton of perceptiveness. Becoming CEO of Apple, Cook understood that few jobs in the world are harder than to be the immediate successor to the founder or a long-lasting icon of an organization.

Imagine being Tim Cook and having to follow Steve Jobs, whom consumers not only loved but also viewed as inseparable from the company he had founded. Jobs publicized Apple in a deeply personal way, encouraging the inseparability. Jobs was always the star of his Apple product launches. Who could blame Apple? No one in business had as much credibility among consumers as Steve Jobs. Highlighting him was about more than ego. Faith in Steve Jobs meant faith in Apple, and faith in Apple meant more money for Apple.

Before he formally took the reins of Apple in 2011, Cook, Apple's then COO, delivered a commencement speech at his alma mater, Auburn University, in May 2010.

"As thrilled as I am to be here," Cook said, "I stand before you with a deep sense of humility both because of how I got here and who is here. I am where I am in life because my parents sacrificed more than they should have. Because of teachers, professors, friends, and mentors who cared more than they had to. And because of Steve Jobs and Apple who have provided me the opportunity to engage in truly meaningful work every day for over 12 years."

Tim Cook knew he couldn't become more Steve Jobs than Steve Jobs. Cook's humility was spot-on: America would not have stomached anything else. But Cook was also perceptive enough to know where he could do better than Jobs in a way the nation would accept.

Steve Jobs was not known for being philanthropic. When he died, he had an estimated $8.3 billion fortune, but, as the *New York Times* wrote, "there is no public record of Mr. Jobs giving money to charity. He is not a member of the Giving Pledge, the organization founded by Warren E. Buffett and Bill Gates to persuade the nation's wealthiest families to pledge to give away at least half their fortunes. (He declined to participate, according to people briefed on the matter.) Nor is there a hospital wing or an academic building with his name on it."

Jobs's widow, Laurene Powell Jobs, on the other hand, has given a tremendous amount of money to noble causes. In 2004, for example, about seven years prior to her husband's passing, Laurene founded the Emerson Collective, which provides funding for education, journalism, health, social justice, and the environment. In 2018, the *Washington Post* called Emerson Collective "perhaps the most influential product of Silicon Valley that you've never heard of." That same year she was worth an estimated $20 billion.

Then Cook became CEO of Apple. In 2012 the *New York Post* reported that Apple gave away $100 million, including $50 million to Stanford University hospitals and $50 million to the African aid organization Product Red, cofounded by U2 frontman Bono.

"You see a real difference under Tim Cook," Stacy Palmer, editor of the *Chronicle of Philanthropy*, told the *Post*. "He has talked more openly about charitable giving by Apple. It sounds like a changed attitude."

In 2012, the *Verge* reported that Cook had recently spent a good deal of time focusing on Apple's charitable contributions and, within weeks of taking the CEO position, instituted a charitable corporate-matching program for Apple employees of up to $10,000 per year. Cook's perceptiveness, realizing that no one could assail him for his philanthropy, has gone hand in hand with his compassion.

Unlike Tim Cook, Dara Khosrowshahi was taking over a broken company when he became CEO of Uber in August 2017. The ride service had earned a terrible reputation for reasons that ranged from dirty business tactics against competitors to underpaying drivers to sexual harassment claims in the workplace. Things were not looking good.

Right off the bat, the *Wall Street Journal* reported that people close to Khosrowshahi described him as a "humble personality at ease with the mounting responsibilities placed on him over the course of his career." Sure enough, he quickly demonstrated his humility at Uber.

In May 2018 the company launched a new ad campaign called "Moving Forward" with Khosrowshahi front and center. "Since joining nine months ago, my priority has been to listen to you—to cities and communities and to my own employees," Khosrowshahi said in the national TV spot. Like Bill Clinton, he knew to listen. Khosrowshahi continues: "I've seen a lot of good. We've changed the way people get around. We've provided new opportunities. But moving forward, it's time to move in a new direction."

And with that, Uber matured into a company more perceptive about its place in the world.

Similarly, Microsoft CEO Satya Nadella has also turned to humility to help his company reach new heights. In his autobiography, *Hit Refresh: The Quest to Rediscover Microsoft's Soul and Imagine a Better Future for Everyone*, Nadella advises all of us take a step back, realize we don't know everything, and evaluate what's going on. Can we as a society find a way to live in peace and harmony as technology, such as artificial intelligence, continues to grow and expand? Can we learn to practice empathy in a meaningful way that steers companies and guides our future? These questions, Nadella argues, need asking. Constantly.

As CEO, Nadella has encouraged his employees and others to adopt a "learn-it-all" attitude as opposed to being a "know-it-all." That's a succinct way of defining the subtrait of humility.

In September 2017, *Fast Company* reported that Microsoft under Nadella "generated more than $250 billion in market value in just three and a half years—more value growth over that time than Uber and Airbnb, Netflix and Spotify, Snapchat and WeWork. Indeed, more than all of them combined."

A *Fortune* headline from early 2019 reads, "How Microsoft CEO Satya Nadella Fueled a Humble Comeback." Perhaps it would be more accurate to say, "How Microsoft CEO Satya Nadella's Humility Fueled a Not-at-All-Humble Comeback."

COMPASSION:
Sympathy + Warmth + Activism

Although perceptiveness is critical to a positive public persona, being able to translate those skills into a compassionate response is equally important in determining overall likeability.

Unlike perceptiveness, compassion involves the ethical impulse to get involved, as opposed to merely being aware of someone's internal state. Compassion is a desire to end suffering and strife wherever it may exist by promoting justice and equality. Compassion is about freeing the oppressed and noticing the unnoticed.

These days there's no shortage of public figures who stake their likeability on compassion, and no shortage of companies seeking to market compassion for consumer consumption. During the 2015 Super Bowl, both McDonald's and Coca-Cola ran advertising campaigns focused on the virtues of compassion. In the McDonald's ad, a friendly cashier tells a customer to "dial up your mom, tell her you love her" as payment for the food.

For the weeks that followed, McDonald's employees selected random customers to pay for their purchases with compassionate acts, like a hug or a compliment. In the Coca-Cola ad, the company urged individuals to be nicer to each other because "the world is what we make it," so naturally we should strive to "#MakeItHappy."

Compassion is such a potent force in enhancing likeability, it even has a daylong extravaganza to put the trait on display. If award shows are equivalent to the Super Bowls of likeability, then the Global Citizen Festival provides the same service for compassion.

Hosted annually since 2012 by the Global Poverty Project, an Australian NGO, the event raises awareness of efforts to end extreme poverty by 2030. Although tickets are free through a raffle, the event is so popular that secondary sales of tickets for the 2015 show sold on average for well over $1,000.

Over the years, the festival has become a who's who for public personalities and an ideal venue for public figures to display their charitable sides. Stars such as Beyoncé, Leonardo DiCaprio, Stephen Colbert, Coldplay, and Hugh Jackman, and large corporations like

Comcast, Citi, YouTube, Google, H&M, and T-Mobile all line up annually to get a piece of the action.

To be sure, several business leaders have made their mark as avatars of compassion, starting with Bill and Melinda Gates. At the Bill & Melinda Gates Foundation, a team of tireless advocates and experts, led by the hands-on management of one of the richest couples on the planet, works with a seemingly bottomless well of financial support to tackle some of the greatest health and development challenges of our time.

Bill and Melinda Gates's interest in helping the less fortunate is rooted in genuine compassion. As Bill Gates noted in a 2013 article in the *Telegraph*, "Money has no utility to me beyond a certain point. Its utility is entirely in building an organization and getting the resources out to the poorest in the world."

And the Gates Foundation has made good on this statement. Bill Gates's lifetime donations total over $29 billion. In 2014, the foundation made a single $50 million gift to aid in the fight against Ebola in West Africa. Most recently the foundation pledged $80 million to close the "data gap" between men and women around the world.

The Gateses have brought their wealthy friends along for the ride. Bill Gates's famous best friend and a Gates Foundation trustee, Warren Buffett, is the second most generous man in the world, with lifetime donations totaling $21.5 billion. In 2006, Buffett pledged to donate 85 percent of his net worth to a number of foundations. In 2013 he gave away $2.6 billion; in 2014 he donated $2.8 billion; and in 2015 he beat his personal best with donations totaling $2.84 billion.

Of the Giving Pledge, founded by the Gateses and Warren Buffett, Marc Benioff, the cofounder of Salesforce.com, noted in 2012: "It is terrific as long as we see an increase in philanthropic projects. It has been two years; what are the 10 or 20 major projects that come out of it? This can't just be a bunch of money going into trusts. It could end up being a bunch of air cover for people who don't want to give away their money."

With a net worth of $6.5 billion, Benioff, a less outrageously wealthy but still equally compassionate CEO, is no stranger to charitable giving. "To be truly successful," he said, "companies need to have a corporate mission that is bigger than making a profit."

At Salesforce, Benioff has done just that. He pioneered the 1–1–1 system, in which one percent of employee hours, equity, and products are donated to charity. The goal of this system is to integrate philanthropic causes into the business culture at Salesforce. It has made him not only loved by his employees but also admired throughout the Bay Area, across which numerous nonprofit institutions have received hundreds of millions in donations from both Salesforce and Benioff personally.

More recently, in 2018, Benioff bought *Time* magazine for $190 million in cash. "I value journalists," Benioff said of his decision to buy the iconic publication. "I value photographers. I value the artists. I actually think that they are the ones that are going to get us through this, not the technologists."

Benioff, in other words, views *Time* as a platform for change, a vehicle for having a positive impact on the world. That's why it was worth protecting.

As for whether he would have a hand in actively managing what the magazine covered and didn't, Benioff said he wouldn't. "I'm not going to be operationally involved at all. I've already met with the management team and told them that. I want them to be unshackled . . . I want those editors and writers and photographers and visionaries to be free. And to really help us and guide us."

Overall, Benioff shows his compassion by preaching the virtues of mindfulness and supporting policies to tackle homelessness. He clearly cares about the people around him, and makes it known.

In presidential politics, perceptiveness and compassion play a critical role. The task for any Democratic nominee is to neutralize the Republicans' typical likeability advantages of protectiveness and reliability—the clincher traits. To do so, Democrats must up their game in communicating those qualities or emphasize the Republicans' lack of them.

Much of the Democrats' advantage in compassion is attributable to the party's historic leadership not only on women's rights but also in championing domestic issues such as education and health that typically resonate more strongly with women. In contrast, protectiveness issues such as national security resonate more strongly with men.

In 1984 the legendary feminist Eleanor Smeal coined the term "gender gap" for the difference in voting patterns between women and men. In a phenomenon we take for granted today, Smeal described how a higher percentage of women, versus the percentage of men, usually vote for Democrats in general elections. But, in fact, the gender gap long predated 1984.

The gender gap has its roots as a compassion gap between the parties, starting with Franklin Roosevelt's New Deal of the 1930s, which did right by the labor movement and seniors. The next several Democratic presidents did right by women, people of color, and LGBTQ people. Especially salient were the Civil Rights Act of 1964 and the Voting Rights Act of 1965, engineered by President Lyndon B. Johnson and civil rights leaders of the time, building on what President Kennedy had begun. Five decades later President Obama would lead the way in repealing "Don't Ask, Don't Tell" and along with Vice President Biden, advocating fiercely for marriage equality.

In several presidential elections the Republicans managed to close the gender gap, but the burden has been the Republicans' to bear. By no accident the Republicans who have won the presidency in recent years have pointedly made compassion a centerpiece of their fall campaigns.

Ronald Reagan promised seniors he'd never be so heartless as to hurt their Social Security or Medicare because he was one of them—mixing compassion and relatability. The first George Bush highlighted his admiration of community organizations as the backbone of the American spirit in which volunteers help the most vulnerable—organizations he called "a thousand points of light."

From his earliest days campaigning, the second George Bush coined the phrase "compassionate conservative" as a central message of his candidacy. It didn't matter that few voters seemed to understand the specifics of "compassionate conservatism," because George W. Bush didn't much care to present them in depth. The reason voters believed him was because he came across with warmth, the third trait of compassion, especially in contrast to the seemingly smarter but stiffer Al Gore. Gore's policies may have been more compassionate than Bush's, but voters were paying more attention to the candidates' demeanor.

And remember: Perceptiveness isn't equal to intelligence. Neither Ronald Reagan nor George W. Bush could count themselves as the intellectual forebears of Barack Obama, former president of the *Harvard Law Review* and constitutional law professor at the University of Chicago.

But progressives who dripped with condescension about the intellect of Reagan or Bush did so foolishly. Both men had enough emotional intelligence to know what made voters beam with excitement or tick with anger.

COMPASSION Subtrait: Sympathy

Sympathy, the subtrait most endemic to compassion, is feeling for others in situations different from yours. Empathy is the ability to put yourself in their shoes, either because you've lived their experience or your heart runs so deep, it goes beyond detached compassion.

In the spring of 2015, Dan Price, the cofounder and CEO of a Seattle credit card processing company called Gravity Payments, was all the rage—at least in the business pages. Price had announced that over the next three years every one of his 120 employees was going to be earning no less than $70,000 per year and that he was willing to decrease his own salary of roughly $1 million to cover the increased cost. At the time the average salary at Gravity Payments amounted to $48,000 per year.

Price became an overnight sensation. Liberals loved him. Conservatives called him a socialist. Résumés poured in. Every media outlet wanted a piece of him to ask what had led to such a drastic decision. Was it just a PR stunt?

"It's not about making money," Price told Hoda Kotb during an interview on the *Today* show. "It's about making a difference."

In a more detailed version of Price's path to a $70,000 minimum wage, he says that one day in late 2011 a thirty-two-year-old phone tech earning $35,000 per year confronted him. "You're ripping me off," the employee told his boss. "You brag about how financially disciplined you are, but that just translates into me not making enough money to lead a decent life."

Price was taken aback. For three days he discussed the encounter with friends and family. He "felt horrible." Ultimately, Price decided to do something with his feelings.

COMPASSION Subtrait: Warmth

Warmth is like pornography: We all know it when we see it. That's probably not the most appropriate metaphor for talking about a subtrait of compassion, but you get it. Warmth usually involves a smile, a slight touch on the arm, and a kind, welcome openness in the eyes. It's the demeanor that communicates our humanness to one another.

Remember when, in April 2017, a United Airlines passenger was forcibly removed from his seat and footage of the man being dragged down the aisle, broken and bleeding, was seen by practically everyone with a connection to the World Wide Web? Things went further south for United when CEO Oscar Munoz released a statement apologizing for having to "re-accommodate" the customer. The response came across as formal, insensitive, and tone-deaf. Twitter had a field day.

Who, on the other hand, knows how to demonstrate warmth? Taylor Swift.

At the young age of fourteen, Swift and her family moved to Nashville, where she began her career as a country music singer. Since then, well, she's become one of the best-selling artists of all time. Some of that, of course, is due to Swift's singing and songwriting abilities. But some of it also stems from her ability to come across as every fan's best friend.

In the music video for 2009's "You Belong with Me"—one of Swift's earlier hit songs—she's depicted as a nerdy high school girl with glasses who longs for the handsome football hero who lives next door. In reference to her secret crush's current girlfriend, the song's lyrics go: "She wears high heels, I wear sneakers / She's cheer captain and I'm on the bleachers."

In 2013, *Vanity Fair* described Swift's persona as follows: "Swift cultivates a gawky adorability in her music videos, in which she often plays the unloved girl alone in her room pining over the cute guy."

Later the article reads: "Swift is a brand. She's been called 'America's Sweetheart': She rarely drinks, doesn't smoke, go clubbing, or get arrested—she's the anti-Lohan, and this squeaky-clean image has made her an attractive advertising partner for Target, Sony, Cover-Girl, Keds, Elizabeth Arden, and, recently, Diet Coke."

In 2014, BuzzFeed published an article titled "23 Times Taylor Swift Was So Adorably Awkward You Wished She Was Your BFF." The list contains GIFs and images of Swift dancing badly at award shows, acting silly in music videos, fooling around on her Instagram account, and making funny faces during interviews.

Like Miley Cyrus and other young celebrities, Swift has been trying to change her image. In the 2017 video for "Look What You Made Me Do," Swift says, "I'm sorry, the old Taylor can't come to the phone right now. Why? Oh, 'cause she's dead." That line is nearly identical to Miley Cyrus's from a couple of years before. And Swift, like Cyrus, will need to evolve yet stick with the basis of her success. For Swift, it will always be about warmth. That's how she's amassed 83 million followers on Twitter and 115 million on Instagram, ranking her at #5 and #8 respectively among thousands of entertainers.

Among men in music, few others come across as warm as singer-songwriter Ed Sheeran. News organizations love to make feel-good lists about him. From MTV: "17 Times Ed Sheeran Made Us Laugh Until We Cried." Another from BuzzFeed: "14 Times Ed Sheeran Was Literally the Nicest Man in Show Business." The latter contains moments of Sheeran visiting a fan in the hospital, helping a man propose to his girlfriend who's battling brain cancer, and crashing a wedding and becoming the wedding singer.

During a 2015 appearance on *Sesame Street*, Sheeran sang a song with Elmo, Abby, Grover, and Cookie Monster about being obedient in school. Sheeran looked genuinely happy. According to *Billboard*,

Sheeran's appearance was "just as sweet as you thought it would be (that is: really, really)." Two "reallys"? You get that from the subtrait of warmth.

COMPASSION Subtrait: Activism

In the early 2000s, Angelina Jolie had public relations disasters that descended like the plagues: first, with a whirlwind marriage to Billy Bob Thornton, after which she wore a vial of his blood around her neck in an awkward statement of affection. Then she became the home-wrecker to a relationship between America's sweethearts, Jennifer Aniston and Brad Pitt.

Today she is a role model for celebrities who travel the world trying to do good, serving as a United Nations High Commissioner for Refugees Goodwill Ambassador, then as a special envoy to the United Nations High Commissioner for Refugees advocating for refugees in areas of conflict.

In that capacity, Jolie has visited the war-ravaged nations of Sudan, Chad, Libya, and Afghanistan, among others. Her focus on displaced persons has sent her to a range of other countries as well, including Cambodia, Iraq, and Syria. Jolie embodies the second subtrait of compassion: activism.

The press follows her on her adventures as an advocate, and *Time* named her "Humanitarian of the Year" in 2014 in recognition of her efforts. Although the positive press might be an added benefit to craft her image, the coverage also draws attention to regions of the world and bloody conflicts that often go unnoticed in the 24/7 news cycle. Jolie's star power helps to bring these tragic stories into the fold. Jolie and her ex-husband Brad Pitt also put their money where their mouths are: In 2006, the couple donated more than $8 million to a range of important causes.

Is Jolie's dedication to activism a construct? Here's my answer: Who cares? She has chosen a route to likeability—compassion—that has helped countless others. Whether or not her philanthropy and social activism are constructs, she has made a difference in the world. She deserves to be acknowledged for her contributions, financial and otherwise, to these causes.

In the corporate world, few other companies are as active for the public good as Patagonia. In 2018, CEO Rose Marcario announced that the company was giving the $10 million it saved from the federal government's "irresponsible tax cut" back to nature. In other words, the money would go to nonprofit environmental groups "committed to protecting air, land and water and finding solutions to the climate crisis." In the grand scheme of things, Marcario wrote in a statement, "our home planet needs it more than we do."

People around the Internet thanked Marcario and cheered her decision to act as though the planet matters more than profits. Marcario became a corporate hero.

When Perceptiveness and Compassion Come Together: The Reverend Dr. Martin Luther King Jr. and Theodora Lacey

Theodora Lacey was a confidante of the Reverend Dr. Martin Luther King Jr. during the civil rights movement of the 1950s and '60s. She and I live in the same town of Teaneck, New Jersey, to which I moved from New York City in 2004. We were brought together by a woman we both love, state Senator Loretta Weinberg, who also lives in Teaneck. It's quite a town, as I'll tell you about in a moment.

Lacey grew up in Montgomery, Alabama, and was Dr. King's lieutenant in organizing the Montgomery bus boycott of December 1955 through December 1956, a turning point in the African-American civil rights movement. Afterward she and her husband, Archie, moved north to Manhattan. Then, in January 1962, they moved five miles away to Teaneck.

By then Dr. King had baptized two of their four children. Archie went on to become the first African-American male professor to receive tenure at Hunter College in Manhattan. He also served as chair of the department of education at Lehman College in the Bronx. Meanwhile, Theodora Lacey became a science teacher at Teaneck's Thomas Jefferson High School.

In 1964 the Laceys successfully led the grassroots campaign that made Teaneck the first municipality in America to come up voluntarily with a plan to integrate its schools. It came ten years after *Brown v. Board of Education*, the U.S. Supreme Court decision that declared school segregation to be unconstitutional.

However, integration didn't follow instantly. Officials across the country had to pressure school districts to do the right thing. But Teaneck created and implemented a school integration plan on its own. Today my town remains a loving model of diversity. People don't move to Teaneck just to own a piece of property. We also move to Teaneck to own a piece of history.

After I told Lacey about this book, I asked her: "Of all eight likeability traits in my paradigm, which two stick out to you as the pair that made Dr. King the extraordinary leader he was?"

I bet nearly all of you, like me, would have guessed it was captivation and hope. After all, hope was the message behind Dr. King's "I Have a Dream" speech at the Lincoln Memorial in 1963. And although he wrote other speeches and treatises equally as captivating, "I Have A Dream" comes to most of our minds first when we think of him.

But Lacey didn't answer with captivation or hope.

"When Dr. King first came to Dexter [Alabama]," she told me, "word spread quickly that he was an outstanding speaker. His sermons were something else. And he was only twenty-seven. But off the pulpit and behind the scenes, he was laid-back and worked to be one voice among many. He focused on giving praise to others and made sure they got their due whenever there was a good idea or good result. He was so generous. He made you not only feel good about the cause but also about yourself. He made you want to *be* better. He made you want to *do* better."

Lacey was talking about Dr. King's perceptiveness and compassion. You may think: Why, of course he had those traits! But I didn't make that assumption as much as I had wanted to. Larger-than-life figures who preach compassion with soaring public oratory don't necessarily have the humility to be perceptive or compassionate in real life.

Lacey described Dr. King as one of the humblest people you could ever meet. He was the kind of person, she said, who would stand in the back of the church and always have something kind and specific to say as you were leaving. He said something unique to each person and about that person. He was a natural at making people feel comfortable, and he listened to *every single word* someone had to say.

"For any of us who worked with him behind the scenes," Lacey said, "he was so perceptive as to each person's needs. Of course he gave us hope. But to know him beyond a public figure was to know how warm and perceptive he was toward other people. I believe *that*, with hope, was the key to his building a movement."

Remember, all this comes from someone who knew the Reverend Dr. Martin Luther King Jr. personally and wasn't influenced by worldwide fame. And Dr. King stayed perceptive to the needs of the moment even when others would have lost their cool. That included the time racists bombed his house in 1956, endangering the life of his wife and eldest daughter, who were both home at the time.

As word of the bombing spread, a crowd of Dr. King's supporters gathered around his house, eager for the command to deliver retribution. However, instead of fueling their justified rage, Dr. King said: "Don't get panicky. Don't do anything panicky at all. Don't get your weapons. He who lives by the sword will perish by the sword. Remember that is what God said. We are not advocating violence. We want to love our enemies. I want you to love our enemies. Be good to them. Love them and let them know you love them . . ."

Dr. King perceived the right path that few others in his shoes might have.

In more recent years researchers at the Yale Center for Emotional Intelligence have praised Dr. King not just for the content of his many famous speeches but also for the clear emotional intelligence contained within them. On his iconic "I Have a Dream" speech, they write: "In naming and harnessing his own emotions, in expressing them with such powerful eloquence, in connecting strongly with the emotions of his listeners, and in convincing them to empathize with others, Dr. King demonstrated emotional intelligence decades before the concept had a name."

Summary: Perceptiveness and Compassion

Perceptiveness and compassion seal the deal of likeability. Without them it's impossible to like someone else entirely. The Reverend Dr. Martin Luther King Jr. wouldn't have achieved all he did in his short life without perceptiveness and compassion. How many would have been willing to march alongside him in the name of nonviolence if he didn't understand them? Who among us can feel good about associating with anyone who lacks perceptiveness and compassion?

To maximize your perceptiveness, give yourself the gift of fluidity. That doesn't mean you shouldn't stand by your convictions. But fluidity does require you to react appropriately to shifts around you. It's one part observation, another part improvisation.

To be fluid, you have to possess a sense of curiosity, which comes from having an open interest in the world. How does this work? Who's that guy over there? Why don't we try doing this instead of that and see what happens? To be curious, in turn, means you have to be humble. Admit you don't know everything. Be open to experiments failing and to learning something better. And credit others for having better ideas. They will only like you more.

To be compassionate, demonstrate compassion. Sympathy requires you to express it, not just feel it. When you do express it, be specific and never let awkwardness for the other person's situation inhibit your warmth. Ideally, compassion should culminate in action. People remember words that made them feel better. But their deeper gratitude will come from actions that reduced their pain.

CHAPTER 9

Public Prejudice and the Perception of Likeability

Each of us views the likeability of others through a prism unlike anyone else's in the world. Our respective likeability prisms are shaped by attributes with which we were born, such as our gender, race, sexual orientation, gender identity, and abilities or disabilities. Many of us know parents who tried to raise their children free of gender stereotypes, only to be astonished that their daughters gravitated to Barbie and their sons to G.I. Joe anyway.

Our likeability prisms are also shaped by life experiences. Prominent among them are the dynamics of our childhood and adulthood families. Then comes religion or its absence, inculcated in each of us since birth by our families and influenced by our own experiences as we age. From there, add ethnicity, education, language, politics, jobs, health, places of residences, and encounters with government and discrimination. Because those experiences are ever changing, each of our likeability prisms is also shaped by the trends in our lives and in the lives of our loved ones.

In short, nature and nurture work together to craft the likeability prism of every human being. Part of nature's influence happens to be idiosyncratic. Who knows why, for example, some of us like orange more than green or vice versa?

When we consider the polarization that plagues our nation and the rest of the world, we can chalk it up to the differences among our likeability prisms. I'd bet the ranch you've distanced yourself from at least one person over the last couple of years, on social media if not beyond, because the person likes or dislikes Donald Trump in the way you do not.

I've been a public figure on the receiving end of Americans' discordant likeability prisms. When President Trump was inaugurated, I was the executive director of the Anne Frank Center for Mutual Respect, the U.S. organization among Anne Frank organizations worldwide. When I took the job, I implemented an expansion in the U.S. organization's mission to include grassroots advocacy aimed at preventing a repeat of history's horrors.

Suddenly I had a platform to take on the Trump administration. I also had a chance to apply to social media the techniques I had developed as Senator Lautenberg's communications director in the late 1990s. To that end I wrote all the Anne Frank Center's tweets and Facebook posts. My mission was to write the boldest, most memorable commentary in social media and for every tweet or Facebook post to induce an emotional reaction, no matter who the reader was. Starting with captivation, I had the eight traits of likeability in mind.

Within months the Anne Frank Center's Facebook likes and Twitter followers jumped from a combined 6,600 to more than 200,000. Among the national profiles that began piling up, the *Forward* ran one that called me "Donald Trump's latest nemesis." I was showered daily with praise from progressives.

Lest you think I got a swollen head, along with the kudos came kicks in the shins. Every week in the media, and in emails and snail mails to our national headquarters, Trump supporters characterized me as evil. I received five death threats, and they scared me.

The hatred was based on one perception about me that some in Trump's base had invented. I'm referring to politically conservative Jewish voters. Keep in mind, the overwhelming majority of American Jews are Democrats, so I was hearing from a minority in my religion. Within that bloc, some individuals branded me as anti-Israel because I was anti-Trump, whom they perceived to be good for Israel. Fact is, my detractors didn't have a clue as to what I stood for. Remember, I'm the guy whom the European edition of the *Wall Street Journal* once described as having "a track record of support for Israeli causes."

The death threats aside, I didn't attribute the distorted views of me to malice. When my detractors focused their likeability prisms on me, their prisms had kaleidoscopic overlays based on life experiences. The result was a massive and unsupported leap in logic from my being anti-Trump to being anti-Israel.

But in too many other cases, distortions of likeability prisms are indisputably nefarious, based on sexism, racism, religious hatred, homophobia, transphobia, and other forms of prejudice. Prejudice is rooted in the likeability prism. A prejudiced person believes you are less likeable because of his or her preconceptions based on your sex or race or other characteristics, but not, as the Reverend Dr. Martin Luther King Jr. said, on the content of your character.

How real is the impact of prejudice on likeability? The fairest analysis requires us to examine how society views the likeability of public figures from disempowered communities and draws a contrast with how society views the likeability of other public figures in similar circumstances. Join me now as I contrast public figures who are African-American, women, and LGBTQ with their well-known counterparts.

Alec Baldwin, Brett Kavanaugh, and Double Standards for African-Americans

Could there be a public figure whose career has survived more publicly reported instances of rage than Alec Baldwin?

In 1995, Baldwin allegedly punched a cameraman in the nose for trying to film Baldwin with his then wife Kim Basinger and their newborn daughter outside their home in Los Angeles.

In 2007 he left an infamous voice mail to his then eleven-year-old daughter calling her a "rude little pig," among other insults and offensive language.

In 2011 he was kicked off an American Airlines flight in Los Angeles for refusing to stop playing Words with Friends on his smartphone as he waited for the plane to take off. When asked to turn off his electronic device, he became belligerent and was thrown off the plane.

In 2012 he had a couple more altercations with news photographers. He punched one and ended up calling another a "little girl." The "little girl" was a man.

In 2013, Baldwin chased a photographer outside his Manhattan apartment and called the man a "c**ksucking f*g."

In November 2018, Baldwin was arrested for assault and harassment for supposedly hitting a man in the face over a parking dispute outside his home in New York City.

The tantrums show remarkable diversity. They include bouts not only with paparazzi, but also with others who don't seek to exploit celebrities at all. But Baldwin—praised for his role as Jack Donaghy on the NBC sitcom *30 Rock* and as Donald Trump on *Saturday Night Live*—remains likeable to a remarkable number of people. He wins Emmys and Golden Globes, appears in movies such as *The Boss Baby* and *Mission: Impossible*, and gets to host television shows such as the prime-time revival of *Match Game*.

Baldwin gets the benefit of the doubt again and again. He even gets to craft his own construct of likeability to distract from his public bouts of rage. That's what his impression of Donald Trump is, aside from being uproariously funny to progressives. Yes, the same progressives who would have otherwise written off Baldwin for his rage years ago.

Lest anyone think Baldwin might be tired of playing Trump, the impression has been the ultimate likeability rescue of Baldwin's career. The actor's real-life rage, which should have destroyed his relatability, protectiveness, reliability, and compassion long ago, has been rescued from the trash heap by the president he hates. Baldwin owes a lot to Donald Trump.

Now imagine if Baldwin were African-American. How would he be able to escape the Angry Black Man label so many African-American males have had to work overtime to avoid? Hint: He wouldn't. His popularity and career opportunities would be zero.

Compare Baldwin with another president, Barack Obama. Even when he faced criticism inextricably mixed with racism, Barack Obama conducted his presidency to avoid coming across as an Angry Black Man. Many of us said to ourselves: How could he not scream in frustration?

At the 2015 White House Correspondents' Association dinner, the guests included Luther, played by Keegan-Michael Key from Comedy Central, as President Obama's so-called anger translator. As Obama delivered his speech at the podium in his typically calm manner, Key stood by Obama's side expressing Obama's inner thoughts to the public in a way Obama never could.

Obama began his speech with this boilerplate: "In our fast-changing world, traditions like the White House Correspondents' dinner are important." Then Key, as Luther, immediately screamed: "I mean, really! What is this dinner? And why am I required to come to it? Jeb Bush, do you really want to do this?!"

Next, Obama: "Because despite our differences, we count on the press to shed light on the most important issues of the day." Then Luther: "And we can count on Fox News to terrify old white people with some nonsense!"

You get the point. Obama, an African-American man, isn't allowed to be authentic. Unlike Alec Baldwin, Obama can't expect forgiveness or ambivalent shrugs for acting out and showing his true feelings. That's the double standard.

For five years Donald Trump attacked Obama with the birther lie that Obama was born in Kenya, not the United States, and therefore was not a constitutionally legitimate president. When Trump admitted, in September 2016, that Obama had been born in the United States, imagine how much Obama wanted to scream.

But Obama didn't. He survived all those years of birther lies by making light of them, often with jokes. Most of the rest of us would have blown a gasket if we were him. Perhaps Obama did behind closed doors. Either way, he had to exercise extreme perceptiveness, aware that the slightest hint of anger would unleash the Angry Black Man stereotype upon him.

Consider this: *USA Today* once stated that Kenneth Chenault, CEO and chairman of American Express from 2001 to 2018, "built his career around being honest and likable." In the article, Chenault says of himself: "Frankly, you can't be a jerk and be successful in the service business for a long period of time. When you're in the service business, reputation is everything. Sometimes when you're very successful, you become arrogant, and what I've tried to instill is a very strong sense of customer needs, respect for your colleagues."

Fair enough. But why did Chenault, an African-American, have to worry about coming across as likeable when many of his peers in the brutal financial industry have not?

Whether on Wall Street, in Hollywood, or in Washington, other leaders don't give a damn about coming across as likeable so long as they come across as convincing and even feared. When Brett Kavanaugh testified before Congress in 2018 as a nominee to the U.S. Supreme Court, he didn't need an anger translator to express his feelings. He responded to Dr. Christine Blasey Ford's allegations of attempted rape with the kind of uncontrolled rage you could imagine coming from a rapist.

Kavanaugh's frightening lack of self-control stood in contrast to the poise and restraint that Dr. Blasey Ford showed during her testimony. The *New Republic* defined Kavanaugh's strategy as follows: "Be mad as hell." When Senator Amy Klobuchar of Minnesota asked Kavanaugh during the hearing if he had ever drank so much that he couldn't remember what he said or did the night before, he stumbled and then snapped: "I don't know, have you?"

Kavanaugh later put on a show of remorse for his conduct. He wrote an opinion piece for the *Wall Street Journal* titled "I Am an Independent, Impartial Judge" in which he admitted that he "might have been too emotional at times" at his confirmation hearings and that he "said a few things [he] should not have said."

But after embarrassing himself with public rage that America had never seen from a Supreme Court nominee—not even from Clarence

Thomas twenty-eight years earlier—Kavanaugh still prevailed. He was confirmed to the U.S. Supreme Court for life.

A cushy job for life is not the expectation of young black men whom police target for Living While Black. African-American males accounted for 22 percent of all people fatally shot by police in 2017 yet comprised just 6 percent of the total population. Researchers at the University of Washington and Cornell University found that "the risk of being killed by police, relative to white men, is 3.2 to 3.5 times higher for black men, and between 1.4 and 1.7 times higher for Latino men."

If white men were killed at a disproportionately higher rate, and white people marched in the streets bringing attention to the issue, they would be seen as protective. Never would they be called radicals seeking to undermine social order, as the backlash against Black Lives Matter has characterized the movement. Besides, what kind of social order prioritizes the survival of some over others?

White people are allowed to be authentic in their anger, but people of color aren't. When Alec Baldwin gets upset because someone stole his parking spot, or when Brett Kavanaugh gets mad that someone would dare to question his assumed right to get a seat on the highest court in the land, millions of Americans can sympathize with their plight. When black people want police officers to stop killing them at higher rates than average, they're out of line and should get their priorities straight.

NFL quarterback Colin Kaepernick had the courage to challenge the double standards. "I am not going to stand up to show pride in a flag for a country that oppresses black people and people of color," Kaepernick told the media near the beginning of his quiet, peaceful protest. "To me, this is bigger than football and it would be selfish on my part to look the other way. There are bodies in the street and people getting paid leave and getting away with murder."

In response, Kaepernick's coach, his team, and the NFL wished he would stand for the national anthem but also respected his right as a free individual in a free land to opt out of participating. That could have been the end of it, but as we all know, it wasn't. Soon after Kaepernick articulated his reasons for protesting, other players around the NFL began doing the same, whether by taking a knee or raising a fist.

Millions debated it. The president tweeted about it. Haters burned Kaepernick's jersey. And by October 2016 a kneeling Kaepernick appeared on the cover of *Time*. Colin Kaepernick became a household name.

Now I ask: What do you think about Seth DeValve? You know, the tight end for the Cleveland Browns drafted in 2016? The name doesn't ring a bell?

In August 2017, about a year after Kaepernick began protesting and just a couple weeks after the Unite the Right rally in Charlottesville, Virginia, where various far-right groups gathered to oppose the removal of Confederate monuments, Seth DeValve reportedly became the first white NFL player to protest during the national anthem, taking a knee prior to a preseason game against the New York Giants. DeValve's wife, Erica Harris DeValve, is African-American, and after the game he told a reporter: "I, myself, will be raising children that don't look like me, and I want to do my part as well to do everything I can to raise them in a better environment than we have right now. I wanted to take the opportunity with my teammates during the anthem to pray for our country and also draw attention to the fact that we have work to do. That's why I did what I did."

After the game, Erica wrote a blog post titled, "I'm Proud of My Husband for Kneeling During the Anthem, but Don't Make Him a White Savior." In it she wrote: "I am grateful for the widespread support and praise that Seth is getting for his actions, but I would like to offer a humble reminder that a man—a black man—literally lost his job for taking a knee, week after week, on his own. Colin Kaepernick bravely took a step and began a movement throughout the NFL, and he suffered a ridiculous amount of hate and threats and ultimately lost his life's work in the sport he loves."

Not only did DeValve get instant credit that had to be swatted away by his own spouse, but he also escaped the hatred that Kaepernick faced for engaging in the same protest.

Another white person, former congressman Beto O'Rourke of Texas, also received praise for defending an athlete's right to take a knee. During his run for the U.S. Senate in 2018, Democrat O'Rourke responded to a town hall question about NFL protests by stating he could "think of nothing more American." The clip went viral as millions of people watched it. The *Atlantic* argued that "by answering a question most Democratic politicians have refused to touch, the Texas Democrat has tapped into a powerful movement."

O'Rourke's answer helped him nearly win his race in Texas, which Republicans always win by statewide landslides. O'Rourke lost by only two and a half points. O'Rourke, too, was able to defend athletes' right to take a knee in a way African-Americans could not have done with similar success.

O'Rourke, committed to racial equality, would be quick to admit it.

Anne Hathaway, Hillary Clinton, and Double Standards for Women

When a talented woman climbs high and reaches the top of her profession, too many others like watching her fall. Think back to late 2012 and early 2013. While receiving praise and multiple award nominations for her role as Fantine in *Les Misérables*, Americans started to hate actress Anne Hathaway for no easily identifiable reason.

Scratch that. There might have been one reason: Hathaway, along with James Franco, hosted the 2011 Oscars. Thanks to Franco, they became the most lambasted Oscar hosts in memory.

Hathaway and Franco, both young dramatic actors, were a revolutionary break from the comedic legends who had hosted the show previously. We're talking Bob Hope, Johnny Carson, and Billy Crystal. This time the Academy of Motion Picture Arts and Sciences tried to lure a new generation of viewers.

From the moment Hathaway and Franco came onstage, Franco was the most visibly disengaged host of any awards show in broadcast television history. It wasn't that he was inept; that would assume he was overwhelmed by the enormity of the task but tried nonetheless. Actually, he did try. He often looked the opposite way when Hathaway spoke. He smirked bitterly when he should have smiled joyously. He smiled when he should have been somber. And he looked as if reading from the teleprompter made him nauseous. He sustained this persona throughout the entire show, hanging Hathaway out to dry for its three-hour-and-sixteen-minute duration.

Deservedly, Franco, not Hathaway, got the bad reviews.

Tim Goodman of the *Hollywood Reporter* wrote: "The 83rd Annual Academy Awards will likely be remembered as the night James Franco couldn't act like a host." Hank Stuever of the *Washington Post* wrote: "Hathaway worked her derriere off, and Franco came off like that lacrosse boy you wish your daughter didn't hang out with so much."

The evening remains unique in Hathaway's career. To this day, no other appearance by her or project associated with her has produced such negative reviews. And the Oscars weren't even her fault.

Moreover, she has done nothing to project an image as out of touch as Gwyneth Paltrow's. But "run a Google search for 'Anne Hathaway' and 'annoying,' and 1.5 million search results are returned," wrote the *Daily Beast* in January 2013. "Try 'Anne Hathaway' and 'hate,' and that number spikes to a mere 28.5 million."

A month earlier, in a December 2012 article titled "Why Do People Hate Anne Hathaway?," BuzzFeed listed the possible reasons, gleaned from social media, for the emerging phenomenon known as "Hathahate." They included everything from complaints that Hathaway thinks she's cool when she's actually boring, to her eyes, mouth, and face being wrong, to her being too perfect, to no real reason at all besides the apparent joy that comes from finding community with others in their hate.

Salon called Hathaway "Hollywood's most polarizing star." One critic said she reminded him of an overcompensating "theater kid" who tries too hard to adapt to the mood of every situation, whether bawdy or classy, silly or somber. Readers of the San Francisco–based website SFGate named Hathaway the Most Annoying Celebrity of 2013. "She took an early lead and there was no looking back," reads the accompanying article.

Hathaway's crime seems to be that she's gifted. Notwithstanding the torrent of hate she had endured, she won the Oscar for Best Supporting Actress, as well as the Golden Globe in 2013 for her performance in *Les Misérables*.

In 2014, during an interview with *Harper's Bazaar* for a cover story, Hathaway recalled the moment she first encountered Hathahate on the Internet. She said she felt "punched in the gut. Shocked and slapped and embarrassed. Even now I can feel the shame. I was in crisis."

Hathaway mentioned that despite winning an Academy Award for Best Supporting Actress for *Les Misérables*, people were hesitant to hire her because her public image was damaged.

"I had directors say to me, 'I think you're great. You're perfect for this role, but I don't know how audiences will accept you because of all this stuff, this baggage,'" she told *Harper's Bazaar*.

Then director Christopher Nolan called and offered her a role in his 2014 sci-fi thriller *Interstellar* alongside Matthew McConaughey. Hathaway had previously worked with Nolan on 2012's *The Dark Knight Rises*, in which she played Selina Kyle/Catwoman.

"Once it was announced that I was doing *Interstellar*, thankfully the phone started ringing again," said Hathaway.

Then, after some time passed and nothing much happened, in August 2015 the *New York Post* declared that Hathahate was finally over. In other words, it ended just about as suddenly and pointlessly as it began.

There was no scandal, crime, or other great offense. There was no end of any scandal, crime, or other offense. Because she is a disposable celebrity—especially a disposable *female* celebrity—it was time for her to entertain us by being the object of our scorn instead of our adoration. Men, including James Franco, have done far worse but never endured what Hathaway has.

For a time, Hathaway became the most analyzed entertainer in America. Or more exactly, her likeability was analyzed more than that of any other entertainer. That's what our society does to women but not to men: We analyze the likeability of women in public life to an extent we rarely analyze the likeability of their male counterparts.

And after we analyze their likeability, we inevitably conclude the women aren't likeable at all. It is sexist, it is cruel, and it is unacceptable.

Look no further than Hillary Clinton, the most analyzed woman in American history.

Is there anything that hasn't been said about her already? As a matter of fact, yes. We've yet to see a fair comparison of Clinton to the man most similar to her in American politics, the late president George H. W. Bush. They present the best possible pair for determining whether a woman running for president faces likeability prisms among Americans that a man does not.

Before we examine the common traits between Secretary Clinton and the first President Bush, let's acknowledge the big difference in how they grew up. She was raised in a typical upper-middle-class family in suburban Chicago. Before moving to Texas, Bush grew up in tony Connecticut as the scion of a rich political dynasty—the son of former U.S. senator Prescott Bush of Connecticut.

But the similarities are greater.

Both grew up in loving homes, with parents whose marriages endured. Both wound up attending Yale University, Bush as an undergraduate and Clinton for law school. Before politics, each had successful careers in the private sector, Bush in the oil business and Clinton in law. Prior to their first runs for president, Bush's in 1980 and Clinton's in 2008, each had attained a significant amount of government experience. Bush had been a member of Congress, U.N. ambassador, liaison to China, and director of Central Intelligence. Clinton had been the first lady of Arkansas, the first lady of the United States, the president's point person on national health care, and a sitting U.S. senator. After losing his 1980 presidential race, Bush served as vice president under Ronald Reagan. After losing hers in 2008,

Clinton served as secretary of state under Barack Obama. In 1988 and 2016, both ran after their respective parties had held the White House for two consecutive terms.

Both stressed a pragmatic way of doing things, not withstanding ideology, that eschewed bravado. Let's return to the 2016 Democratic National Convention, when Clinton said she always found the "public" part more difficult than the "service" part. The same for Bush. He once quipped: "Fluency in English is not something I'm often accused of." In early 1987, *Time* also reported that Bush was aware he didn't have a solid grasp on the whole "vision thing"—big, charismatic ideas that inspire the masses. Both candidates understood they weren't captivating.

When they ran for president for the second time, Bush in 1988 and Clinton in 2016, they were the most accomplished and qualified non-incumbents to run for president in the histories of their parties. But Bush won and Clinton lost. He did not have to face what she did. Yes, I'm talking about the double standard of likeability called sexism.

When Hillary married Bill Clinton in 1975, controversy swirled around whether she should or should not take his last name as her own. She decided to remain Hillary Rodham. A few years later, a *New York Times* write-up of her husband, soon after he became governor of Arkansas, noted he was "married to an ardent feminist, Hillary Rodham, who will certainly be the first First Lady of Arkansas to keep her maiden name."

When Bill lost his reelection bid in 1980, Hillary's last name had played a role in his defeat. Arkansans didn't like it. Who was this strange woman asserting herself as a fully independent person? It certainly didn't help that Bill's opponent, Republican Frank D. White, reminded people along the campaign trail that his wife was named "Mrs. Frank White." Years later, Hillary wrote of the experience, "I

learned the hard way that some voters in Arkansas were seriously offended by the fact that I kept my maiden name."

Two years later, in 1982, Bill Clinton ran again. This time, however, he and Hillary presented themselves as Mr. and Mrs. Bill Clinton. "I don't have to change my name," Hillary told a reporter at
the time. "I've been Mrs. Bill Clinton. I kept the professional name
Hillary Rodham in my law practice, but now I'm going to be taking
a leave of absence from the law firm to campaign full time for Bill,
and I'll be Mrs. Bill Clinton. I suspect people will be getting tired of
hearing from Mrs. Bill Clinton."

Sure enough, the Clintons reclaimed the governorship of Arkansas
from Mr. and Mrs. Frank White, and Bill held the office until he was
elected president in 1992.

Since then, Hillary has gone by the names Hillary Rodham Clinton, Hillary Clinton, and just plain Hillary, depending on the writer,
the news organization, and the campaign. But from day one in the
public spotlight, her choice of name—and the pressure upon her to
change it—presented questions of authenticity, relatability, and perceptiveness that no man in her shoes, including George H. W. Bush,
has ever had to face. Heck, the elder Bush was given four names from
his upper-crust Connecticut family—hardly a construct of relatability to everyday Americans—and no one questioned his name or his
choice to shorten it to George Bush. In making that choice, was he
disrespecting his family in the way Arkansans believed Hillary was
disrespecting her husband? It never came up.

Every candidate for president, including natural campaigners like
Bill Clinton and unlike Hillary Clinton and the first President Bush,
makes mistakes on the campaign trail. During the summer of 1988,
for example, Bush introduced his three grandchildren to President
Reagan as "the little brown ones." The three kids—Jeb Jr., Noelle,

and George P.—belong to son and former governor of Florida Jeb Bush and his wife, Columba Bush, who is Mexican-American. George Bush got in trouble for that one, especially among Latinos and Latinas. He was criticized for setting those particular grandchildren apart from, you know, regular grandchildren.

"For anyone to suggest that that comment of pride is anything other than what it was, I find it personally offensive," Bush said at a news conference, in defense of his description. "This is my family and I'm going to protect them. This heart knows nothing but pride and love for those three children, and you're going to see them with me every inch of the way."

That Bush called his grandchildren "little brown ones" is largely forgotten to history. America forgave him for his "little brown ones" in a way it couldn't forgive Hillary's "basket of deplorables." But Hillary has never been forgiven easily. In early 1992, for example, when discussing Bill's alleged infidelity during a joint interview on *60 Minutes* on CBS, Hillary said: "I'm not sittin' here some little woman standin' by my man like Tammy Wynette. I'm sittin' here because I love him and I respect him and I honor what he's been through and what we've been through together and, you know, if that's not enough for people, then heck, don't vote for him." The line landed her in a pot of boiling water. Her attempt at authenticity and protectiveness ended up sounding like an unperceptive put-down to traditional stay-at-home women across the country.

Later in 1992, Clinton responded to a question about her legal career with her infamous answer: "I suppose I could have stayed home and baked cookies and had teas, but what I decided to do was to fulfill my profession, which I entered before my husband was in public life." Again the answer was authentic, but lacked perceptiveness and compassion for women without the means or opportunities to pursue a profession outside the home. But did George H. W. Bush have to deal with the tension between being an obedient husband by staying home to bake muffins versus having a career and running for office? Of course not.

In a *New York Times* column, "Why Is Clinton Disliked?," David Brooks argued that Clinton's low likeability ratings stemmed from a perception of her as a workaholic. "At least in her public persona," he wrote, "Clinton gives off an exclusively professional vibe: industrious, calculated, goal-oriented, distrustful. It's hard from the outside to have a sense of her as a person; she is a role."

Glamour responded to Brooks a couple days later with an article titled "Male Pundit Accidentally Lays Out the Sexist Reasoning Behind Hillary Clinton's Likability Problem." In it writer Krystal Marie Ball argued: "According to David, Hillary never seems to have fun, and that's why she has dismal approval ratings." Later, Ball notes: "To put it simply, we tend to dislike powerful women. Of course we would never frame our distaste for a particular woman that way. Instead we might say that she's imperious or bitchy or lacking 'gravitas,' as was said about Fed Reserve Chair Janet Yellen. But dig a little deeper and you'll find that the same qualities that make a woman bitchy and unlikable make a man commanding and authoritative. When Bernie Sanders yells to make a point he's passionate, but when Hillary raises her voice she's told by condescending male TV hosts that she needs to 'smile more.'"

For George H. W. Bush, his lifetime in public service, along with never losing sight of the next rung to climb, was an attribute. He was ready to be president. For Hillary, having experience became dangerously uncool during the 2016 presidential elections. When Kate McKinnon played Hillary on *Saturday Night Live*, she recounted Hillary's decades of experience—as Hillary—to laughs. Why, exactly, did America find it funny that Hillary Clinton was the most experienced non-incumbent Democratic nominee in history? Why didn't Dana Carvey, who had played the elder Bush a generation earlier, try for laughs by making fun of Bush's experience?

Both the elder Bush and Hillary Clinton had behind-the-scenes likeability machines. In February 2015 the *Washington Post* published "The Making of Hillary 5.0: Marketing Wizards Help Re-imagine Clinton Brand." As Philip Rucker and Anne Gearan reported: "Clinton has tapped some of the Democratic Party's star strategists as well as two of corporate America's branding wizards: Wendy Clark, who specializes in marketing age-old brands such as Coca-Cola to younger and more diverse customers; and Roy Spence, a decades-long Clinton friend who dreamed up the 'Don't Mess With Texas' anti-littering slogan as well as flashy ad campaigns for Southwest Airlines and Wal-Mart." The article implied that Clinton's hiring of experts to remake her image somehow made her less authentic.

When Bush was running for president in 1988, he also had an image problem: He was seen as lacking protectiveness. In October 1987, *Newsweek* ran a cover story titled "George Bush: Fighting the 'Wimp Factor.'" It was an especially damaging article coming just a week after Bush announced his plans to run for president. To combat the public perception, Bush had an ace up his sleeve: longtime Republican media adviser Roger Ailes, who later became the chairman and CEO of Fox News. Ailes embarked on a comprehensive rebranding.

Bush's campaign, and independent groups that supported it, aired a biographical ad with footage of Bush being pulled out of the Pacific Ocean and onto a submarine after his plane was shot down during World War II, emphasizing his hero veteran status.

In January 1988, at Ailes's urging, Bush got angry on national television. During an interview with CBS News anchor Dan Rather,

Bush accused Rather of misrepresenting the purpose of the interview, which Bush claimed was to be about why he wanted to be president. It's hard to imagine that any credible news organization would consent to such puffery. On air, Rather pushed Vice President Bush to reveal his role in the Iran-Contra Affair, which occurred in the second term of the Reagan administration. "I want to talk about why I want to be President," Bush said at one point. "It's not fair to judge my whole career by a rehash on Iran. How would you like it if I judged your career by those seven minutes when you walked off the set in New York?"—referring to an earlier incident when Rather walked off set during a live broadcast.

According to reports, Ailes and Bush campaign director Lee Atwater had planned the entire on-air confrontation as a likeability construct for Bush to show off his toughness. They had convinced Bush prior to the CBS interview that the conversation with Rather was a trap and that the Iran-Contra Affair questions were coming. The event turned into a great moment to display Bush as the exact opposite of a wimp.

Although many might have taken offense to Bush's tactics, few seemed to consider his image makeover to be phony. He was a wimp, and then he was tough—or tough enough to win the election, at least. Why was the same image-makeover grace not lent to Clinton? Why couldn't she change her hair without our noticing? Why? Because she's a woman.

If any of us were Hillary Clinton, it would be hard not to take the critical double standards personally. But when six women announced in late 2018 and early 2019 that they were running for president in 2020, they, too, had their likeability analyzed and bashed as Hillary Clinton had experienced throughout her career. And the men who announced their candidacies for 2020 did not.

Freeheld and Double Standards
for LGBTQ People

If you ever wind up being portrayed by an actor in a movie, you'll find it painful to watch how Hollywood fictionalizes your life. The movie's phony version of you is the only version that thousands will meet and come to believe is the real you.

Steve Carell, you'll recall, played me in the 2015 film *Freeheld*. It chronicled Garden State Equality's months-long battle on the streets and in the halls of power to allow a dying police officer, Lieutenant Laurel Hester, to give her death benefits to her partner, Stacie Andree. As soon as the documentary *Freeheld* had won the Oscar for Best Documentary Short in 2008, some of Hollywood's most seasoned producers looked to turn the story into a full-length film with actors.

Hollywood infused the script of the fictionalized *Freeheld* with a homophobic bias the documentary hadn't had, and it impacted how Steve Carell played me. The evolution occurred even though everyone associated with the fictionalized film was pro-LGBTQ and intent on advancing LGBTQ equality. Some of the producers were LGBTQ themselves, as was costar Ellen Page and screenwriter Ron Nyswaner, a celebrated LGBTQ activist previously nominated for an Oscar for his screenplay for the film *Philadelphia*.

So what the hell happened?

The script and Carell's portrayal made me out to be the Jewish clone of Just Jack from *Will & Grace*, the gayest character in all of television. By now you know how out and proud I am. And I'd have no self-awareness if I didn't acknowledge the funny gay side of me. But that was the only dimension of me the script allowed. The producers and screenwriter crafted a fictionalized "Steven" as if they were on a simplification acid trip. Worse than Just Jack, a character to whom the producers of *Will & Grace* have given more nuance in that series' reboot, I became Cardboard Just Jack.

The powers behind the movie told me they had a challenge. They didn't want a movie with a lesbian couple and a gay man as the three leads. It would make for "too gay" a movie and lack appeal to straight audiences. So not only did the script make me a flamingly gay sidekick, but it also transferred much of my real-life activism to another character in the movie, Laurel's former partner on the police force, the straight Dane Wells. The movie also portrayed the character of Dane as a hard-nosed political conservative, which the real Dane isn't, to reinforce the storyline of an unlikely hero coming to the rescue of two lesbians.

Freeheld, the fictionalized movie, got awful reviews. Critics called it flimsy, inauthentic, and filled with offensive stereotypes. Critics who had seen and loved the documentary were angry at the opportunity the fiction film had squandered. The U.S. box office take wound up being $573,000, representing about 50,000 theatergoers in a nation of 320 million. Garden State Equality, serving just one state, has 150,000 members.

The failure of *Freeheld* confirmed everything I've lived and taught about coming across as likeable. Likeability, as manufactured and contrived as it may be, is still rooted in reality. The fiction *Freeheld* veered so far from reality, its likeability was dead on arrival.

A Sign of Hope

Will prejudice always exist in some form or another? Yes, but we are seeing signs of its diminution. The #MeToo movement suggests Americans are increasingly fed up with people failing to judge others by the content of their character. Although the movement has focused on the exploitation of women, no doubt it will make powerful people think twice about how they treat members of all oppressed communities— and, hopefully, how they portray members of oppressed communities in public life.

CHAPTER 10

Scandals, Killer Scandals, and Likeability Comebacks

P onder these names: Roseanne Barr, Bill Cosby, Matt Lauer, Lindsay Lohan, Charlie Sheen, Kevin Spacey, Martha Stewart, Anthony Weiner, and Brian Williams. They were all likeable people who became unlikeable, at least to enough of us. Their careers came to a screeching halt because of scandals of their own making. And in most cases their careers came to an end.

Likeability is an ever-changing construct, as is each of its eight traits. Likeability is not invincible. It can be damaged by mistakes, bled by crises, and killed by enemies. In a matter of seconds, public figures can watch their carefully cultivated likeability slip, then tumble, then crash and burn.

The likeability of people in the three fields of public life that have been our focus—politics, business, and entertainment—are sensitive to scandals in different ways, depending on the field.

Across all three, the #MeToo movement has made public figures' sexual abuse of women a killer of likeability after decades in which America's industries of power disgraced our nation by giving sexual abusers a pass. It's hard to imagine comebacks for Bill Cosby, Matt Lauer, or Charlie Rose. But the impact of other scandals is varied.

A CEO, even if all parts of his or her life are in order, could do no worse than lie or be caught as corrupt, as other people's money is at stake. Bernie Madoff will never be seen as likeable again. Sometimes others' health is at stake. Hedge fund manager Martin Shkreli not only drained innocent people of their money, but he also risked their lives as he did it. He gouged the price of the drug Daraprim, used to help people with HIV/AIDS, from $13.50 to $750 per pill. The media began calling him "the most hated man in America." He, too, will never be seen as likeable in the future. And his years of boasting about preying on other people made him unlikeable in the first place.

Americans are more understanding about drug use, certainly when a star is so public about his or her struggles, as Robert Downey Jr. has been. His career is roaring, and his transparency has only made him more likeable. Infidelity, in contrast, can hurt likeability to various degrees, depending on the public figure's depth of preexisting likeability and whether the infidelity harmed the basis upon which the public figure presented himself as likeable. None of us who supported Bill Clinton for president did so because we thought he was a saint.

Making prejudiced statements against others because of their race, religion, sexuality, or other characteristics hurts a public figure's likeability to various degrees. Though Mel Gibson's drunken rampage of anti-Semitism in 2006 brought his career to a grinding halt, it has shown signs of recovery as his likeability in the eyes of the American public has improved. Roseanne Barr's racism, when she tweeted in 2018 that former President Obama's friend and adviser Valerie Jarrett would be the result if "muslim brotherhood & planet of the apes had a baby," led ABC to fire her and cancel the series *Roseanne.*

However, prejudiced statements by Kevin Hart didn't hurt his career for years. In a 2010 live show for video, Hart said one of his "biggest fears is my son growing up and being gay." In a 2011 tweet, he wrote: "Yo if my son comes home & try's 2 play with my daughters doll house I'm going 2 break it over his head & say n my voice 'stop that's gay,'" The Academy of Motion Picture Arts and Sciences still hired Hart to host the Oscars in 2019, and fired him only when a public uproar brought the old quotes to light. His career in movies continues.

Scandal impacts the likeability of politicians the fastest. Political figures don't have the zones of privacy that business leaders and entertainers do. As for CEOs and other high-level executives in major corporations, the public doesn't know most of them to adjust the perception of their likeability up or down. And although entertainers face brutal pressure from tabloids and social media that look for scandals even where they don't exist, entertainers and their handlers can still ratchet access up or down depending on the stars' latest movie, television series, or sporting endeavor.

But in politics, the news coverage is 24/7, magnifying every likeability mistake into a potential likeability crisis. Unlike in business or entertainment, likeability in politics is a zero-sum game where one politician's likeability in an election depends on destroying another's. When you do something unlikeable, your opponents won't merely portray you as a likeable man or woman with mortal flaws; they will portray you as one of the most unlikeable people in the world.

The worst scandal for any politician is to insult American voters. A politician is supposed to represent the people rather than resent them. To be sure, Donald Trump got a pass in 2016, having made an astonishing number of statements that insulted women, people of color, and people with disabilities. He was the exception to the rule because enough voters liked what they considered to be his flawed authenticity. To understand how insulting statements can damage the likeability of almost anyone else who runs for office, you only have to look to Mitt Romney in 2012 and Hillary Clinton in 2016.

On May 17, 2012, Mitt Romney spoke at a fund-raiser at the home of private equity manager Marc Leder in Boca Raton, Florida. It was a private fund-raiser, with no journalists present. Here's what Romney said about President Obama and his supporters:

"There are 47 percent of the people who will vote for the president no matter what. All right, there are 47 percent who are with him, who are dependent upon government, who believe that they are victims, who believe the government has a responsibility to care for them, who believe that they are entitled to health care, to food, to housing, to you-name-it. My job is not to worry about those people. I'll never convince them they should take personal responsibility and care for their lives."

A guest at the fund-raiser recorded Romney on video and sent it to *Mother Jones*, which released it to the world. In the days after the video went public, Romney tried to rationalize his remarks every which way short of a retraction and an apology. The more he rationalized, the more his poll numbers plunged.

You would think Hillary Clinton, cautious and self-controlled, would not make a mistake such as the one Mitt Romney made years earlier.

On September 9, 2016, Clinton addressed a fund-raising gala of LGBTQ supporters at the Cipriani Club in Manhattan. "To just be grossly generalistic," she said, "you could put half of Trump's supporters into what I call the basket of deplorables. Right? The racist, sexist, homophobic, xenophobic, Islamophobic—you name it. And unfortunately there are people like that. And he has lifted them up."

Although her division of Trump voters into two baskets had not gone public until her LGBTQ fund-raiser, she had been developing the meme in previous appearances that summer. True, there was a difference between Romney's "47 percent" and Clinton's "basket of deplorables." Romney insulted all of Obama's voters, while Clinton had a more complex view of Trump voters. She categorized her non-deplorable basket of Trump voters as good-intentioned people who simply "feel that the government has let them down" and are "desperate for change," as she said at the LGBTQ fund-raiser. But the press didn't report the distinction. Remember what I told you a while back? The stories that captivate us the most are the simplest, and the media knows it.

The remarks by Romney and Clinton accelerated their perceived unlikeability with the speed of sound. Romney's remarks were reported on September 17, 2012. Just one day later—a day in which American voters heard television news outlets play Romney's remarks constantly—Gallup took a national poll to measure the impact. Thirty-six percent of registered voters, and a significant 29 percent of independent voters, said the comment made them less likely to support Romney.

In 2016, Clinton's likeability went into a similarly fast tailspin. After the election, one of Clinton's pollsters, Diane Hessan, wrote in the *Boston Globe*:

"There was one moment when I saw more undecided voters shift to Trump than any other, when it all changed, when voters began to speak differently about their choice. It wasn't FBI Director James Comey . . . it wasn't Benghazi or the emails or Bill Clinton's visit with Attorney General Loretta Lynch on the tarmac. No, the conversation shifted the most during the weekend of Sept. 9, after Clinton said,

'You can [sic] put half of Trump supporters into what I call the basket of deplorables.'"

What made "47 percent" and "basket of deplorables" two of the worst likeability crises in presidential campaign history? Both sets of remarks eviscerated each of our likeability traits:

1. The remarks were **captivating** in the most negative way. Americans thought of Romney and Clinton: *Stop! Who the hell do you think you are?*

2. The remarks showed the candidates were not people in whom voters could invest their **hope**: *If you don't have faith in me, how could I have faith in you?*

3. The remarks revealed the candidates to be **inauthentic**: *So that's what you think backstage?*

4. The remarks showed the candidates were unable to **relate** to voters: *You view me as a parasite upon the public treasury, or a racist.*

5. The remarks made voters think the candidates would never **protect** them: *If something happens to me, I'm out of luck because I'm not among the voters you like.*

6. The remarks revealed the candidates to be **unreliable**: *My goodness, what are you going to say next?*

7. The remarks showed the candidates unable to **perceive** the reality voters wanted to hear: *Just how ignorant about my life can you get?*

8. The remarks gave the impression the candidates lacked **compassion**: *What kind of unfeeling jerk are you?*

Although the presidential campaigns of Romney and Clinton never recovered from their self-inflicted likeability wounds, some other public figures do bounce back from scandal. To figure out who and why, I asked the creators of the Celebrity DBI, Jeff Chown and Matt Delzell of TMA in Dallas, for some of the company's most revealing time lines of likeability for various scandal-ridden celebrities. Let's look at the case studies now.

Who Recovers? Tiger Woods
Versus Lance Armstrong

In 1997, Tiger Woods became the youngest golfer and the first person of color to win the Masters Tournament, golf's premier event. From there the world fell in love and Woods kept on winning. By 2008 he had won fourteen championships. In December 2009, however, more than a dozen women came forward claiming to have had sexual relations with Woods, who was married with two children at the time. Sponsors began to distance themselves, and his wife, Elin Nordegren, divorced him the following year.

In February 2010, Woods offered a public apology. "I was unfaithful. I had affairs. I cheated," he said at a news conference. "What I did is not acceptable, and I am the only person to blame. I stopped living by the core values that I was taught to believe in. I knew my actions were wrong, but I convinced myself that normal rules didn't apply. I never thought about who I was hurting. Instead, I thought only about myself."

Like Tiger Woods, bicyclist Lance Armstrong was a peerless athlete in his sport who brought scandal about himself. He won seven consecutive Tour de France titles between 1999 and 2005. After surviving testicular cancer, he founded the Livestrong Foundation, a nonprofit organization that has raised hundreds of millions of dollars to aid cancer survivors.

Although rumors long existed that Armstrong was doping his way to victory, it had never been proven—that is, until 2012, when the United States Anti-Doping Agency formally accused Armstrong of not only using performance-enhancing drugs but also leading the "most sophisticated, professionalized, and successful doping program that sport has ever seen." Soon after, officials stripped Armstrong of his seven Tour de France titles and he resigned from the Livestrong Foundation. In January 2013, Armstrong went on *Oprah* and confessed to doping. He apologized to everyone.

How did the scandals impact the likeability of Tiger Woods and Lance Armstrong, and which of the two rebounded? Let's look at TMA's numbers. Keep in mind, scores range from 0 to 100, and the ranking places each public figure among approximately 4,500 public figures in all. Unless noted, the scores and rankings are for TMA's category of appeal, the equivalent of likeability.

	TIGER WOODS	LANCE ARMSTRONG
Pre-scandal appeal score	82.22	77.05
Pre-scandal appeal rank	#76	#409
Post-scandal appeal score	56.91	48.89
Post-scandal appeal rank	#1,498	#2,694
January 2019 appeal score	61.12	56.41
January 2019 appeal rank	#4,404	#4,563

The likeability trajectory of Woods and Armstrong has had a similar pattern. Both men endured a precipitous drop after scandal. And the likeability of each has rebounded in part, but is nowhere near its peak. Woods, however, crossed a 60 percent score for likeability, as desirable for an entertainer or sports figure as 60 percent would be for a candidate in an election. To be sure, few public figures caught in scandal can hope to recover their likeability entirely. The American public is forgiving, but it does not have amnesia. Indeed, the best for which mere mortals in public life can hope is a partial recovery with realistic expectations for a future public career.

Why, then, has Tiger Woods rebounded? The lessons inherent in his likeability comeback apply to the likeability comebacks of all public figures. We need to ask three questions.

1. *How well liked was the public figure before the crisis?*

   The best-liked public figures have the greatest reservoir of goodwill from the American public and are the most likely to rebound. Before the public revelation of his scandals, Tiger Woods's likeability was in the stratosphere. He had a cushion upon which to fall.

2. *Did the public figure's mistakes hurt his or her likeability strengths, or did the mistakes merely exacerbate weaknesses that were never important to the public figure's likeability?*

   Mistakes that undercut a public figure's strengths are more damaging to his or her likeability and more difficult from which to recover. Tiger Woods's behavior in his marriage had nothing to do with his golfing skills that captivated the world. Lance Armstrong's doping, in contrast, went to the heart of his achievement in sport.

3. *Has the public figure apologized or atoned sufficiently to recover his or her likeability traits?*

   The public will buy only an apology that seems sincere, delivered in clear language or through acts of atonement that show he or she has learned a lesson. Tiger Woods offered a textbook example of a perfect apology, and he did it with comparative speed. Lance Armstrong refused to apologize for months. That said, his likeability rebounded when he finally offered a full-throttled mea culpa, free of hedging, on *Oprah.*

No Chance at a Comeback:
Bill Cosby and Kevin Spacey

For five consecutive seasons beginning in 1985, *The Cosby Show* was the highest rated show on television, with an audience of 63 million viewers at the peak of the sitcom's popularity. To give you an idea of how massive a rating that is—and how popular Bill Cosby as Dr. Cliff Huxtable was—*The Big Bang Theory* was the highest rated show for the 2017–18 television season with 18.6 million viewers.

Over the years, dozens of women came forth to state that Cosby had sexually assaulted them and in some cases had plied them with drugs without their knowledge. In one case in September 2018, a judge sentenced Cosby to three to ten years in prison. To this day Cosby has never admitted guilt or apologized. He is a remorseless predator, the opposite of protective Dr. Huxtable.

As with Bill Cosby, multiple people have accused Kevin Spacey of sexual assault and harrassment—fifteen men, to be exact, though Massachusetts prosecutors dropped charges in one case in July 2019. What Cosby once achieved in ratings, Spacey has achieved in critical acclaim. He has won two Academy Awards, a Golden Globe, a Tony, a Drama Desk Award, and four Screen Actors Guild awards. All in all, he has been nominated for eighty-one awards and won fifty-five times.

In October 2017, Broadway actor Anthony Rapp said Spacey made a sexual advance to Rapp when Rapp was only fourteen. Other men came forth with their own stories. Unlike Cosby, Spacey offered an apology—sort of, for it was far from an apology without equivocation. "I honestly do not remember the encounter" with Rapp, Spacey said. "But if I did behave then as [Rapp] describes, I owe him the sincerest apology for what would have been deeply inappropriate drunken behavior, and I am sorry for the feelings he describes having carried with him all these years." When we strip away the softer words, Spacey blamed the bottle.

Have a look at Cosby and Spacey's numbers from TMA:

	BILL COSBY	KEVIN SPACEY
Pre-scandal appeal score	85.14	82.79
Pre-scandal appeal rank	#19	#41
Post-scandal appeal score	48.03	53.76
Post-scandal appeal rank	#4,228	#4,602
January 2019 appeal score	41.52	53.15
January 2019 appeal rank	#4,661	#4,605

When it comes to Cosby and Spacey, America has its priorities right. The nation is unforgiving and offers no chance of a likeability comeback for either.

When Journalists Breach Our Trust: Brian Williams and Matt Lauer

Journalists must have our trust. More than any other likeability trait or subtrait it is essential if they are to succeed in public life. From late 2004 to early 2015, Brian Williams had our trust as anchor of *NBC Nightly News*. During nearly that entire period, Williams kept *Nightly* #1 in the ratings. He was beloved not only as a news anchor but also as an engaging talk show guest. He was on top of the world.

In late January 2015, Williams retold a story of his flying aboard a Chinook helicopter in Iraq in 2003 that was hit by fire and forced to land. Several service members began challenging his version of the story, saying he was in another helicopter about an hour behind the one that received enemy fire. Rather than correct his error instantly, as any journalist is supposed to, Williams blamed his mistake on the passage of time making the details blurry in his mind. "I don't know what screwed up in my mind that caused me to conflate one aircraft with another," he said. It was ridiculous.

On Twitter, users mocked Williams with satirical tweets that saluted him for being on location for everything from the moon landing to the founding of the United States of America. A common hashtag was #BrianWilliamsMisremembers.

Matt Lauer had an equally successful career at NBC. He had been cohost of *Today* from 1997 to 2017 and, like Brian Williams, anchored a show usually tops in the ratings. For all the stories about Lauer's having gotten Ann Curry fired in June 2012—leading to her heart-wrenching goodbye and monstrous news coverage for Lauer—he survived nonetheless. His appeal score before Curry's firing was 77.74. After her firing, his appeal decreased to 70—still impressively high.

In November 2017, NBC fired Lauer after numerous allegations of inappropriate sexual behavior with employees. In a statement he said: "Some of what is being said about me is untrue or mischaracterized, but there is enough truth in these stories to make me feel embarrassed and ashamed. I regret that my shame is now shared by the people I cherish dearly."

Immediately after Lauer was fired, his appeal dropped to 42.36, about where it remains today.

Because our trust in journalists plays an outsized role in their credibility, the good folks at TMA suggest their numbers for trust are the most telling of all. Let's look at the numbers now.

	BRIAN WILLIAMS	MATT LAUER
Pre-scandal trust score	72.59	67.20
Pre-scandal trust rank	#9	#55
Immediate aftermath trust score	51.29	38.39
Immediate aftermath trust rank	#3,256	#4,603
Early 2019 trust score	56.49	41.74
Early 2019 trust rank	#3,985	#4,621

Oddly, Brian Williams has seen less of a fall in trust than Matt Lauer has. Williams's scandal stemmed directly from the very basis for which Americans trusted him: his news reporting. Lauer's scandal had nothing to do with his news reporting. However, NBC has gone to great lengths over the years to promote the *Today* cast as a family, including a promotional campaign that called Matt Lauer and his colleagues "America's First Family." In short, they are supposed to be part of our family as much as they are there to tell us the news. That's how our trust in Matt Lauer fell so fast. His scandal did go to the heart of why Americans watched him in the first place. As for Brian Williams, the shocker is that NBC kept him at all—these days at MSNBC—when his numbers for trust are unacceptable for anyone in public life, and a journalist especially.

The Jury's Still Out: Roseanne Barr and Mel Gibson

The revival of *Roseanne* was a top-rated series on television in 2018 and looked as if it could have a run as long as the original one, which aired from 1988 to 1997. Then came Barr's racist tweet in May 2018 and ABC's near-instant cancellation of her show.

Years earlier, Mel Gibson had made slurs of his own. In July 2006, after he was arrested for driving under the influence, he delivered an anti-Semitic rant to the arresting officer. He issued an apology, but its potential impact never got a chance to register. In July 2010, racist-and profanity-laced audio recordings of Gibson surfaced. During an angry phone conversation with his former romantic interest, Oksana Grigorieva, he used the *n*-word and equated African-Americans with rapists.

Here's a look at Barr's and Gibson's appeal numbers from TMA:

	ROSEANNE BARR	MEL GIBSON
Pre-scandal appeal score:	57.25	70.75
Pre-scandal appeal rank:	#1,732	#1,170
Immediate aftermath appeal score:	[Not in survey]	57.15
Immediate aftermath appeal rank:	[Not in survey]	#4,514
Early 2019 appeal score:	52.53	65.68
Early 2019 appeal rank:	#4,613	#4,166

Mel Gibson, whom you might have thought could never recover after his slurs, has seen his likeability recover after several years. His appeal score, even if not what it was, is remarkably high for someone who made anti-Semitic and racist statements. This leaves hope for Roseanne, as improbable as that might seem so soon after her own racist remarks. Roseanne's likeability numbers have been above average, but not great, for years, suggesting she has always polarized America. Odds are, she always will. And that leaves room for a comeback.

The Teflon Man of Likeability: Morgan Freeman

In February 2010, Freeman had an appeal score of 89.75, earning the #1 spot on Celebrity DBI's index of 4,500 celebrities.

In May 2018, CNN reported that multiple women came forward accusing Freeman of sexual harassment, inappropriate touching, and making them feel on edge, whether on set, at his production company, or while promoting his films. Responding to the #MeToo moment, Freeman said in a statement, "Anyone who knows me or has worked with me knows I am not someone who would intentionally offend or knowingly make anyone feel uneasy. I apologize to anyone who felt uncomfortable or disrespected—that was never my intent."

That's hardly what you'd call a full-throttled, unambiguous apology. But Freeman's appeal was virtually unscathed. It took a dip after the scandal but remained in the stratosphere nonetheless, and now it's rebounded even further. It seems as if nothing Freeman does can hurt him. Take a look at these numbers from TMA:

	MORGAN FREEMAN
Pre-scandal appeal score:	89.75
Pre-scandal appeal rank:	#1
Immediate aftermath appeal score:	78.51
Immediate aftermath appeal rank:	#295
Early 2019 appeal score:	82.22
Early 2019 appeal rank:	#29

A Lesson for Rebuilding
Your Own Likeability

Our examination of celebrity scandals, including their numerical assessments from TMA, can be instructive to all of us. You can fall flat on your face, even if it's a scandal of your own making, so long as it didn't destroy the core of why others liked you in the first place. Say, for instance, you messed up at work and your project didn't produce the revenue you promised. Own up to it immediately and broadly through a public apology to all the relevant stakeholders.

That will maximize your ability to maintain your authenticity and your chance to rebuild your reliability. If others have always considered you to be authentic and relatable, you will have acted to protect your likeability strengths and thereby stop your likeability from spiraling further.

If you said or did something beyond the pale, be it rooted in unethical or unlawful conduct, you will have to own up to a different reality. It will be time for you to move on and consider the possibility of rebuilding your likeability at another time and place in your life.

CHAPTER 11

The Global Turn-On: Comparing Eight World Leaders

The likeability of presidents, prime ministers, and other world leaders has played a heightened role in international diplomacy since 1918. President Woodrow Wilson, ever confident in his erudition and persuasion, sailed to Europe to meet with Allied leaders to craft terms successfully for the end of World War I. Previous presidents had not much engaged directly with other leaders, leaving diplomacy to the secretary of state and other advisers. During World War II, FDR and Churchill, each smitten with the other's likeability, cemented a relationship that came to be known as the friendship that saved the world.

Since then, every advancement in travel and communications technology has put the likeability of world leaders increasingly front and center in shaping the times in which they lived. "Shuttle diplomacy" would become common parlance for the airplane travels of U.S. secretaries of state, for whom countless diplomatic skills rest on likeability. From there, the ultimate faceoffs in likeability, summits between leaders of adversarial powers, sometimes changed the world.

President Reagan and his successor, the first George Bush, had enough rapport with Mikhail Gorbachev to hasten the end of the Cold War and of the Soviet Union itself. During his 2008 presidential campaign, Barack Obama flew to Berlin to deliver an electrifying showcase of his likeability to 250,000 Germans who greeted him as a rock star, helping him to win over allies in Europe even before he entered the White House.

Just as social media has revolutionized the role of likeability in electoral politics, so, too, has social media revolutionized the role of likeability in diplomacy. Today it is commonplace for leaders to engage publicly in the kind of diplomacy that once would have remained behind closed doors. In fact, leaders now use social media to advance or end some of the most heated conflicts in the world. Through social media, Vladimir Putin and other Russian officials sought to portray protectiveness—or alleged protectiveness—in their unilateral annexation of Crimea from Ukraine. In Russia's presentation, Crimeans wanted to unite with Russia, so Russia acted out of compassion. Leaders of Ukraine, in turn, appealed for global concern and protectiveness by adopting the Twitter hashtag #CrimeaIsUkraine.

If no world leader has used Twitter as aggressively as Donald Trump has—and as refreshingly or erratically, depending on your politics—nowhere has Trump's unique style of tweeting been more apparent than in his intentional diplomacy. "Why would Kim Jong-un insult me by calling me 'old,' when I would NEVER call him 'short and fat?'" [*sic*] Trump tweeted on November 11, 2017. "Oh well, I try so hard to be his friend—and maybe someday that will happen!"

Lest any of us laugh or groan, Trump's tweet was a classic case of "soft" power, which, you'll remember, is the power of countries to persuade other countries rather than to coerce them. The first part of Trump's tweet was about captivation, because—let's face it—who the hell ever heard a previous president of the United States communicate like that? The second part of the tweet offered Kim, the supreme leader of North Korea, hope for friendship with Trump and the United States more broadly.

Trump turned to coercion, the basis of "hard" power, in a tweet on January 2, 2018. "North Korean Leader Kim Jong Un," Trump tweeted, "just stated that the 'Nuclear Button is on his desk at all times.' Will someone from his depleted and food starved regime please inform him that I too have a Nuclear Button, but it is a much bigger & more powerful one than his, and my Button works!"

Never have the likeability traits of presidents, prime ministers, and other world leaders mattered more, whether for the benefit for their respective countries or for peace around the world. With that in mind, I'll now examine the likeability of eight of the most important leaders in the world. The eight leaders I've chosen each excel most in one particular trait of likeability, with enough likeability in each of the other traits to have gotten them to the top.

CAPTIVATION: Prime Minister Narendra Modi of India

For Prime Minister Narendra Modi, clothes make the man, or at least his popularity. By his own admission, he bases much of his leadership on his clothes and other elements of physical presentation. And it works. With an approval rating of 88 percent after three years in office, Modi is the world's most popular democratically elected leader. Sure, the leaders of Russia, China, and North Korea win elections nearly unanimously, but they don't rule democracies.

Modi changes his bold and colorful outfits up to four times a day—the most for a public figure, perhaps, since Bob Mackie dressed Cher for her variety series in America. We'll talk more about Modi's clothes in a moment.

Of a bit more gravitas, Modi's high approval comes in the most difficult nation in which to achieve it. India has 1.4 billion people, four times that of the United States, and twenty-two languages to which the Indian constitution confers official status—in effect, a recognition of twenty-two different cultures.

Compare Modi to other leaders in India. Rahul Gandhi, chief opposition leader and chair of India's Congress Party, which essentially founded modern India, has a 58 percent approval rating. Sonia Gandhi, who leads a center-left coalition of parties, gets 57 percent. Both Gandhis come from the Nehru-Gandhi family tree, which has had political dominance in India from before India's independence in 1947. Yet Modi is more popular.

Were it not for an improving, if uneven economy, no leader would have an 88 percent approval rating, particularly in diverse India, because of his or her clothes. Under Prime Minister Modi, India has overtaken China as having the fastest-growing economy in the world. Modi's policies have had an impact. Modi has done what leaders before him would not: He implemented deregulation, ending many barriers to foreign investment, and moved India's economy closer to a free market.

But India's high poverty and income inequality remain, and Modi's opponents on the left have attacked him relentlessly. They are especially frustrated that Modi bases his charisma on broad, unifying themes without getting into the sticky wicket of details. That was the criticism Ronald Reagan faced when he was president.

In that context, perhaps Modi would fear that news coverage of his wardrobe would make him seem shallow and prompt him to change the subject. Far from it. Modi embraces his wardrobe as the centerpiece of his likeability.

"God has gifted me the sense of mixing and matching colors," said Modi. "So I manage everything on my own. Since I'm God-gifted, I fit well in everything. I have no fashion designer but I'm happy to hear that I dress well."

Colorful though it may be, Modi's wardrobe is based on a simple foundation: the kurta. It's a tunic shirt without a collar that extends below the waist seamlessly, all as one garment, and stops at a man's knee. Kurtas are made of raw silk and other traditional Indian fabrics, and range from earthy pastels to bright Indian colors. Kurtas typically come with long sleeves, but Modi wears a short-sleeved version that's become a national sensation.

What's the big deal about a kurta? India's iconic leaders, Nehru and Gandhi, were known across the world for their jackets and loincloths respectively, and the couture became a source of national pride. Modi's clothes are a politically savvy nod to India's past as Modi transforms India for the future.

Along the way, Modi's tailor, Bipin Chauhan, has become a celebrity throughout India. With Modi's blessing, Chauhan has trademarked the term "Modi Kurta." It is likely just one of two trademarks around the world for a national leader's construct of likeability. The U.S. Patent and Trademark office approved Donald Trump's application for "Make America Great Again" in 2015.

Modi's likeability is produced by "Narendra Modi's image factory," as the *Economist* described it in 2018. To keep the focus on the clothes, not the issues, Modi does not bring journalists with him when he travels. When he ran into journalists during a visit to the southern state of Tamil Nadu, his team told them they could not ask questions about politics.

Surprisingly in populous India, it's not hard to meet Modi in person. Since at least 2012, Modi has used 3-D holographic technology to appear "live" all over the country. A life-size Modi, with feet perfectly touching the stage, is a hologram in full color that speaks to a crowd of thousands.

We're not talking 1970s Disneyland animatronics. The real Modi speaks live at a remote location, usually at a large rally, as the holograph captures his face and body. The holographic Modi, a 3-D figure to scale that has a front, back, and sides, walks around the stage with hand movements and body turns just as if Modi were there. From a distance at a rally, you could not tell the difference between the real and fake Modis.

In 2015, the British magazine the *New Statesman* reported that Modi's holographic self once appeared simultaneously at 1,400 rallies, many in remote villages where no one even owned a television. Or, as *Bloomberg* quoted a spokesperson for Modi the year before, the holographic Modi is "just like the Hindu mythology where the God was omnipresent. So he is everywhere."

There is, however, one difference between the real Modi and the holographic one. As the real prime minister has gained weight over the years, the holograph Modi is projected as a substantially thinner version. I don't know about you, but I want one of those for sure.

HOPE: Pope Francis

Until a couple of years ago, Pope Francis was the only world leader to have mastered all eight traits of likeability. In contrast to his predecessor, the more traditional and staid Pope Benedict XVI, Pope Francis actually seemed to lift people's spirits. As soon as he assumed the papacy in March 2013, the man from Argentina formerly known as Jorge Mario Bergoglio gave the Catholic Church, and the world, a rejuvenated vision of what a religious leader could be.

During the first years of his papacy, Francis embodied all eight of our likeability traits more than other leader in the world. He demonstrated the traits of captivation and hope when in St. Peter's Square, he kissed and embraced a severely disfigured man suffering from neurofibromatosis, a rare disease that causes tumors all over the body. The pope displayed authenticity and relatability by choosing the papal name Francis to pay tribute to Saint Francis of Assisi, a thirteenth-century friar known for living in poverty and preaching to ordinary people in the streets.

Pope Francis showed protectiveness and reliability not only by taking on wealth inequality and climate change but also by applying his criticism of systemic injustice and uncaring bureaucracy to his own institution, the Catholic Church. When a little boy walked on-stage during a message Pope Francis was giving about the importance of family, he revealed his perceptiveness and compassion by patting the boy on his head, hugging him, and letting him stay by his side instead of getting security guards to remove the child.

No wonder *Time* named Pope Francis the magazine's Person of the Year in 2013. A year later *Fortune* named him #1 on its list of the World's 50 Greatest Leaders. At the time, the Pew Research Center found that Pope Francis "enjoys broad support across much of the world." Heck, even atheists liked the guy. Thanks to his clear possession of all eight traits of likeability, which he managed to amplify through both traditional and social media, Pope Francis's popularity soared.

The trait Pope Francis embodies above all else is hope. After all, if there's anything clergy are supposed to do, it's to paint a relentlessly positive picture of reality through optimism, resilience, and goal-oriented thinking. And most members of the clergy do it well.

While the Catholic Church can be slow to change, the hope of Pope Francis has been his ability to transform it into something warmer, more relaxed, and more alive. Something deeply devoted to tackling today's most pressing problems.

In March 2013, for instance, Pope Francis washed and kissed the feet of twelve prisoners incarcerated at a youth prison in Rome. The group included two women—and two Muslims. Although previous popes conducted the same rite, Francis was the first to include women. This was a clear signal that everyone was welcome, everyone was worthy.

While Pope Francis is opposed to marriage equality for same-sex couples, he has shown a lot more acceptance of the LGBTQ community than his predecessors. In 2013, for example, Pope Francis argued that LGBTQ people should be integrated into society, as opposed to marginalized. "If a person is gay and seeks God and has good will, who am I to judge?" he said. Later that year, the LGBTQ-focused magazine the *Advocate* named Pope Francis its Person of the Year.

Also in 2013, Pope Francis wrote a letter to an Italian newspaper telling a nonbeliever to follow his conscience and that God's mercy "has no limits." That's the opposite of despair. That's hope.

But then, in 2018, things changed. Pope Francis's likeability and resulting poll numbers declined dramatically, although they remain above 50 percent in all demographics. Unlike what we saw of the pope in the first couple of years of his papacy, he has been slow, secretive, and defensive in handling the Catholic Church's response to priests who sexually abused children.

In 2018, an ideological rival of the pope's, the right-wing archbishop Carlo Maria Viganò, wrote an eleven-page public letter that
accused the pope of knowing about and covering up sexual abuse for
years, including abuse by former cardinal Theodore McCarrick, previously archbishop of Newark, New Jersey, and Washington, D.C.,
that dates to when McCarrick was a priest in Boston.

Viganò's letter, released on August 25, 2018, made a worldwide
splash. Lest it seem Viganò had an axe to grind—which he probably
does—earlier that month Pennsylvania attorney general Josh Shapiro revealed the results of his two-year investigation of sexual abuse
within the Catholic Church. Shapiro and his staff uncovered abuse by
300 priests of 1,000 victims over a period of 70 years.

A Pew poll released in October 2018 showed only 51 percent of
Americans rated Pope Francis favorably, a stunning fall of 19 percentage points since January 2017.

Should we count out the pope's likeability comeback? Never count
out a man with the skill to have dominated all eight traits as no other
living leader in the world has. Indeed, he has already begun to act.

In February 2019, the pope expelled Archbishop McCarrick from
the priesthood after the Church found him guilty of decades of sexual abuse. It was the first time any pope had turned a cardinal into a
former cardinal because of sexual abuse. It was a morally triumphant
moment for the pope, the Church, and the Church's victims of sexual
abuse, although the action was but one small step in the context of far
greater systemic abuse.

But the pope's move provided hope that he was turning a corner.
It demonstrated that he still knows the trait on which his popularity
rests the most. So long as the pope is able to provide hope when millions want it so badly, they will find him likeable enough to give him
another chance.

AUTHENTICITY: Queen Elizabeth II

Remember when Queen Elizabeth danced with a Hula-Hoop during its 1950s craze? And did it again in the 1960s with her bouffant hairdo that rivaled Jackie Kennedy's?

The queen didn't disappoint us in the 1970s. Her sensible shoes gave her an earthy dimension. And never ignoring fashion trends, she rocked those shoulder pads in the 1980s.

Who looked better in the 1990s than the queen, with her Rachel haircut from *Friends*? In the 2000s the queen's appearances as a *Pop Idol* judge proved to be unforgettable.

Let's not forget her selfies. The queen takes the best selfies you've seen this decade.

None of those things happened, of course, and that's what makes Queen Elizabeth authentic. She doesn't reinvent herself for the cultural whims of the moment.

But wait: Why am I discussing the queen, who, unlike all the other leaders in this chapter, is not the head of her country's government? Simple. Any leader who has held on to power since 1953, even if she ascended through a coronation rather than election, has likeability that compels our attention. She is the longest-serving monarch in the recorded history of the world. In contrast, Britain's prime ministership is likely to be in flux in the immediate years ahead because of the nation's internal divide over Brexit.

However much herself the queen remains, she still knows when to give in to popular culture when it looks more enduring than a fad. She was smart enough to meet the Beatles in 1965 and to knight Paul McCartney in 1997.

The key to Queen Elizabeth's popularity is, as Sir Paul sang, to "Let It Be." She just is. She is Coca-Cola Classic. Anyone who would think of changing the formula, whether at Buckingham Palace or in Atlanta, knows nothing about likeability.

When you don't reinvent yourself over seventy-five years in power, you put at risk other likeability traits, such as captivation. But you can take your authenticity to the bank. In the queen's case, her bank includes a net worth estimated to be $530 million. Her annual income in 2017 was estimated to have doubled to £76.1 million, or $97.2 million. Her income comes from receiving 15 percent of the profit generated by a trust called the Crown Estate, the collection of all lands and holdings in the United Kingdom belonging to the British crown. As for the queen's petty cash, she's won a cumulative $9.4 million from horse racing.

The queen is so authentic, she doesn't hide her wealth at all—not even when it would be a public relations mistake. In her 2018 year-end address, broadcast on the BBC and other channels and spread virally around the world, she offered: "Some cultures believe a long life brings wisdom. I'd like to think so. Perhaps, part of that wisdom is to recognize some of life's baffling paradoxes such as the way human beings have a huge propensity for good, and yet a capacity for evil. Even the power of faith, which frequently inspires great generosity and self-sacrifice, can fall victim to tribalism."

There was the queen, compassionately relating to common folk about their struggles as she sat by her piano, every inch of it dripping in gold but the keys. The Twitterverse went insane.

"Ah, the Queen's message," wrote a user named Josh. "I love getting yelled at by an old publicly-funded billionaire with a gold piano that we should all be happier and less angry." Josh's tweet was one of hundreds of others like it.

Was it possible that the queen or her staff didn't notice the piano in the room? No. Her video message was carefully produced. Did they not care about the gold piano as one of the negative likeability constructs of the year? Who knows. But the queen and her staff certainly didn't overcompensate with false humility. She would have gotten worse criticism had she delivered a speech in jeans, walking along the Thames. She expressed her authenticity at the expense of her relatability.

In fact, the queen, notwithstanding all her money, has relatability to spare. Much of it has to do with her silence. All these years after her 1953 coronation, we know next to nothing about what she thinks, be it her family or the state of her country and the rest of the world. We know what the tabloids say she thinks, but not what she really thinks.

Occasionally articles appear that describe Prince Charles's political views as center-left. But the queen's politics? She speaks not a hint. She has offered not an ounce of public friction between her and her prime ministers. They've included the center-right Winston Churchill, the defiantly liberal Harold Wilson, the immovably conservative Margaret Thatcher, the center-left Tony Blair, and others across the ideological spectrum.

None of them rattled Queen Elizabeth. She has never betrayed her responsibility to be the monarch of a constitutional monarchy, which is to be a figurehead.

Knowing little about the queen allows us to believe we know a lot about her. We can project onto her our own experiences. Suddenly the royal family becomes ours, as relentless news coverage of her family means we get to hear from them, or at least about them, every day. Many of us cannot say that about our families.

Identifying with Queen Elizabeth's family would be impossible if we knew and rejected the queen's politics as vastly different from our own. Not knowing the queen's thoughts on politics and policy means we'll never argue about her, or surely with her, at holiday dinners. She's the great-grandmother we all love.

That the queen places no political roadblocks in the way makes her largesse palatable—she's family, after all—and the stories about her family are something to which we can relate.

Do Kate Middleton and Meghan Markle not get along? Who knows if it's true, but we all know in-laws who don't. Has there been friction between William and Harry? Again, who knows, but we've all been privy to sibling rivalries. Have we attended fairy-tale weddings like Kate or Meghan's? Not quite like theirs, but we've attended weddings that brought us joy, and we are grateful to the royal family for letting us attend others through television.

The over-the-top events somehow make the royal family seem more real. The pieces of gossip, rather than besmirch the queen and her family, make them more familiar and therefore relatable. Everyone has family troubles.

When the queen herself makes a misstep, as when she waited five days after Princess Diana's death in 1997 to deliver public remarks about it, she pisses us off, as family members occasionally do. Our tolerance for the mistakes of family members is high so long as the mistakes are not frequent.

And the queen's mistakes are rarer than occur among our families in real life. Or at least, that's what we get to see.

The height of the queen's relatability came in 1992 when she delivered a speech marking her forty years on the throne. The queen and her family had had a horrible year, one the queen described in Latin as "annus horribilis." It would seem strange to relate to a queen who uses Latin, which no one speaks as a living language, to describe her emotions. But all of us relate because we have all endured such awful years and said to ourselves: Next year will be better.

But what a year the queen had. Prince Andrew separated from Sarah. Anne divorced Captain Mark Phillips. Author Andrew Morton revealed intimate details of Prince Charles's extramarital affair with Camilla Parker Bowles. And Windsor Castle, one of the queen's homes, caught fire.

Without going into detail and keeping her neutralism, the queen became a family member many drew closer to and loved more.

RELATABILITY: President Xi Jinping of China

On Friday, December 27, 2013, Xi Jinping, president of the People's Republic of China and general secretary of the Communist Party, walked into the jam-packed Qingfeng Dumpling Shop in Beijing and joined the long line of customers waiting to select lunch items at the cafeteria-style restaurant. Neither Xi nor his staff had notified the Dumpling Shop. So here he was, standing patiently in line, just another hungry customer without an entourage or visible security.

As he reached the front, with a shocked crowd having gathered around him, Xi ordered Chinese comfort food: pork buns, a dish of fried pig liver, and a dish of vegetables, all for just 21 renminbi, equal to $3.50, which he paid in cash.

News and photos of the lunch spread so fast across all of China, it was as if Neil Armstrong landed on the moon in 1969 and enthralled the entire adolescent-through-adult population of the United States—times five.

Food has long been a construct of likeability for public figures. Because everyone eats and presumably loves food, the construct comes down to relatability. Among politicians, Bill Clinton set the standard in 1992, when he visited various McDonald's restaurants throughout his first campaign for president—and he continued to do so as president. If some Americans consider fast food to be unhealthy, so what?

Those voters weren't the people the Clinton campaign was targeting. Clinton went to McDonald's to come across as relatable to everyday blue-color voters. Forget that he was a Yale Law graduate who had attended Oxford on a Rhodes scholarship. Bubba Bill eats McDonald's just like you.

When Hillary Clinton embarked on a listening tour right after she declared for president in 2016, she stopped at a Chipotle. In 2018, Barack Obama and Joe Biden ordered lunch at a bakery in Washington, D.C., that supports military veterans. Both men were two years out of office, but Biden was planning a run for president. A photo op with Obama couldn't have hurt.

China's president Xi took the concept of going to a restaurant one better. Once Xi got his food from the counter, he remained at the restaurant to eat. The Clintons and Biden didn't dare. Xi even sat at a communal table. Call him Bubba Xi, man of the people.

Given's Xi's role in the nation's politics, he has plenty of platforms where he can be omnipotent but not necessarily relatable. As the *New York Times* called him, Xi is the Chairman of Everything. Aside from being president of the People's Republic and Communist Party general secretary, he is also core leader of the Party, chairman of China's Central Military Committee, and chairman of even more. Intimidating, right? But under communist regimes such as China and in the old Soviet Union, leaders are inflated to untouchable degrees that run diametrically opposed to communism's self-professed premium on a people's government. The Soviet Union had its imposing statues and portraits of Lenin. In China, a towering portrait of Mao Zedong still hangs over Tiananmen Square.

What a contrast from Xi. As the *Wall Street Journal* reported: "Chinese citizens, who have grown up with the image of emperors surrounded by servants and concubines, are accustomed to thinking that their leaders' lifestyles are nothing like their own, full of privilege and pomp." And although Xi's lunch appeared to be spontaneous, the *Journal* also reported that "photos released on state media suggest that the drop-by was intended to portray the leadership as being in touch with common concerns."

Xi's likeability machine runs nonstop to reach Chinese and foreigners alike. With the help of official Chinese government media, he has taken on the name of Xi Dada, or Big Daddy Xi. "Dad" or "Daddy" in Chinese is pronounced "Ba Ba," and father is *fu qin*, so "Xi Dada" is clearly meant for foreign audiences. YouTube even has a video called Xi Dada produced by the *People's Daily*, the main Communist newspaper, in which young visitors to China, including many young Americans, praise Xi as if they know him personally. The video is in English. A young man from Africa says, "He is not just another leader. He is like part of the family." A young woman says, "I read in the English press he is called Uncle Xi."

I don't know about you, but I've never heard anyone in the United States, Canada, England, or any other English-speaking country who calls Xi their uncle. Wait, you mean to tell me Uncle Xi came to your house for Thanksgiving? I'm ashamed. My family never invited Uncle Xi to break matzo at our seders.

China's likeability machine is aware of the careful balance between portraying Xi as modern versus steeped in tradition. Like China itself, Xi honors both—or so the story goes. Chinese propaganda often portrays Xi as a Confucian father whose job is to guide the country as a good patriarch should. Xi "regularly quotes Confucius and other ancient sages, stressing their teachings on obedience and order," the *New York Times* reports, and "promoting the idea that the party is the custodian of a 5,000-year-old civilization."

When the Chinese government decides it doesn't like a portrayal of Xi, it bans the portrayal. The government turned hostile to comparisons between Xi and cute Winnie the Pooh, which the *People's Daily* had earlier included in the "Xi Dada" video. Apparently, Pooh was way too cute, coming at the expense of Xi's gravitas. The government then banned poor Pooh on social media.

PROTECTIVENESS:
President Vladimir Putin of Russia

Perhaps you've seen the portrayal of Vladimir Putin on *Saturday Night Live*. Putin, played by Beck Bennett, pops up mid-scene wearing no shirt, even when he visits the Oval Office. Indoors or outdoors on *SNL*, Vladimir Putin is always puffing out his chest.

That doesn't come close to the machinations of the real Putin to appear as his country's studly savior in Russia. He certainly rides shirtless on horses for all the media to see. But his stunts to show off his virility are way more complex.

News video of Putin in 2008 showed him hunting and shooting an endangered tiger in the wild with a tranquilizer. Multiple men attended to the sleeping cat, and Putin, in full camouflage, was in the huddle with them. So strong, yet so caring. One version of the story claimed Putin saved the lives of the TV crew by pacifying the beast. Four years later the *Guardian* reported the whole ordeal was a fraud: The tiger was apparently taken from a zoo and transported into the woods, only to die from the tranquilizers Putin shot.

But why stop at equating Putin with Superman? Putin is also Aquaman. In 2011 he went scuba diving in the Black Sea and, according to state television, discovered two ancient Greek vases. After some pressure, an official spokesperson later admitted the event was staged and the artifacts planted. So what? By land or by sea, Putin is the hero of the world, and there is no room for dispute or subtlety. A Moscow art gallery displayed twelve paintings of Putin as Hercules, including one of Putin holding the world on his shoulders. Another painting portrayed Putin as triumphantly fighting the United States over its sanctions on Russia.

Putin will go to any lengths to portray himself as the tough, protective guardian of the Russian people. Fashioning himself a martial arts expert, apparently with a black belt in judo, he has coauthored a book on judo and released an instructional DVD titled *Let's Learn Judo with Vladimir Putin*. But in televised displays, Putin is shown only taking down people. He is never flipped or dropped. A narrator intones: "Who needs bodyguards when you're this good at self-defense? Vladimir Putin shows he's a politician not to be messed with."

Putin's protectiveness has flowed deep into the Russian psyche. In "Someone Like Putin," a song that hit YouTube in 2016, the Russian pop group Zlachnoe Mesto sang about a young woman who dreams of dumping her ne'er-do-well boyfriend. And whom does she want her next boyfriend to be like?

> *Someone like Putin, so full of strength,*
> *Someone like Putin who doesn't get drunk,*
> *Someone like Putin, who wouldn't hurt me,*
> *Someone like Putin who won't run away.*

To understand why the Russian people so eagerly embrace Putin's over-the-top construct of protectiveness, we need to understand how history permeates Russia's psyche.

During World War II, an estimated 22 million to 28 million citizens of the Soviet Union, including soldiers and civilians, died in battle or because of war-related famine and disease. They represented 14 percent of the total Soviet population.

Russia's casualties during World War I numbered as high as 3.3 million. The Russian famine of 1921–22 killed an estimated 5 million Russians. And as many as 14 million Russians died during the famine of 1932–33. Russia and the former Soviet Union have endured through mind-boggling pain.

Add to the mix the collapse of the former Soviet Union in 1991. It was the end of an oppressive system but of a nation nonetheless, and of a superpower unlike the Russia that followed. No wonder Russians seek a protective leader.

As the *Washington Post* reports, Putin's spokesman Dmitry Peskov is only too happy to call his boss a "strongman." To us in the West, "strongman" has the negative connotations of a dictator or thug. But the word furthers Putin's image metaphorically and physically. For years, most leaders of the former Soviet Union looked like dowdy old bears who, notwithstanding the country's military prowess, looked as if they slept all day long in a cave and were vulnerable to attack. But not Vladimir.

Putin makes Russians forget their economy ranks eleventh in the world in terms of gross domestic product. That's one-twelfth the size of the American economy and one-eighth the size of China's. But when your country is blessed to have Superman as president, it's impossible to believe you live in anything but a superpower.

RELIABILITY:
Chancellor Angela Merkel of Germany

No ceremony exists to transfer power from one leader of the free world to another. I'm not talking about presidential inaugurations.

Rather, I'm referring to a ceremony in which the president of the United States, having isolated himself from our NATO allies, hands the gavel of global democracy to the leader of a different nation.

But in June 2018 we came close to that moment through a photo seen around the world. It was taken at the annual G7 summit, held in Quebec in 2018. Participants included the leaders of Canada, France, Germany, Italy, Japan, the United Kingdom, and the United States, along with observers from the European Union.

In the photo Donald Trump sat at a table, his arms folded and his face overwhelmed by all the other world leaders who remained standing and huddled around him. Except for one leader, they stood straight or nearly so, and peered down at Trump with faces of dismay, exasperation, and resignation. If ever there were a portrait that showed how Trump had alienated himself from the rest of the free world, this was it.

But one world leader positioned herself differently. Angela Merkel, chancellor of Germany, leaned forward with both hands on the table with a petulant-looking Trump on the other side and stared at him firmly but without emotion. She did not glare, nor did she look as if she had sighed. She simply gave Trump a calm and understatedly confident look, one that didn't grab for power but was based in responsibility, that seemed to tell Trump and all of us: "I've got this. I've got the mantle of the free world for now, and we'll all be okay."

That's the steadiness—indeed, the reliability—that Angela Merkel has given Germany and the rest of the world since she became chancellor in 2005.

Her reliability is rooted in her personality and personal history. A research scientist by trade, she is fact-based rather than emotion-driven. Her charisma is what you might expect from a PhD in quantum chemistry: She's low-key, to say the least. But in a world where nationalistic movements have produced chest-thumping, self-important leaders filled with hot air, she sets the standard for normalcy in personality. In today's world, her anti-charisma is charisma in spades.

As the *Herald* of Scotland describes her: "There is no image consultant orchestrating her coiffeur or clothes, no makeover artist employed to shape her style. The combination of blandness, painstaking thoroughness, shyness, a passion for data, and a boring wardrobe has resulted in an astonishing product, which could be labelled political gold."

Of course, Merkel's consistency in refusing visible likeability constructs *is* a construct. But she's not immune to one in a traditional sense. Her staff immediately recognized the value of the G7 photo of Merkel peering down at Trump, taken by her official photographer, and pounced to post it on social media. To be sure, Merkel's staff had a choice of photos to post. Other photos of the event, taken by journalists from around the world, showed each of the other world leaders variously looking as if he were in charge at the same scene. One photograph portrayed Trump as the dominant leader, with the others hovering over him as if they were hanging on his every word.

At home, Merkel has run as the candidate of the center-right Christian Democratic Party but governs as decidedly centrist. On the one hand, she has made Germany a welcoming place for immigrants and refugees. On the other hand, she has issued stern warnings about not requiring them to speak German at an early age to integrate with the rest of society. On the one hand and on the other—that balance of logic—is the Merkel mind. Like a metronome, the balance works reliably.

No wonder Germans call her *Mutti*, or "Mom," and news outlets call her the Decider. She makes wise decisions for her country and, these days, on behalf of allies, consistently. Merkel, not Trump, has remained steadfast in her criticism of Vladimir Putin. Where Trump professes his love for Putin, Angela Merkel never forgets Putin is an anti-West schoolyard bully who constantly needs scolding from Mom. That was the case even before Trump became president. In 2014, when Barack Obama was still president, Merkel took Putin to task at the annual G20 summit over his annexation of Crimea. According to the *Guardian*, she engaged Putin in a marathon meeting that didn't end until 2:00 a.m.

With Angela Merkel, Germany's future is in good hands, or so her reelection slogan went in 2013. Splattered all over Germany were campaign posters that featured only Merkel's hands. No one in Germany needed to see Merkel's face to figure out whose hands they belonged to, and many outside Germany wouldn't have needed to see her face, either. On the posters, Merkel posed her hands in the famous "Merkel Diamond," the unique hand gesture in which she points both index fingers forward but at angles toward each other, with her thumbs also touching. The diamond is the space in the middle.

"There was always the question, what to do with your arms, and that's how it came about," Merkel told *Brigitte* magazine. The gesture, she said, "contains a certain symmetry." There she goes again: Symmetry equals balance equals reliability. Indeed, good hands are the ultimate construct of reliability, and Merkel, as much as she has cast aside other constructs of political likeability, has always been wise enough to keep this one.

PERCEPTIVENESS:
President Emmanuel Macron of France

Imagine if Jill Stein, the Green Party's nominee for U.S. president in 2016, had defeated Donald Trump and Hillary Clinton to win the general election. Then imagine if Stein carried enough congressional Green Party nominees to victory for her party to take control of the U.S House of Representatives. She would be considered one of America's all-time political geniuses.

That kind of success, going from nowhere to national takeover through democratic means, is what happened in France when voters elected Emmanuel Macron president in 2017. To be sure, Macron was more mainstream than Jill Stein was. He had been minister of the economy in the incumbent government. But he was a backroom player hardly known to everyday citizens. In fact, Macron's victory was way more improbable than Donald Trump's the year before.

Trump used his high name recognition to run for the nomination of one of America's two major parties, completely within the political system, to capture a Republican base that had been moving to the far right and was ripe for the taking. As Macron set out to win the presidency, he had neither a political party or a base. He created his own party, La République En Marche!, and defeated the two parties that had had a stranglehold on French electoral politics for years: the Socialists, and the center-right French Republican Party and its predecessor parties.

In June 2017, a month after Macron won the presidency, his party won a clear majority of 308 of 577 seats in France's National Assembly, an increase from zero seats because the party had not existed prior to the election before that.

How does a leader transform a country's politics to that extreme and with such speed? The leader starts a violent revolution or demonstrates political savvy unlike what the world has seen before—a perceptiveness, if you will, unique to Emmanuel Macron.

Macron made a series of decisions in which he viewed French politics more presciently than anyone else in the world had done. Rather than run for the nomination of his Socialist Party, he rejected the party as hopelessly weak because of the unpopularity of Socialist president François Hollande. Macron, moreover, resigned as Hollande's minister of the economy and renounced the government's policies in protest—a neat trick for an economics minister who would have been inextricably linked to an economy in trouble.

Rather than run as an angry nationalist-populist—riding the far-right wave of Donald Trump and Brexit, both successful in 2016—Macron bet French voters would never move to the extreme right. As the *Guardian* would describe it, France, the bastion of *"Liberté, Egalité, Fraternité,"* prefers equality to freedom if given the choice. Thus the extreme right-wing Marine Le Pen never got off the ground as Trump did, and extreme left-wing candidates who adopted her angry rhetoric became just as unappealing. French leaders on the far left and far right may have read the populist-nationalist trend across the world correctly, but they were wrong in how they read their own country.

Macron alone was accurate. He saw the vacuum and came up the center lane. Stylistically, where others immolated in frightening ideological tantrums, Macron offered a mixture of solutions from the center-left and center-right with intellectual brilliance and sophisticated élan—qualities that play well among the French, who have never sought a Bubba president any more than they spray Cheez Whiz in Paris. Although Macron was only thirty-nine, he came across as the only grown-up in the room, and an extraordinarily handsome one at that.

Once in office, his early relationship with Donald Trump offered promise that Macron's perceptiveness in French politics would carry the day on the world stage. Macron showered Trump with so much public love during Trump's 2017 Bastille Day visit, Trump said: "People don't realize, he loves holding my hand!" Macron didn't stop there. He threw a military parade that knocked Trump's socks off, and arranged for a private dinner for the Trumps and the Macrons in the Eiffel Tower restaurant—tackier and far less gastronomic than hundreds if not thousands of other restaurants around Paris but, for Trump, simply perfect.

Watching the scene of the two leaders in France might have made any Trump skeptic, well, a bit nauseous. Macron's play to Trump's ego was that gaudy and that obvious, as if it were a wink to the entire world but Trump. But it worked. The two seemed to become genuine friends, however much Trump's withdrawal of the U.S. from the Paris Agreement on climate change would cause a schism.

But that's where Macron's perceptiveness ended. More than any other leader in this chapter, Macron's near undoing could be attributed to a complete reversal of the trait that played the greatest role in making him likeable.

By borrowing ideas from the left and the right when he ran for president, Macron reinforced an expression he often used publicly: *en même temps,* or "on the other hand." He had run as the French Angela Merkel, someone not bound by ideology but by rational assessment of ideas—or, as his detractors would put it, with no deep beliefs except for winning. He was a fierce proponent of globalism yet an equally committed guardian of French national pride. He promised programs to help the poor yet a reduction of taxes on the rich to spur investment. He promised worker retraining programs even as he promised to lift regulations on how employers treated their workers.

In his first year as president, however, Macron focused on his free-market proposals and forgot the others, apparently believing he would stimulate economic growth to kick off his presidency. The French were enraged. They stopped seeing him as their own JFK and started seeing him as president of the rich.

Just as damaging, Macron made stylistic errors that oozed contempt for everyday people. As seen on a YouTube video in 2018 that went viral and became a national nightmare for Macron, he came upon a line of French citizens outside Paris, all gushing with excitement to meet him. They included a teenager who exclaimed in French with youthful innocence: "How's it going, Manu?" in the same way a young American might shout, "We love you, Barack!"

Macron, who has signed letters using the nickname Manu, went incomprehensibly ballistic. "No, you can't do that, no, no, no, no," he scolded the teen. "You can play the fool, but . . . you call me 'Mr. President' or 'sir.'" Even as the teen apologized, Macron continued with full-on humiliation, making the assumption that the teen was some kind of bum. "First obtain a degree," Macron told him, "and learn how to feed yourself, okay?"

In another viral video, Macron met a twenty-five-year-old unemployed gardener and told him he could easily find the gardener work. "There are loads of jobs, go on!" Macron said. "Hotels, cafes, restaurants—I'll find you one just by crossing the road!"

Almost overnight, it seemed, Macron was no longer an elegant symbol of national pride. Suddenly he demonstrated a lack of emotional intelligence that made people wince. News reports about his spending $31,000 of taxpayers' money on cosmetics in his first three months in office surely didn't help.

By the end of 2018, Macron's popularity dipped to 29 percent, and tens of thousands of protesters wearing bright yellow vests of rage flooded Paris streets week after week. The Yellow Vest movement was part left-wing, part right-wing, and entirely anti-Macron. He retreated quickly by prioritizing the progressive safety net he had forgotten since taking office.

Could Macron's likeability rebound? It depends on whether his perceptiveness during the campaign was a fluke, demonstrating a level of electoral brilliance that strangely had nothing to do with emotional intelligence.

COMPASSION: Prime Minister
Justin Trudeau of Canada

If *Family Feud* asked any one hundred Americans who oppose Donald Trump which leader they find the most likeable, the number one answer would be Justin Trudeau of Canada. Trudeau is not only the anti-Trump in substance but also in likeability construct. Trudeau and his team continuously invoke Trudeau-versus-Trump comparisons to maximize Trudeau's popularity in Canada.

The construct works for a couple of reasons: First, Canadians are, by and large, to the left of Americans, albeit with the political cycles of change that exist in every country. But the change in Canada sways from center-right to center-left to left, by American standards, and remains left on social issues. Secondly, most Canadians get American television and deal with Donald Trump as part of their lives to an extent other non-Americans do not. There is always an American president to which Canadians get to compare their own prime minister.

To Justin Trudeau's credit, his likeability is both a construct and an instinct with which he was born. He's the oldest son of the most revered prime minister in modern Canadian history. Former prime minister Pierre Elliott Trudeau was a dashing, cosmopolitan, virtually peerless intellectual on the world stage whose popularity generated "Trudeaumania" in the 1960s. To picture the elder Trudeau, think of Emmanuel Macron, who became president of France with similar goodwill, but who, unlike Macron, did everything possible to remain likeable in office. That would make such a leader a legend, and his family royalty. Justin Trudeau entered office as Canadian royalty.

Justin Trudeau's reintroduction to Canadians in his adulthood came when he eulogized his father in 2000. At age twenty-eight, with the entire nation watching, Justin gave the eulogy of a lifetime. In it he revealed the compassion that dominated his father's worldview and the compassion that would become Justin's own salient trait in politics. "Simple tolerance, mere tolerance, is not enough," the future prime minister recalled his dad saying. "We need genuine and deep respect for each and every human being notwithstanding their thoughts, their values, their beliefs, their origins. That's what my father demanded of his sons and that's what he demanded of his country."

Likeability constructs succeed when they are based on reality, as we've seen time and again. For instance, Trudeau has tied his model good looks to advancing causes with compassion. In 2011, when he was a member of Parliament but not yet prime minister, he performed a striptease at a fund-raiser for liver disease in Ottawa. He ultimately earned $1,900 that went to the Canadian Liver Foundation, and he didn't even have to remove his undershirt. He engaged in harmless fun to support a good cause, only to see the rival Conservative Party use footage of the event in an attack ad that the party aired less than twenty-four hours after Trudeau was elected leader of his own Liberal Party. The ad had no impact other than to expose the Conservatives' frustration over Trudeau's destiny.

In 2016, as Donald Trump ran in the Republican primaries and spewed put-downs of seemingly every constituency that could not fight back powerfully enough, Prime Minister Trudeau recorded a video in which he wore a pink T-shirt on Canada's Pink Shirt Day to combat school bullying. As Trudeau explained in the video, the day came about after a student in Nova Scotia was bullied for wearing a pink shirt, not masculine enough for his classmates. Trudeau's T-shirt was fluorescent pink and featured the slogan "Kindness Is One Size Fits All."

Trudeau ended his video message with "You are supported. You are loved. It's about respect. It's about being Canadian." And therein lay his compassion construct writ large. Trudeau not only draws a distinction between his compassion and Trump's, but he also draws a parallel distinction between the compassion of Canada and that of the United States. He makes Canadians feel good about themselves and, by extension, feel good about him.

The world refugee crisis has given both Canada and Trudeau their greatest compassion construct. In December 2015, as a planeload of 163 Syrian refugees arrived at Toronto Pearson International Airport, news footage showed Trudeau welcoming refugees as brand-new Canadians. He gave out new winter jackets to beaming children and helped them into the jackets. "This is a wonderful night," Trudeau said. "We get to show not just a planeload of new Canadians what Canada's all about, but we get to show the world how to open our hearts and welcome in people who are fleeing extraordinarily difficult situations." A year later, when he was reunited with one of those Syrian refugees, Trudeau cried.

The Toronto *Globe and Mail*, Canada's largest newspaper, even ran a feature in 2017, "Politics and Tears: For Trudeau, It Works." Columnist Gary Mason counted at least seven times Trudeau cried in public since becoming prime minister. "To this point," Mason wrote, "no one has questioned his sincerity or suggested these episodes have been calculated in any way."

As unafraid as Trudeau is to cry, he is equally unafraid to offer apologies for the mistreatment of vulnerable peoples in Canada's past.

On behalf of the nation, he has issued formal apologies for how Canada did wrong by indigenous Canadians, LGBTQ Canadians, and Jewish refugees whom Canada, like the United States, turned away during World War II. Unlike Donald Trump, famously opposed to apologizing for anything, Trudeau does not see weakness in apologies or, for that matter, in breaking down gender stereotypes.

In 2017, for instance, Trudeau wrote an essay for *Marie Claire* magazine, "Why I'm Raising My Kids to Be Feminists." Trudeau insisted: "I want my sons to escape the pressure to be a particular kind of masculine that is so damaging to men and to the people around them. Feminism is not just the belief that men and women are equal. It's the knowledge that when we are all equal, all of us are more free." That is Justin Trudeau's Canada, the construct of compassion in today's troubled world.

CHAPTER 12

How You Can Be
The Turn-On

O ur discussion of nearly three hundred stars in politics, business, and entertainment has presented the eight personality traits and twenty-four subtraits through which public figures present their likeability. Now you know how the stars turn us on. You know how some turn us off. And you've learned how some turn us on again after scandal has knocked them down.

Along the way, you've surely wondered how our model can help your own likeability. How can you invoke the traits and subtraits to shape how others perceive you? And how can you invoke them to reshape your likeability when it has fallen on rough times?

In short, tailor the traits and subtraits to your strengths and your audience. Don't get me wrong: None of the eight traits is unimportant. People reveal them in stages of two traits at a time, as if each stage were a link to the next, giving each trait a connective role and a symbiotic role with the other trait in the pair.

But none of us is equally likeable across all eight traits. That's our aspiration, but not the reality, for ourselves and those we date, live with, or work with, as well as for the public figures we welcome into our lives. We just saw how eight world leaders each have maximum likeability in a particular trait, and in a trait different from the other world leaders. The bottom line: Develop enough likeability through each trait, but cut yourself slack in aiming for perfection across the eight. Don't let the perfect be the enemy of the terrific.

Even our most likeable public figures are imperfectly likeable. Ben Franklin, Madonna, Lady Gaga, and Miley Cyrus captivated us even as they reinvented themselves in ways that would defy reliability. They placed a bet that their reliability lay in the consistency of their being entertaining. The ups and downs of Angelina Jolie's personal life have been a public roller coaster—one on which she has sometimes invited us along for the ride. But through her activism she's been able to anchor her public reliability in compassion.

Steve Jobs was no walk in the park to employees who fell short of his genius. He was hardly the model of compassion. But he overflowed with the symbiotic trait of perceptiveness in his uncanny ability to understand what we in the marketplace would crave next. Consumers who had endured computer crashes on their PCs would experience far less of a problem, as well as far less anxiety, after switching to Apple computers. Apple's customers had reason to consider Steve Jobs compassionate to them.

Similarly, John Legere of T-Mobile, with his ferocious dress and frequent Twitter threats against the competition, hardly comes across a softie. But he's been betting successfully that grateful consumers would find T-Mobile compassionate in reducing their phone bills.

When I recommend developing enough likeability in each trait, how, exactly, would you do that? One way, as I just described, is to use your strongest traits to lift up your weakest.

Another way is to use the twenty-four subtraits. Whereas our like-ability model requires you to be proficient in each of the eight main traits—allowing for you to be stronger in some traits than others—you do not have to be proficient in all twenty-four subtraits. Who among us would come across as authentic or relatable if we had all twenty-four? That's not a human being. That's a deity.

Think of each subtrait as an entry point to its larger trait. For instance, the three subtraits of relatability—similarity, physical proximity, and vulnerability—represent three different opportunities for you to project relatability.

If you have just one of those subtraits, consider yourself proficient in relatability. If you have two of the three subtraits, your relatability is outstanding. And if you have all three, you must be Oprah. The same standard applies to the other seven likeability traits: Having one subtrait makes you proficient in the trait. Two subtraits make you outstanding.

Few if any of the public figures we've encountered have all twenty-four subtraits. Take Gwyneth Paltrow, whose likeability has been at perpetual risk. Her elitism and unawareness of it—which makes her more elitist—seem to put all three relatability subtraits out of her reach. Right off the bat, we can eliminate from Paltrow's repertoire the subtrait of similarity. Elitism is the opposite of similarity. Next we can disqualify her from the subtrait of physical proximity. Hardly any of us is bound to bump into Paltrow at the five-star hotels around the world that she recommends for relaxation. Heck, the mere thought of them is distancing. As for the third subtrait of relatability, vulnerability, the utopia she presents on her website, Goop, precludes it.

All that said, Paltrow is similar to enough of us in her aspirations for a better life. But note my qualifier: *enough* of us. Public figures like

Paltrow, Donald Trump, and Sarah Palin prove that coming across as likeable, whereby they convince others they have the eight traits and sufficient subtraits, doesn't mean the entire public has to be on board.

Many of us don't consider Donald Trump or Sarah Palin to be erudite, one of three subtraits of captivation. But their political base thinks they're erudite. I'm not being snarky. The two politicians articulate the frustrations of enough people in the hard-core Republican base to come across as erudite in ways few others do.

Am I suggesting you heed a lesson from Donald Trump and Sarah Palin? My goodness, I suppose I am. Whenever you need to come across as likeable to a group of people, be it your family, your workplace, or an audience of strangers, you need only to convince a sizeable minority that you have all eight traits and enough of the twenty-four subtraits. For candidates and elected leaders, that core of true believers is called their political base. For you, it's your likeability base. So long as you prioritize your likeability base and convince its members to see likeability traits and subtraits in you that other people may not see, you will avoid a likeability crisis.

Immediately after this chapter, you will find a chart that lists all eight traits and twenty-four subtraits. The chart will ask you to assess your ability in each trait and subtrait as "fair," "proficient," or "outstanding." If you check "proficient" or "outstanding" for one subtrait under a broader trait, check "proficient" for the broader trait. If you check "proficient" or "outstanding" for two or three subtraits under a broader trait, check "outstanding" for the broader trait.

Use the chart to keep your presentation of likeability rooted in reality. Likeability, as you know, is something public figures manufacture for our public consumption—what I've called a construct. When a public figure creates a likeability construct that strays too far from real life, the leap doesn't work, or it certainly doesn't last.

It will feel more authentic to others—and be easier for you—if you work to improve your likeability in a trait or subtrait from "fair" to "proficient" than from "fair" to "outstanding" in one leap. To advance from "fair" to "outstanding," you will need enough time to internalize the dramatic change and present it to others. Otherwise, your shift in likeability will come across as the construct it is. Don't become the New New Nixon.

Mark Cuban and Judge Judy have demonstrated the importance of not rushing the biggest likeability leaps. They both came to public attention with red-hot tempers that radiated protectiveness rather than compassion. But each has softened gradually and believably. Cuban has come to show us his more compassionate side on *Shark Tank*. And over the last few years Judge Judy has ruled her courtroom with poignant moments of kindness that would have been unimaginable in the show's premiere season in 1996.

Along with my model of traits and subtraits, I'd like to provide you with an insurance policy that will all but guarantee your success in enhancing your likeability. For that, let's return to our food chain of likeability.

You'll recall that Pete Seyfer of Magid, the company that pioneered likeability consulting, set out to evaluate the likeability of the newscasts produced by Magid's client station in Shreveport, Louisiana. Seyfer's well-honed instinct, borne out by Magid's quantitative research, concluded that Stephen Parr didn't project the infectious energy to convince viewers he loved his job—and, by extension, his audience. After Seyfer worked with Parr and the station to hone Parr's on-air style, his joy of performance burst through the television screen and he became the #1 weather forecaster in the market.

Projecting the joy of performance is as important as any trait or subtrait in our likeability model. The joy of performance is how you convey gratitude to others for the honor they have bestowed upon you by allowing you to enter their world. Surely the alchemy involves the time-honored techniques of language, body language, and facial expressions. But the major ingredients come from our likeability model: captivation and hope.

When you pull out all the stops to captivate others, you are telling them they're worth it. You make them feel valued. When you communicate hope to others, showing them your desire to keep them from despair, you are expressing concern for their welfare. You make them feel loved.

After all, how we fall in like is how we fall in love. And that, my likeable reader, is The Turn-On.

The Turn-On: A Self-assessment
of Your Likeability

	FAIR	PROFICIENT	OUTSTANDING
CAPTIVATION (P. 67)			
Passion (p. 73)			
Presence (p. 76)			
Erudition (p. 80)			
HOPE (P. 83)			
Optimism (p. 86)			
Resilience (p. 87)			
Goal-Oriented Thinking (p. 91)			
AUTHENTICITY (P. 100)			
True to Origins (p. 109)			
Coolness and Self-possession (p. 110)			
Self-disclosure (p. 114)			
RELATABILITY (P. 117)			
Similarity (p. 120)			
Physical Proximity (p. 122)			
Vulnerability (p. 125)			
PROTECTIVENESS (P. 136)			
Toughness (p. 137)			
Courage (p. 139)			
Self-confidence (p. 141)			
RELIABILITY (P. 143)			
Trust (p. 145)			
Stability (p. 148)			
Accountability (p. 150)			
PERCEPTIVENESS (P. 160)			
Fluidity (p. 162)			
Curiosity (p. 165)			
Humility (p. 168)			
COMPASSION (P. 171)			
Sympathy (p. 177)			
Warmth (p. 178)			
Activism (p. 180)			

ACKNOWLEDGMENTS

Though I conceived of *The Turn-On* twenty-five years ago, my friend and sister of the heart, Julia Sweig, pushed me to write it. Without her advice and relentless encouragement, this book would not exist. Julia, my love and enduring gratitude.

Among those who have blessed my life with unconditional love are my brother Richard and you, Loretta Weinberg, to whom I have dedicated this book. Loretta, God gave me a gift when we met twenty years ago.

Just as Loretta has been a second mother to me, U.S. Senator Frank Lautenberg of blessed memory, for whom I worked, was my father figure. I think of him every day. I also think of Salena Lesniak of blessed memory every day. Salena, the former chair of the New Jersey Civil Rights Commission, was one of my closest friends in the world. She passed away shortly before publication of this book.

I wrote *The Turn-On* during an unusual period in my life, but one also filled with resilience and renewal. I owe so much to my mom, Carole, and my separated-at-birth siblings: my cousins Marion Stein and Craig Savel, and Liz Sak, Yoav Sivan, Leah Binder, Francine Weinberg Graff, Rabbi Lori Schneide Shapiro, Hetty Rosenstein, Heidi Block Barishman, and Raymond Lesniak. You are my family, and I love and cherish you.

I hit the jackpot with my editor, Hollis Heimbouch of Harper-Business, and my agent, Mel Berger of William Morris Endeavor. Hollis, your remarkable instincts improved the book with every edit and big-picture suggestion. Working with you has been thrilling. Mel, you set the standard among agents for being a mensch among mensches. And thank you, Rebecca Raskin of HarperBusiness and David Hinds of WME. What a joy to work with all of you and your spectacular teams.

My researcher, Paul Hiebert, was indispensable. Paul, no other author could have had a finer or more devoted researcher, and we can be proud of this book together. For your valuable input, I'm grateful to you Judith R. King, Marianne Szegedy-Maszak, Herb Schaffner, Laura Schenone, Arielle Eckstut, and especially you, Kerri Kolen, who made such a difference.

My boundless appreciation goes to the two companies with which I worked closely, TMA (formerly The Marketing Arm) and Magid. At TMA, my thanks go to Jeff Chown, Matt Delzell, and Jean Scheidnes, and alum Jordis Rosenquest. At Magid, my thanks go to Brent Magid, Steve Ridge, Pete Seyfer, Bill Daddi, and to alum Kate Loor. Thanks to Stephen Parr, the former weather forecaster at KSLA-TV in Shreveport, Louisiana, for allowing me to profile him, and to KSLA news director Jayne Ruben. Thank you for your insightful interviews as well, Bruce Cohen, Richard Fischoff, Bobby Florsheim, and Jason Springer.

You have added immense joy to my life, William Saab, and Armaan, Trudi, and Leila Jazayeri, Manigeh Jazayeri, and Marsha Sherman. I love all of you deeply. Thank you, Michele Weinberg, Andrea Hurwitz, Lauren Hurwitz, and Lucy and Bill O'Brien, for your shoulders during the roughest times. For the magic of insight, thank you, Merle Rosenfelt.

My gratitude goes to others among my family, friends, colleagues, and educators who have added so much to my life and work over the years. They include Aunt Thea Flaum and Robert Hill, Dr. Tony Aizer, Congressman John Adler of blessed memory, Stacie Andree, Bear Atwood, Les Barenbaum, Ed Barocas, New Jersey Senator Bill Baroni, Mia Barricini and Adam, Rebecca, Mollie and Naomi Gross, AnnLynne Benson, New Jersey Assemblyman Dan Benson, Lynne Bernabei, Bonnie Bernstein, Alan and Anne Block, Margaret Bonafide, Aliza Bloom, U.S. senator Cory Booker, Aunt Sheila Brooks, Rosemary Bruno, Marilyn Canda, Cantor Lisa Klinger-Cantor, Bill Caruso, Illinois Representative Kelly Cassidy, Ron Chen, Ben Chevat, Alice Cohan, Clare Coleman, Congresswoman Bonnie Watson Coleman, Amy Cores, Sara Cross, Jean Cummings, Joyce Daniels of blessed memory, Reverend Bruce Davidson, Sharon Douglas, Reverend L.L. DuBreuil, E. Vaughn Dunnigan, Congresswoman Donna Edwards, David Eichman, Sam Elowitch, Dr. Yakir Englander, Cecilia Fasano, John Finnerty of blessed memory, Aviva Fintz, June Fischer, Jamie Fox of blessed memory, Debbie Francica, Charles Garner, Linda Geczi and Joan Hervey, Jaimee Gilmartin, Emily Goldberg, Rabbi Dr. Matthew Goldstone, Dr. David Golomb, Lela Goren, Robert Green, Matt Gross, Peter Hakel, Rabbi Dr. Jill Hammer, Reverend Rose Hardy, Reverend Rose Hardy, TJ Helmstetter, Rabbi Jeff Hoffman, Jennifer Holdsworth, Varda Hubara, New Jersey Assemblywoman Valerie Vainieri Huttle, Kerry Isham, Jennifer Jackman, Christy Davis Jackson, Deborah Jacobs, Susan Jester, Dr. Job Jindo, Cindy Joseph, Dr. Tamar Kamionkowski, Cantor Michael Kasper, Andrea

Katz, Cantor Lois Kittner, Matt Klapper, Rabbi Sharon Kleinbaum, Cantor Lisa Klinger-Cantor, Beth Knobel, Reverend Harry Knox, Reverend Bob Kriesat, and Ed Mather, Rabbi Charles Kroloff, Theodora Lacey, Jeannine LaRue, Jay Lassiter, Rabbi Len Levin, Jan Ellen Lewis of blessed memory, Cantor Jeremy Lipton, Eve Lubalin, Lily Lucey, Larry Lustberg, Jack Lynch, Congresswoman Carolyn Maloney, Barbara and Herb Marion, both of blessed memory, Dr. Harvey Mazer, Karen Nicholson McFadden, Phil Meisner, U.S. Senator Bob Menendez, Marie Moussignac, Juan Melli, Jo Miller, Tom Moran, Cantor Michael David McCloskey, Patti McGuire, Michael Murphy, Dr. Adina Newberg, Andrea Packer, Divij Pandya, Susan Petrizzo, Suzannah Porter, Rabbi Amber Powers, Tom Prol, Dorothy Dordelman Pearson, Cheryl Plumly, Dr. Ora Horn Prouser, Ayal Prouser, Rabbi Joseph Prouser, Dr. Peter Rapaport, Arnon and Diane Rieger, Linda Ripps, Julie Roginsky, Ruth Rosen, Cheryl Appel Rosenfeld, Dr. Louis Albert Ross, Mary Rother, Rabbi Lois Ruderman, Bari Alyse Rudin, Lisa Rosen Sanders, Beryl Satter, Rishika Satyarthi, Uncle Norman Savel of blessed memory, Rabbi Robert Scheinberg, John Schultz, U.S. Senator Chuck Schumer, Freeholder Patricia Sebold, Rabbi Jeffrey Segelman, Sally Shore-Wittenberg, Alex Silets, Rabbi Steven Sirbu, Eleanor Smeal, David M. Smith, Rob Snyder, Marc Solomon, Sushma Soni, Devon Spier, Alan Steinberg, Rabbi David Steinberg, Nancy Sutley, Nathan Tabak, Elder Reverend Kevin E. Taylor, Rabbi Elliott Tepperman, David Thau, Mary Theroux, Frank Vespa-Papaleo, Elizabeth Volz, Cynthia Wade, Del Walters, Rabbi Dr. Deborah Waxman, Karin Elkis Weinstein, Danny Weiss, Dane Wells, Ann Whelan, David Wildstein, Audrey Wilf, Tom Wilson, Evan Wolfson, Peter Yacobellis, David Yassky, Chancellor Dr. Phil Yeagle, Rabbi Dr. Tzemah Yoreh, Thalia Zepatos, and Sharon Zezima.

I could never forget my first partner, Tom Whelan of blessed memory, and his belief in me decades ago that continues its force in my life. The same goes for my grandparents of blessed memory: Herman Goldstein, Frances and Sam Ray. And my great-aunt of blessed memory, Adele Leimsider.

Thanks to the 150,000 members of the organization I founded in 2004, Garden State Equality, including Marty Finkle, Laurel Hester and Babs Siperstein, all of blessed memory; and my wives in activism, as I fondly call them, Marsha Shapiro and Louise Walpin. Thanks also go to the undergraduate and law students at Rutgers University to whom I have taught concepts in this book, and who provided invaluable feedback.

My deepest thanks go to all the students, faculty members, and administrators at my rabbinical school, the Academy for Jewish Religion in New York. AJR, the most inspirational community I've ever known, has introduced me to serenity and thankfully broadened my view of wisdom. To everyone at AJR, *ani ohev etchem*. Love also to the clergy in nineteen religions, denominations, and movements with whom I have worked for equality, all of whom inspired me to pursue my childhood dream of becoming a rabbi.

Special gratitude goes to Daniel Gross, with whom I lived much of this book in real time. Daniel, thank you with loving respect for the years we shared.

NOTES

Chapter 1: Discovering The Turn-On

2   America's support for Israel: Dominic Tierney, "The Twenty Years' War," *Atlantic*, August 23, 2016, https://www.theatlantic.com/international/archive/2016/08/twenty-years-war/496736/.

2   "support for Israeli causes": Yaroslav Trofimov, "Attack on America: Saudi Arabia's Bin Laden Clan Loses Support of Royal Family," *Wall Street Journal* (Europe; Brussels), October 2, 2001, ProQuest Central.

3   fifty-three siblings and half siblings: Kurt Eichenwald, "Bin Laden Family Liquidates Holdings with Carlyle Group," *New York Times*, October 26, 2001, https://www.nytimes.com/2001/10/26/business/bin-laden-family-liquidates-holdings-with-carlyle-group.html.

3   repeatedly distanced themselves from Osama: Daniel Golden, James Bandler, and Steve LeVine, "Bin Laden Is 'Black Sheep' of a Blue-Chip Family," *Wall Street Journal*, September 19, 2001, https://www.wsj.com/articles/SB1000849911107474240.

4   "never consider working for them": Betsy Rothstein, "Bin Laden Kin Turns to Former Hill Staffer," *Hill*, September 26, 2001, Nexis Uni.

5   bin Ladens had chartered a jet: Eric Lichtblau, "White House Approved Departure of Saudis After Sept. 11, Ex-Aide Says," *New York Times*, September 4, 2003, https://www.nytimes.com/2003/09/04/us/white-house-approved-departure-of-saudis-after-sept-11-ex-aide-says.html.

5   "likeable enough": Patrick Healy and Jeff Zeleny, "At Debate, Two Rivals Go After Defiant Clinton," *New York Times*, January 6, 2008, https://www.nytimes.com/2008/01/06/us/politics/06dems.html.

8   organization of 150,000 members: "Garden State Equality: About," Garden State Equality, accessed March 16, 2019, https://www.gardenstateequality.org/about.

9   violated the sanctity of marriage: Damien Cave, "Gay Officer, Dying, Is Pulled into Rights Issue," *New York Times*, November 24, 2005, https://www .nytimes.com/2005/11/24/nyregion/gay-officer-dying-is-pulled-into-rights-issue .html.

10   support for marriage equality had grown: "New Jersey Divided on Same-Sex Marriage," Monmouth University, February 19, 2009, https://www.mon mouth.edu/polling-institute/reports/monmouthpoll_nj_021909/.

10   freeholders voted to allow her: Michael Wilson, "Lieutenant Who Won Pension Rights for Her Domestic Partner Dies at 49," *New York Times*, February 20, 2006, https://www.nytimes.com/2006/02/20/obituaries/lieutenant-who -won-pension-rights-for-her-domestic-partner-dies.html.

10   Oscar for Best Documentary Short: "The 80th Academy Awards: 2008," Academy of Motion Picture Arts and Sciences, accessed March 16, 2019, https:// www.oscars.org/oscars/ceremonies/2008.

12   seventeen Republican candidates for president: Carl Bialik, "How the Republican Field Dwindled from 17 to Donald Trump," FiveThirtyEight, May 5, 2016, https://fivethirtyeight.com/features/how-the-republican-field-dwindled-from -17-to-donald-trump/.

12   most diverse in the country: "Campus Ethnic Diversity: National Universities," *U.S. News & World Report*, accessed March 15, 2019, https://www.usnews .com/best-colleges/rankings/national-universities/campus-ethnic-diversity.

Chapter 2: Wear Your Hard Hats: Likeability Is a Construction Industry

15   telling stories in a conversational fashion: Walter Isaacson, *Benjamin Franklin: An American Life* (New York: Simon & Schuster, 2003), 28–29.

15   played dozens of characters: Ibid., 2.

15   When Ben was twelve: Gordon S. Wood, *The Americanization of Benjamin Franklin* (New York: Penguin Press, 2005), 19.

15   founded the *New-England Courant*: H. W. Brands, *The First American: The Life and Times of Benjamin Franklin* (New York: Anchor Books, 2002), 24.

15   Mrs. Silence Dogood: Ibid., 26–27.

16   sent marriage proposals: Madeline Bilis, "Throwback Thursday: The Debut of Silence Dogood," *Boston*, March 31, 2016, https://www.bostonmagazine .com/news/2016/03/31/silence-dogood/.

16   both very rich and a voice of authority: H. W. Brands, *The First American: The Life and Times of Benjamin Franklin* (New York: Anchor Books, 2002), 5.

16   Franklin-mania among the intellectual elite: "Benjamin Franklin: In His

Own Words," Library of Congress, accessed March 17, 2019, https://www.loc .gov/exhibits/franklin/franklin-congress.html.

16   Franklin's fur hat became as popular: Walter Isaacson, *Benjamin Franklin: An American Life* (New York: Simon & Schuster, 2003), 325–28.

16   Franklin outlined the thirteen virtues: H. W. Brands, *The First American: The Life and Times of Benjamin Franklin* (New York: Anchor Books, 2002), 97–98.

16   Franklin was a slave owner: "Benjamin Franklin Petitions Congress," National Archives and Records Administration, accessed March 17, 2019, https://www.archives.gov/legislative/features/franklin.

16   freeing his own slaves: "Citizen Ben: Abolitionist," PBS, accessed March 17, 2019, https://www.pbs.org/benfranklin/l3_citizen_abolitionist.html.

17   "A benevolent man": Benjamin Franklin, *The Autobiography of Benjamin Franklin* (Boston: Houghton Mifflin, 1906), 93.

17   but also simplified: Walter Isaacson, *A Benjamin Franklin Reader* (New York: Simon & Schuster, 2005), 400.

18   Franklin produced creations: "Benjamin Franklin's Inventions," Franklin Institute, accessed March 17, 2019, https://www.fi.edu/benjamin-franklin /inventions.

18   God gave it magical powers: Exodus 4:1–5 (King James Version).

18   God told Moses to lift up his rod: Exodus 14:1–31 (King James Version).

19   God prohibited the disobedient Moses: Numbers 20:1–12 (King James Version).

19   "dissent collar": Megan Uy, "Ruth Bader Ginsburg's 'Dissent Collar' Necklace Is Being Reissued by Banana Republic," *People*, January 8, 2019, https://people.com/style/ruth-bader-ginsburg-dissent-collar/.

19   producers put glasses filled with wine: Tim Teeman, Lachlan Cartwright, Maxwell Tani, and Lloyd Grove, "Kathie Lee Gifford Just Broke Up Daytime TV's Best Double Act on NBC's 'Today,'" *Daily Beast*, December 11, 2018, https://www.thedailybeast.com/kathie-lee-gifford-just-broke-up-daytime-tvs -best-double-act-on-nbcs-today.

19   made a show of passing a box of peanut brittle: "Morning Session—2018 Berkshire Hathaway Annual Meeting," CNBC, May 5, 2018, https://buffett .cnbc.com/video/2018/05/05/morning-session--2018-berkshire-hathaway-annual -meeting.html.

20   Bruce Springsteen has insured his voice: Claire Suddath, "Top 10 Oddly Insured Body Parts," *Time*, September 1, 2010, http://content.time.com/time /specials/packages/article/0,28804,2015171_2015172_2014894,00.html.

20   Jennifer Lopez has insured her derriere: Diana Pearl, "J. Lo's $27 Million Booty, Julia's $30 Million Smile and More Insured Star Body Parts," *People*, March 18, 2015, https://people.com/celebrity/celebrities-insured-body-parts -jennifer-lopezs-butt-insured/.

20   Dolly Parton insuring her cleavage: Hollie McKay, "Pop Tarts: How Much Are Rihanna's Legs and J-Lo's Bottom Really Worth?" Fox News, May 18, 2015, https://www.foxnews.com/story/pop-tarts-how-much-are-rihannas-legs-and -j-los-bottom-really-worth.

20   more highly rated than Oscar ceremonies since: Sarah Whitten, "Hostless Oscars Ceremony Sees Viewership Jump 12%, the First Gain in 5 Years," CNBC, February 25, 2019, https://www.cnbc.com/2019/02/25/host-less-oscars-sees -viewership-jump-12percent-first-gain-in-5-years.html.

20   take a selfie amidst a constellation of other Hollywood stars: "If only Bradley's arm was longer. Best photo ever. #oscars," (@TheEllenShow, March 2, 2014), https://twitter.com/theellenshow/status/440322224407314432?lang=en

20   One hundred thousand people retweeted the photo instantaneously: Ryan Broderick, "Ellen DeGeneres' Oscars Selfie Is the Most Retweeted Tweet of all Time, Breaks 2 Million Retweets," BuzzFeed, March 2, 2014, https://www .buzzfeed.com/ryanhatesthis/ellen-degeneres-just-took-a-selfie-at-the-oscars-so -epic-tha.

20   breaking the previous all-time retweet record: Caspar Llewellyn Smith, "Ellen DeGeneres' Oscars Selfie Beats Obama Retweet Record on Twitter," *Guardian*, March 2, 2014, https://www.theguardian.com/film/2014/mar/03 /ellen-degeneres-selfie-retweet-obama.

20   ABC had signed a $20 million deal: Suzanne Vranica, "Behind the Preplanned Oscar Selfie: Samsung's Ad Strategy," *Wall Street Journal*, March 3, 2014, https://www.wsj.com/articles/behind-oscar-selfie-samsungs-ad-strategy -1393886249.

21   guaranteed ten celebrity selfies: Cotton Delo, "ABC Taps Twitter to Broadcast Celebrity Selfies During Oscars," *Ad Age*, February 27, 2014, https://adage .com/article/media/abc-taps-twitter-broadcast-celebrity-selfies-oscars/291891/.

21   "Twitter for iPhone": Helen Davidson, "Ellen's Oscars Selfie That Went Viral Was Not a Marketing Stunt, Samsung Insists," *Guardian*, March 3, 2014, https://www.theguardian.com/film/2014/mar/04/ellens-oscars-selfie-that-went -viral-not-marketing-stunt-samsung-insists.

21   showing Ellen how to use a Samsung phone: Suzanne Vranica, "Behind the Preplanned Oscar Selfie: Samsung's Ad Strategy," *Wall Street Journal*, March 3,

2014, https://www.wsj.com/articles/behind-oscar-selfie-samsungs-ad-strategy -1393886249.

21   "organically": Anthony Ha, "Samsung to Donate $3M to Charities Chosen by Ellen, Says It Was Included 'Organically' in Her Oscar Selfie," TechCrunch, March 3, 2014, https://techcrunch.com/2014/03/03/samsung-ellen-selfie -donation/.

21   gave away free Samsung Galaxy Note 3 phones: "I gave everyone in my audience a @SamsungMobileUS Galaxy Note 3. Anyone else want one? http:// ellen.tv/1cozqtZ," (@TheEllenShow, March 3, 2014), https://twitter.com/The EllenShow/status/440585470880141312.

21   Her 77.8 million Twitter followers: "Top 500 Twitter Profiles: Sorted by Most Followed," Social Blade, accessed March 17, 2019, https://socialblade.com /twitter/top/500/followers.

22   the gig that changed political campaigning forever: David Zurawik, "Bill Clinton's Sax Solo on 'Arsenio' Still Resonates," *Baltimore Sun*, December 27, 1992, https://www.baltimoresun.com/news/bs-xpm-1992-12-27-1992362178 -story.html.

22   worried whether his formal communication style: Michael Beschloss, "Eisenhower, an Unlikely Pioneer of TV Ads," *New York Times*, October 30, 2015, https://www.nytimes.com/2015/11/01/upshot/eisenhower-an-unlikely-pioneer -of-tv-ads.html.

22   first political likeability guru: Ibid.

22   commercials of twenty to sixty seconds: Kathryn Cramer Brownell, "This Is How Presidential Campaign Ads First Got on TV," *Time*, August 30, 2016, http://time.com/4471657/political-tv-ads-history/.

22   Roy Disney, brother of Walt: Michael Beschloss, "Eisenhower, an Unlikely Pioneer of TV Ads," *New York Times*, October 30, 2015, https://www.nytimes .com/2015/11/01/upshot/eisenhower-an-unlikely-pioneer-of-tv-ads.html.

22   *Tonight Starring Jack Paar*: Frank Rich, "Paar to Leno, J.F.K. to J.F.K.," *New York Times*, February 8, 2004, https://www.nytimes.com/2004/02/08/arts /paar-to-leno-jfk-to-jfk.html.

22   Nixon appeared with Jack Paar: Robert Nedelkoff, "The Road to 'Sock It . . . to Me?,'" Nixon Foundation, August 5, 2011, https://www.nixonfoundation .org/2011/08/the-road-to-sock-it-to-me/.

22   writer on the show, Paul Keyes: Stepen Hess, "What It Was Like to Work for Richard Nixon," History News Network, November 4, 2018, https://history newsnetwork.org/article/170105.

23   "Sock it to me": Ryan Lintelman, "In 1968, When Nixon Said 'Sock It to Me' on Laugh-In, TV Was Never Quite the Same Again," Smithsonian.com, January 19, 2018, https://www.smithsonianmag.com/smithsonian-institution/1968 -when-nixon-said-sock-it-me-laugh-tv-was-never-quite-same-again-180967869/.

23   having won Nixon the election: Marc Freeman, "'Laugh-In' at 50: How the Comedy Helped Elect Nixon and Set the Stage for 'SNL,'" *Hollywood Reporter*, January 22, 2018, https://www.hollywoodreporter.com/live-feed/laugh-at-50 -how-comedy-helped-elect-nixon-set-stage-snl-1074575.

23   appearance pushed by Clinton adviser Mandy Grunwald: Howard Kurtz, "The Woman Who Put Clinton on 'Arsenio,'" *Washington Post*, August 10, 1992, https://www.washingtonpost.com/archive/lifestyle/1992/08/10/the-woman-who -put-clinton-on-arsenio/6b29669b-4daf-4063-8c20-810993d13193.

23   likeability numbers among young voters rose: Steve Johnson, "Voters Under Age 25 Go for Clinton, Democrats," *Chicago Tribune*, November 5, 1992, https:// www.chicagotribune.com/news/ct-xpm-1992-11-05-9204100226-story.html.

23   winning the position of first chair in saxophone: President Bill Clinton, "It All Began in a Place Called Hope," White House, accessed March 19, 2019, https://clintonwhitehouse4.archives.gov/WH/EOP/OP/html/Hope.html.

23   *Dancing with the Stars*: "Bill Clinton: I Turned Down 'Dancing with the Stars,'" *Huffington Post*, September 21, 2011, https://www.huffingtonpost .com/2011/09/21/bill-clinton-i-turned-down-dancing-with-the-stars_n_973443 .html.

24   nonprescription versions of Jobs's glasses: Christina Binkley, "And Now You Can Own Steve Jobs' Quirky Eyeglasses," *Wall Street Journal*, November 9, 2011, https://blogs.wsj.com/runway/2011/11/09/and-now-you-can-own-steve-jobs -quirky-eyeglasses/.

24   black turtleneck had been an icon: Maisie Skidmore, "How Beatnik Style Made the Underground Mainstream," *AnOther Magazine*, February 18, 2016, http://www.anothermag.com/fashion-beauty/8395/how-beatnik-style-made-the -underground-mainstream.

24   make him some turtlenecks: Elizabeth Snead, "Steve Jobs on His Issey Miyake Black Turtlenecks: 'I Have Enough to Last for the Rest of My Life,'" *Hollywood Reporter*, October 11, 2011, https://www.hollywoodreporter.com/news /steve-jobs-his-issey-miyake-black-turtlenecks-i-have-last-rest-my-life-246808.

24   Jobs was far from a dream to work for: David Coursey, "Steve Jobs Was a Jerk, You Shouldn't Be," *Forbes*, October 12, 2011, https://www.forbes.com/sites /davidcoursey/2011/10/12/steve-jobs-was-a-jerk-you-shouldnt-be/#7ff661a14045.

25   who would later apologize: Brooks Barnes, "Pixar Co-Founder to Leave Disney After 'Missteps,'" *New York Times*, June 8, 2018, https://www.nytimes .com/2018/06/08/business/media/john-lasseter-leaves-disney.html.

25   his signature look was born: Yoni Heisler, "When Steve Jobs Isn't Wearing Jeans and a Black Turtleneck," Network World, May 19, 2011, https://www .networkworld.com/article/2229288/when-steve-jobs-isn-t-wearing-jeans-and-a -black-turtleneck--photos-.html.

26   an estimated 40 million Americans owned a television: Michael Beschloss, "Eisenhower, an Unlikely Pioneer of TV Ads," *New York Times*, October 30, 2015, https://www.nytimes.com/2015/11/01/upshot/eisenhower-an-unlikely -pioneer-of-tv-ads.html.

26   "I'll never lie to you": Sam Roberts, "Patrick Caddell, Self-Taught Pollster Who Helped Carter to White House, Dies at 68," *New York Times*, February 16, 2019, https://www.nytimes.com/2019/02/16/obituaries/patrick-caddell-dead.html.

27   attacked Obama for his celebrity: Alexander Mooney, "McCain Ad Compares Obama to Britney Spears, Paris Hilton," CNN, July 30, 2008, http://www .cnn.com/2008/POLITICS/07/30/mccain.ad/index.html#cnnSTCVideo.

27   Twitter had grown: Lahle Wolfe, "Twitter User Statistics 2008 Through 2017," Balance Careers, November 4, 2018, https://www.thebalancecareers.com /twitter-statistics-2008-2009-2010-2011-3515899.

27   Facebook had reached slightly more: Associated Press, "Number of Active Users at Facebook over the Years," Yahoo Finance, October 23, 2012, https:// finance.yahoo.com/news/number-active-users-facebook-over-years-214600186 --finance.html.

28   accelerated unemployment to a staggering 10 percent: Peter S. Goodman, "U.S. Unemployment Rate Hits 10.2%, Highest in 26 Years," *New York Times*, November 6, 2009, https://www.nytimes.com/2009/11/07/business/economy /07jobs.html.

28   unemployment was 7.9 percent: "Unemployment Rate Edges Down in November 2012," Bureau of Labor Statistics, December 11, 2012, https://www.bls .gov/opub/ted/2012/ted_20121211.htm?view_full.

28   Unemployment had fallen to 5.7 percent: "Unemployment Rate in the United States in the Month Before Midterm Elections from 1970 to 2018," Statista, accessed March 19, 2019, https://www.statista.com/statistics/933352 /us-unemployment-rate-month-before-midterm-elections/.

29   Unemployment had dropped to 4.9 percent: Vernon Brundage Jr. and Evan Cunningham, "Unemployment Holds Steady for Much of 2016 but Edges Down

in the Fourth Quarter," Bureau of Labor Statistics, March 2017, https://www.bls
.gov/opub/mlr/2017/article/unemployment-holds-steady-for-much-of-2016-but
-edges-down-in-fourth-quarter.htm.

30   startlingly low 3.7 percent: "Official Unemployment Rate Was 3.9 Percent
in December 2018; U-6 was 7.6 Percent," Bureau of Labor Statistics, January 9,
2019, https://www.bls.gov/opub/ted/2019/official-unemployment-rate-was-3
-point-9-percent-in-december-2018-u-6-was-7-point-6-percent.htm?view_full.

31   would have generated $6,295: Damian Davila, "Berkshire Hathaway Stock
Prices," Investopedia, October 4, 2018, https://www.investopedia.com/articles
/markets/020916/if-you-had-invested-right-after-berkshire-hathaways-ipo
-brka.asp.

31   online survey of 1,700 senior executives: "The CEO Reputation Premium:
A New Era of Engagement," Weber Shandwick, March 5, 2015, https://www.weber
shandwick.com/news/the-ceo-reputation-premium-a-new-era-of-engagement/.

32   in a ranking *Forbes* calls the "Just 100": Maggie McGrath, "The Just 100,"
Forbes, December 10, 2018, https://www.forbes.com/just-companies/#42533
ef72bf0.

32   most recent year by which a Glassdoor ranking is available for the CEO
(2017): "Highest Rated CEOs 2017," Glassdoor, accessed March 19, 2019, https://
www.glassdoor.com/Award/Highest-Rated-CEOs-2017-LST_KQ0,23.htm.;
"Top CEOs 2018," Glassdoor, accessed March 19, 2019, https://www.glassdoor
.com/Award/Top-CEOs-LST_KQ0,8.htm.

33   potential to use force: Joseph S. Nye Jr., *Soft Power: The Means to Success in
World Politics* (New York: Public Affairs, 2004).

33   rather than to coerce them: G. John Ikenberry "Soft Power: The Means to
Success in World Power," *Foreign Affairs*, May/June 2004, https://www.foreign
affairs.com/reviews/capsule-review/2004-05-01/soft-power-means-success-world
-politics.

34   "(when others see them as legitimate and having moral authority)": Joseph
S. Nye Jr., "Think Again: Soft Power," *Foreign Policy*, February 23, 2006, https://
foreignpolicy.com/2006/02/23/think-again-soft-power/.

34   ranked #1 in soft power: "Overall Ranking 2016," Soft Power 30, accessed
March 19, 2019, https://softpower30.com/?country_years=2016.

34   the U.S. fell to #3: "Overall Ranking 2017," Soft Power 30, accessed
March 19, 2019, https://softpower30.com/?country_years=2017.

34   U.S. ranked #4: "Overall Ranking 2018," Soft Power 30, accessed
March 19, 2019, https://softpower30.com/?country_years=2018.

34   cultural soft power, the U.S. ranked #1: "Culture Ranking 2016, Culture Ranking 2017, Culture Ranking 2018," Soft Power 30, accessed March 19, 2019, https://softpower30.com/?country_years=2016%2C2017%2C2018&sort_by=culture.

34   clear leader in movie exports: "Top 2018 Movies at the Worldwide Box Office," Numbers, accessed March 18, 2019, https://www.the-numbers.com/box-office-records/worldwide/all-movies/cumulative/released-in-2018.

34   top ten movie stars through March 2019: "Top 100 Stars in Leading Roles at the Worldwide Box Office," Numbers, accessed March 18, 2019, https://www.the-numbers.com/box-office-star-records/worldwide/lifetime-acting/top-grossing-leading-stars.

35   "My doctors estimated": Angelina Jolie, "My Medical Choice," New York Times, May 14, 2013, https://www.nytimes.com/2013/05/14/opinion/my-medical-choice.html.

35   nearly three in four American adults: Dina L. G. Borzekowski, Yue Guan, Katherine C. Smith, Lori H. Erby, and Debra L. Roter, "The Angelina Effect: Immediate Reach, Grasp, and Impact of Going Public," Genetics in Medicine 16, no. 7 (December 2013): 516–21.

36   Harvard Medical School researchers: Sunita Desai and Anupam B. Jena, "Do Celebrity Endorsements Matter? Observational Study of BRCA Gene Testing and Mastectomy Rates After Angelina Jolie's New York Times Editorial," BMJ 355: i6357 (December 2016).

36   Canada: "'Angelina Jolie Effect' Sparks Surge in Genetic Testing," CBC, October 17, 2013, https://www.cbc.ca/news/canada/nova-scotia/angelina-jolie-effect-sparks-surge-in-genetic-testing-1.2101587.

36   Australia: Kate Hagan, "Breast Cancer: Genetic Testing Soars After Angelina Jolie's Double Mastectomy," Sydney Morning Herald, November 13, 2013, https://www.smh.com.au/healthcare/breast-cancer-genetic-testing-soars-after-angelina-jolies-double-mastectomy-20131112-2xelm.html.

36   the UK: D. Gareth R. Evans, Julian Barwell, Diana M. Eccles, Amanda Collins, Louise Izatt, Chris Jacobs, Alan Donaldson, Angela F. Brady, Andrew Cuthbert, Rachel Harrison, Sue Thomas, Anthony Howell, the FH02 Study Group, RGC teams, Zosia Miedzybrodzka, and Alex Murray, "The Angelina Jolie Effect: How High Celebrity Profile Can Have a Major Impact on Provision of Cancer Related Services," Breast Cancer Research 16, no. 5, article no. 442 (September 2014).

36   Research from Cornell University: Jialin Mao, Louisa Jorm, and Art Sedrakyan, "Trends in Use of Risk-Reducing Mastectomy in a Context of Celebrity

Decisions and Media Coverage: An Observational Study in the United States and Australia," *Health Services Research* 53, no. S1 (August 2018): 2682–95.

36   climbing from an average: Timothy Malcolm, "Breast Cancer Study Confirms 'Angelina Jolie' Effect," *Cornell Chronicle*, September 25, 2017, http://news.cornell.edu/stories/2017/09/breast-cancer-study-confirms-angelina-jolie-effect.

36   "Please, please educate yourself": "I'm writing this post about the upcoming midterm elections on November 6th . . ." (@taylorswift, October 7, 2018), https://www.instagram.com/p/BopoXpYnCes/.

36   the site received 65,000 registrations: Claudia Rosenbaum and Michael Blackmon, "Taylor Swift's Instagram Post Has Caused a Massive Spike in Voter Registration," BuzzFeed, October 9, 2018, https://www.buzzfeednews.com/article/claudiarosenbaum/taylor-swift-voter-registration-spike.

36   the figure topped 240,000: Evan Real, "Taylor Swift's Political Post Sparks Voter Registration Surge," *Hollywood Reporter*, October 9, 2018, https://www.hollywoodreporter.com/news/taylor-swifts-political-instagram-post-sparks-voter-registration-surge-1150521.

36   In August 2018, 56,669 had registered: Claudia Rosenbaum and Michael Blackmon, "Taylor Swift's Instagram Post Has Caused a Massive Spike in Voter Registration," BuzzFeed, October 9, 2018, https://www.buzzfeednews.com/article/claudiarosenbaum/taylor-swift-voter-registration-spike.

37   The decisions cost Netflix: Jill Serjeant and Lisa Richwine, "Netflix Takes $39 Million Charge After Kevin Spacey Scandal," Reuters, January 22, 2018, https://www.reuters.com/article/us-netflix-results-spacey/netflix-takes-39-million-charge-after-kevin-spacey-scandal-idUSKBN1FC072.

37   grossing $57 million: "All the Money in the World," Box Office Mojo, accessed March 18, 2019, https://www.boxofficemojo.com/movies/?id=allthemoneyintheworld.htm.

37   cost of $50 million: Carolyn Giardina, "Ridley Scott Reveals How Kevin Spacey Was Erased from 'All the Money in the World,'" *Hollywood Reporter*, December 18, 2017, https://www.hollywoodreporter.com/behind-screen/ridley-scott-reveals-how-kevin-spacey-was-erased-all-money-world-1068755.

37   Spacey's crime drama *Billionaire Boys Club*: Pamela McClintock, "Box Office: Kevin Spacey's 'Billionaire Boys Club' Earns Abysmal $126 on Opening Day," *Hollywood Reporter*, August 18, 2018, https://www.hollywoodreporter.com/news/box-office-kevin-spaceys-billionaire-boys-club-earns-126-friday-1135816.

Chapter 3: America's Food Chain of Likeability, Starting with Marion in Iowa

40   one of the two institutions: cmarcucci, "In Memory: Frank N. Magid," *Radio and Television Business Report*, February 7, 2010, https://www.rbr.com/in-memory-frank-n-magid/.

41   began to coach the on-air newscasters: Ibid.

41   the "news doctor": Johanna Steinmetz, "'Mr. Magic'—The TV Newscast Doctor," *New York Times*, October 12, 1975, https://www.nytimes.com/1975/10/12/archives/mr-magicthe-tv-newscast-doctor-mr-magicthe-newscast-doctor.html

42   developed ABC's *Good Morning America*: Ibid.

45   ninetieth largest television market: "Local Television Market Universe Estimates," Nielsen Company, Estimates as of January 1, 2019, accessed March 19, 2019, https://www.nielsen.com/content/dam/corporate/us/en/public%20fact sheets/tv/2018-19-dma-ranker.pdf.

50   evaluating celebrity likeability: David Finkle, "Q-Ratings: The Popularity Contest of the Stars," *New York Times*, June 7, 1992, https://www.nytimes.com/1992/06/07/arts/television-q-ratings-the-popularity-contest-of-the-stars.html?src=pm.

50   the field had expanded: Brian Steinberg, "Omnicom Unit to Enter Game of Valuing Stars," *Wall Street Journal*, February 13, 2006, https://www.wsj.com/articles/SB113979992994972159.

50   Davie Brown Entertainment had started in 1982: Scott Donaton, *Madison And Vine: Why the Entertainment and Advertising Industries Must Converge to Survive* (New York: McGraw-Hill, 2004), 166.

50   focused on product placement: Marty Swant, "How Pepsi Landed the Perfect Product Placement, Then Made It a Reality," *Adweek*, October 9, 2015, https://www.adweek.com/brand-marketing/how-pepsi-landed-perfect-product-placement-then-made-it-reality-167515/.

50   Omnicom bought Davie Brown: Allison Fass, "Omnicom Acquires Davie Brown," *New York Times*, September 11, 2001, https://www.nytimes.com/2001/09/11/business/the-media-business-advertising-addenda-omnicom-acquires-davie-brown.html.

50   absorbed the Davie Brown Index: Marty Swant, "How Pepsi Landed the Perfect Product Placement, Then Made It a Reality," *Adweek*, October 9, 2015, https://www.adweek.com/brand-marketing/how-pepsi-landed-perfect-product-placement-then-made-it-reality-167515/.

52   "Before Mr. Williams apologized": Emily Steel and Ravi Somaiya, "Brian Williams Loses Lofty Spot on a Trustworthiness Scale," *New York Times*, February 9, 2015, https://www.nytimes.com/2015/02/10/business /media/under-fire-brian-williams-loses-lofty-spot-on-a-trustworthiness-scale .html.

56   "plead for a nap": Laurence Arnold, "The Selling of Sen. Lautenberg: Publicity Machine in Overdrive," Associated Press, March 9, 1998, via news retrieval.

57   "collecting baseball cards": Mary Jacoby, "The Senator and the Showman," Transom column, *New York Observer*, November 10, 1997, via news retrieval.

Chapter 4: How We Fall in Like Is How We Fall in Love

65   Abraham Maslow's hierarchy of needs: A. H. Maslow, "A Theory of Human Motivation," *Psychological Review* 50, no. 4 (July 1943): 370–96.

Chapter 5: The Gateway Traits: Captivation and Hope

68   headline for the ages: Tom Moran, "He Was No Cher, and Democrats Were Not Sunny," *Newark Star-Ledger*, September 13, 2006, A1, http://www.edmecka .com/articles/2006-nj-us-senate-election-he-was-no-cher-and-democrats-were -not-sunny.html.

70   Goldman Sachs CEO David Solomon: Kate Kelly, "At Goldman, He's David Solomon. At the Club, He's D.J. D-Sol," *New York Times*, July 13, 2017, https://www.nytimes.com/2017/07/13/business/dealbook/goldman-sachs-david -solomon-dj-d-sol.html.

70   entered the *Billboard* dance charts: Gordon Murray, "Billboard Dance Chart Upstarts: D-Sol, Excision & Illenium and Said the Sky," *Billboard*, July 26, 2018, https://www.billboard.com/articles/news/dance/8467209/billboard-dance -chart-upstarts-d-sol-excision-illenium-said-the-sky.

70   "David's always believed": Kate Kelly, "At Goldman, He's David Solomon. At the Club, He's D.J. D-Sol," *New York Times*, July 13, 2017, https://www.ny times.com/2017/07/13/business/dealbook/goldman-sachs-david-solomon-dj-d -sol.html.

71   Branson crossed the Atlantic: "Exclusive: Richard Branson Reminisces About Achieving the First Transatlantic Crossing in a Hot Air Balloon," *Telegraph*, December 9, 2014, https://www.telegraph.co.uk/news/newstopics/howabout that/11281268/Exclusive-Richard-Branson-reminisces-about-achieving-the-first -transatlantic-crossing-in-a-hot-air-balloon.html.

71   dressed up as a giant soda can: Catherine Clifford, "What Richard Branson Learned When Coke Put Virgin Cola out of Business," CNBC, February 7, 2017, https://www.cnbc.com/2017/02/07/what-richard-branson-learned-when-coke-put-virgin-cola-out-of-business.html.

71   jumped off a hotel in Las Vegas: Tahira Yaqoob, "Branson Takes a Leap and Flies by the Seat of His Pants . . . but Then Rips Them," *Daily Mail*, October 11, 2007, https://www.dailymail.co.uk/news/article-486997/Branson-takes-leap-flies-seat-pants--rips-them.html.

71   dressed in drag: "Virgin's Sir Richard Branson Turns Stewardess After Losing Bet," BBC, May 12, 2013, https://www.bbc.com/news/av/world-22499827/virgin-s-sir-richard-branson-turns-stewardess-after-losing-bet.

71   "If you are willing to make a fool of yourself": "Richard Branson Biography," *Entrepreneur*, October 10, 2008, https://www.entrepreneur.com/article/197616.

71   homage to Batman: "John Legere," (@JohnLegere), Twitter, accessed March 18, 2019, https://twitter.com/JohnLegere.

72   "greedy bastards": Justin Wm. Moyer, "Has T-Mobile's Foul-mouthed CEO Crossed the Line?," *Washington Post*, June 20, 2014, https://www.washingtonpost.com/news/morning-mix/wp/2014/06/20/whos-americas-most-foul-mouthed-ceo-hint-his-companys-slogan-is-listen-without-limits/.

72   "these high and mighty duopolists": Steve Kovach, "T-Mobile's CEO Went Off and Said AT&T and Verizon Are 'F——' That Are 'Raping You,'" Business Insider, June 19, 2014, https://www.businessinsider.com/john-legere-profanity-2014-6.

72   "The drawback to having no filter": "The drawback to having no filter when I speak . . ." (@JohnLegere, June 19, 2014), https://twitter.com/JohnLegere/status/479704470646173696.

72   "I don't walk closely up against the line": Steve Kovach, "T-Mobile's CEO Went Off And Said AT&T and Verizon Are 'F——' That Are 'Raping You,'" Business Insider, June 19, 2014, https://www.businessinsider.com/john-legere-profanity-2014-6.

73   Legere explained to CNBC: Abigail Stevenson, "T-Mobile CEO to Cramer: 'Shut Up and Listen,'" CNBC, April 28, 2015, https://www.cnbc.com/2015/04/28/t-mobile-ceo-to-cramer-shut-up-and-listen.html.

73   Photos of Legere: Photos by Mike McGregor, "John Legere, Bloomberg BusinessWeek," Getty, May 14, 2010, https://www.gettyimages.com/detail/news-photo/businessman-john-legere-ceo-of-global-crossing-poses-at-a-news-photo/103356069.

73   leaning over a chessboard in a stately corporate office: Photos by Jon Ro-emer, "Level Crossing," Roemer Film, April 11, 2011, http://blog.jonroemer.com/2011/04/level-crossing/.

73   merciless Twitter attack: Daniel Cooper, "Sprint's CEO Is Tired of T-Mobile's 'Uncarrier Bullshit,'" Engadget, July 2, 2015, https://www.engadget.com/2015/07/02/sprint-ceo-uncarrier-bullshit/.

74   national fame through his passion: Catherine Clifford, "Mark Cuban on Buying the Mavs: 'I Did It Because I Love Basketball,'" CNBC, January 4, 2019, https://www.cnbc.com/2019/01/04/mark-cuban-bought-nba-dallas-mavericks-because-hes-a-basketball-fan.html.

74   Cuban has faced $2 million: Ben Gollive, "NBA Fines Mavericks Owner Mark Cuban $100,000 for Confronting Referees After Loss," *Sports Illustrated*, January 18, 2014, https://www.si.com/nba/point-forward/2014/01/18/mark-cuban-fined-nba-confronting-referees-mavericks-clippers.

74   to manage a Dairy Queen: "Mark Cuban's Most Notable NBA Fines," *Chicago Tribune*, December 2, 2014, https://www.chicagotribune.com/sports/ct-spt-1202-smack-list-cuban-20141201-story.html.

74   Dairy Queen invited Cuban: Ali Montag, "Warren Buffett and Mark Cuban Met for Lunch at Dairy Queen—Here's What Happened," CNBC, June 12, 2018, https://www.cnbc.com/2018/06/12/warren-buffett-and-mark-cuban-met-for-lunch-at-dairy-queen.html.

75   SEC were "idiots": Sarah Whitten, "This Is the Next Big Thing According to Mark Cuban," CNBC, May 20, 2015, https://www.cnbc.com/2015/05/20/this-is-the-next-big-thing-according-to-mark-cuban.html

75   "I've got a 5-year-old son": Ibid.

75   "Who the fuck do you think you are?": Mark Cuban, "At Age 25 Mark Cuban Learned Lessons About Leadership That Changed His Life," *Forbes*, March 28, 2013, https://www.forbes.com/sites/monteburke/2013/03/28/at-age-25-mark-cuban-learned-lessons-about-leadership-that-changed-his-life/#2a69237b6ade.

76   one spirited exchange: Rebecca Shapiro, "CNN's Ana Navarro Demolishes Trump in 2 Languages: 'He Is a Flat-out Racist!'" *Huffington Post*, October 6, 2016, https://www.huffingtonpost.com/entry/ana-navarro-cnn-trump-racist-two-languages_us_57f7016ee4b068ecb5dd80a6.

76   "We're going to impeach the motherfucker": Ryan Bort, "Rep. Rashida Tlaib Calls Trump a 'Motherf-cker' While Promising Impeachment," *Rolling Stone*, January 4, 2019, https://www.rollingstone.com/politics/politics-news/tlaib-trump-motherfucker-774901/.

76   "I fully understand urge to cuss": Ana Navarro, "I fully understand urge to cuss in public to describe Trump," (@ananavarro, January 5, 2019), https://twitter.com/ananavarro/status/1081621520374472706.

77   "worth a million dollars": Dale Carnegie, *How to Win Friends and Influence People* (New York: Simon & Schuster, 2010), 63.

77   best way to become likeable: "The Best Summary of How to Win Friends and Influence People," Farnam Street, accessed March 18, 2019, https://fs.blog/2012/07/how-to-win-friends-and-influence-people/.

77   *People*'s 2018 Sexiest Man Alive: Julie Jordan, "Idris Elba Is People's Sexiest Man Alive 2018," *People*, November 5, 2018, https://people.com/movies/idris-elba-sexiest-man-alive-2018-reveal/.

77   be the next James Bond: Michael Sebastian, "Idris Elba Says Bond Producers Haven't Formally Talked to Him," *Esquire*, March 11, 2019, https://www.esquire.com/entertainment/movies/a26785952/idris-elba-bond-hollywood-reporter-interview/.

79   personal income: Natalie Robehmed, "The World's Highest-Paid Actresses 2018: Scarlett Johansson Steals the Spotlight with $40.5 Million," *Forbes*, August 16, 2018, https://www.forbes.com/sites/natalierobehmed/2018/08/16/the-worlds-highest-paid-actresses-2018-scarlett-johansson-steals-the-spotlight-with-40-5-million/#8a3eb873667d.

79   box office revenue: "People Index," Box Office Mojo, accessed March 18, 2019, https://www.boxofficemojo.com/people/?view=Actor&sort=sumgross&order=DESC&p=.htm.

79   The *New Yorker* once noted: Anthony Lane, "Her Again," *New Yorker*, March 24, 2014, https://www.newyorker.com/magazine/2014/03/24/her-again.

79   *Rolling Stone* called Johansson's performance: Peter Travers, "Her," *Rolling Stone*, December 18, 2013, https://www.rollingstone.com/movies/movie-reviews/her-102516/.

79   originally voiced by actor Samantha Morton: Kevin Jagernauth, "It Turns Out That Scarlett Johansson Replaced Samantha Morton in Spike Jonze's 'Her,'" *IndieWire*, June 21, 2013, https://www.indiewire.com/2013/06/it-turns-out-that-scarlett-johansson-replaced-samantha-morton-in-spike-jonzes-her-96743/.

80   "Her voice—breathy, occasionally cracking": Christopher Orr, "Why *Her* Is the Best Film of the Year," *Atlantic*, December 20, 2013, https://www.theatlantic.com/entertainment/archive/2013/12/why-em-her-em-is-the-best-film-of-the-year/282544/.

80   year's top fashion statements: Belinda Luscombe, "Lady Gaga: Top 10

Fashion Statements," *Time*, December 9, 2010, http://content.time.com/time/specials/packages/article/0,28804,2035319_2034464,00.html.

80 "Be fearful when others are greedy": Warren Buffett, "Buy American. I Am," *New York Times*, October 16, 2008, https://www.nytimes.com/2008/10/17/opinion/17buffett.html?_r=0.

81 1,000 pages per day: Shana Lebowitz, "21 Books Billionaire Warren Buffett Thinks Everyone Should Read," Business Insider, November 2, 2016, https://www.businessinsider.com/warren-buffett-favorite-books-2016-10

81 "I insist on a lot of time being spent": Chris Winfield, "This Is Warren Buffett's Best Investment Advice," *Time*, July 23, 2015, http://time.com/3968806/warren-buffett-investment-advice/.

81 lives in the same Omaha house: "Warren Buffett, Billionaire, Still Lives In Modest Omaha Home Which Cost $31,500 In 1958," *Huffington Post*, January 18, 2013, https://www.huffpost.com/entry/warren-buffett-home_n_2507179.

81 "This is the one Alexander Graham Bell gave me": Jason Kurtz, "Warren Buffett on Cell Phones, Email, and Material Goods," *Piers Morgan Live*, CNN, October 22, 2013, http://piersmorgan.blogs.cnn.com/2013/10/22/warren-buffett-on-cell-phones-email-and-material-goods/.

81 "No matter how great the talent or efforts": Catherine Taibi, "The 16 Best Things Warren Buffett Has Ever Said," *HuffPost*, December 6, 2017, https://www.huffingtonpost.com/2013/08/30/warren-buffett-quotes_n_3842509.html.

81 doesn't like the word "sexy": "Helen Mirren's Sex-Symbol Status, 'Woman In Gold' | TODAY," YouTube, April 1, 2015, https://www.youtube.com/watch?v=TwS1BbVTZ84.

82 free a Canadian journalist: "Mohamed Fahmy's Lawyer Amal Clooney Says Canada Has Formally Applied for a Pardon," CBC, August 30, 2015, https://www.cbc.ca/news/world/mohamed-fahmy-amal-clooney-1.3209075.

82 reporters jailed in Myanmar: Foster Klug, "Amal Clooney: Pardon Reuters Reporters Jailed in Myanmar," Associated Press, September 28, 2018, https://www.apnews.com/c08477ed5fc847048ac0d84cf44b7281.

82 "politically motivated show trial": Joanna Crawley, "Amal Clooney Blasts Maldives Human Rights as She Meets with the Former President in His High-Security Jail Cell Just Days After Her Local Lawyer Was Ambushed and Stabbed," *Daily Mail*, September 8, 2015, https://www.dailymail.co.uk/tvshowbiz/article-3226705/Amal-Clooney-arrives-Maafushi-jail-Maldives-meet-jailed-former-president-Mohamed-Nasheed.html.

82 cover of *Vogue*: Nathan Heller, "Inside the World of Amal Clooney," *Vogue*,

April 10, 2018, https://www.vogue.com/article/amal-clooney-vogue-cover-may
-issue-2018.

82   "I'm wearing Ede & Ravenscroft": Bruno Waterfield, "Amal Clooney and
Her Robes: A Tale Told in Tweets," *Telegraph*, January 29, 2015, https://www
.telegraph.co.uk/news/worldnews/europe/armenia/11376127/Amal-Clooney-and
-her-robes-A-tale-told-in-tweets.html.

83   "intellectual heft delights": R.J.E., "The Meaning of Kendrick Lamar,"
Economist, April 20, 2017, https://www.economist.com/prospero/2017/04/20
/the-meaning-of-kendrick-lamar.

83   won the Pulitzer Prize for Music: Joe Coscarelli, "Kendrick Lamar Wins
Pulitzer in 'Big Moment for Hip-Hop,'" *New York Times*, April 16, 2018, https://
www.nytimes.com/2018/04/16/arts/music/kendrick-lamar-pulitzer-prize-damn
.html.

84   made his condition public: Karen S. Schneider, "After the Tears," *People*,
December 7, 1998, https://people.com/archive/cover-story-after-the-tears-vol-50
-no-21/.

84   "deep, dark secret": Ibid.

84   starred in a television ad: "Michael J. Fox," McCaskill4Missouri, YouTube,
October 20, 2006, https://www.youtube.com/watch?v=a9WB_PXjTBo.

85   accused Fox of exaggerating: "Ass Rush Limbaugh Mocks Michael J. Fox.
sickhorses.com," tmabomb, YouTube, January 19, 2009, https://www.youtube
.com/watch?v=xpFC9uziVhE.

85   Fox responded during an interview: "Michael J Fox Takes Down Limbaugh," Kevin Spidel, YouTube, October 26, 2006, https://www.youtube.com
/watch?v=5INPn9lCNp4.

85   roots in Downey's drug addiction: Luchina Fisher, "Robert Downey Jr.
Talks About Addiction and Passing It to His Son," ABC News, September 9, 2014,
https://abcnews.go.com/blogs/entertainment/2014/09/robert-downey-jr-talks
-about-addiction-and-passing-them-to-his-son/.

86   That's what BuzzFeed called him: Lauren Yapalater and Dave Stopera, "21
Reasons Robert Downey Jr. Is the Most Perfect Man in the Universe," Buzzfeed,
April 25, 2013, https://www.buzzfeed.com/lyapalater/reasons-robert-downey-jr
-is-the-greatest-man-who-ever-liv.

86   29.2 million Americans watched: Associated Press, "Nielsen Says 29 Million
People Watched Wedding in US," *Washington Post*, May 21, 2018, https://www
.washingtonpost.com/business/nielsen-says-29-million-people-watched-wedding
-in-us/2018/05/21/30a29c5c-5d0b-11e8-b656-236c6214ef01_story.html.

86 the *Guardian* put it: Afua Hirsch, "Meghan Markle's Wedding Was a Rousing Celebration of Blackness," *Guardian*, May 20, 2018, https://www.the guardian.com/uk-news/2018/may/19/meghan-markles-wedding-was-a-celebra tion-of-blackness.

87 attract the attention of the SEC: Gretchen Frazee, "Why Elon Musk's Tweets Matter to the SEC," PBS, March 11, 2019, https://www.pbs.org/news hour/economy/making-sense/why-elon-musks-tweets-matter-to-the-sec.

87 "There's no point in being pessimistic": Neal E. Boudette, "Tesla Shaken by a Departure and What Elon Musk Was Smoking," *New York Times*, September 7, 2018, https://www.nytimes.com/2018/09/07/business/tesla-stock-elon -musk.html.

88 erect a model of resilience: John W. Reich, Alex J. Zautra, and John S. Hall, eds., *Handbook of Adult Resilience* (New York: Guilford, 2010), xi.

89 shot in the head: Mishal Husain, "Malala: The Girl Who Was Shot for Going to School," BBC, October 7, 2013, https://www.bbc.com/news/magazine -24379018.

89 win a Nobel Peace Prize: Liam Stack, "Malala Yousafzai, Nobel Peace Prize Laureate, Starts at Oxford," *New York Times*, October 10, 2017, https://www .nytimes.com/2017/10/10/world/europe/malala-yousafzai-oxford.html.

89 pursuing her education at Oxford: Malala Yousafzai, "Malala on Life at Oxford University and Why Every Girl Deserves the Same Chance," *Vogue*, October 22, 2018, https://www.vogue.co.uk/article/malala-yousafzai-interview-2018.

89 "I forgive them because that's the best revenge": Robert Fulford, "Malala's Nemesis Is Dead, and Locals Hope He's Gone to Hell," *National Post*, June 22, 2018, https://nationalpost.com/opinion/robert-fulford-malalas-nemesis-is-dead -and-locals-hope-hes-gone-to-hell.

89 undergoing a sports drought: Mark Bechtel, "The Curse Is Dead: Cleveland Fans Can Finally Breathe a Sigh of Relief," *Sports Illustrated*, June 20, 2016, https://www.si.com/nba/2016/06/20/lebron-james-cavs-nba-finals-cleveland -championship-drought.

90 "I got a goal": Marc Berman, "LeBron Warns He Won't Leave Cleveland Without Title," *New York Post*, April 2, 2010, https://nypost.com/2010/04/02 /lebron-warns-he-wont-leave-cleveland-without-title/.

90 "This fall I'm going to take my talents": Henry Abbott, "LeBron James' Decision: The Transcript," ESPN, July 8, 2010, http://www.espn.com/blog/true hoop/post/_/id/17853/lebron-james-decision-the-transcript.

90   "our former hero": "Dan Gilbert's Open Letter to Fans: James' Decision a 'Cowardly Betrayal' and Owner Promises a Title Before Heat," Cleveland.com, July 9, 2010, https://www.cleveland.com/cavs/2010/07/gilberts_letter_to_fans _james.html.

90   "In Northeast Ohio, nothing is given": LeBron James, "I'm Coming Home," *Sports Illustrated*, July 21, 2014, https://www.si.com/vault/2014/07/21/106615402 /im-coming-home.

90   "Cleveland, this one's for you!": Zach Harper, "LeBron James After Winning the 2016 NBA Finals: 'Cleveland, This Is for You!,'" CBS Sports, June 19, 2016, https://www.cbssports.com/nba/news/lebron-james-after-winning-the -2016-nba-finals-cleveland-this-is-for-you/.

91   a photo of Fonda surfaced: Colby Itkowitz, "How Jane Fonda's 1972 Trip to North Vietnam Earned Her the Nickname 'Hanoi Jane,'" *Washington Post*, September 21, 2018, https://www.washingtonpost.com/news/retropolis /wp/2017/09/18/how-jane-fondas-1972-trip-to-north-vietnam-earned-her-the -nickname-hanoi-jane/.

91   *Journal of Social and Clinical Psychology*: Lorie Ritschel, "Lessons in Teaching Hope: An Interview with C. R. Snyder," *Teaching of Psychology* 32, no. 1 (2005): 74–78, https://www.tandfonline.com/doi/abs/10.1207/s15328023top3201_15.

91   pioneer in positive psychology: "Chancellor, Colleagues Issue Statements on Death of KU Professor Rick Snyder," University of Kansas, January 18, 2006, http://archive.news.ku.edu/2006/january/18/statement.shtml.

91   hope requires goal-oriented thinking: C. R. Snyder and Shane J. Lopez, eds., *Handbook of Positive Psychology* (Oxford, UK: Oxford University Press, 2001), 257–58.

91   Snyder posits that hope leads to: C. R. Snyder, "Hope Theory: Rainbows in the Mind," *Psychological Inquiry* 13, no. 4 (2002): 249–75.

91   "This nation should commit itself": Robert R. Gilruth, "I Believe We Should Go to the Moon," National Aeronautics and Space Administration, accessed March 18, 2019, https://history.nasa.gov/SP-350/ch-2-1.html.

92   Kennedy's "Man on the Moon" goal: Morten T. Hansen, "The 'Man on the Moon' Standard," *Harvard Business Review*, May 25, 2011, https://hbr .org/2011/05/the-man-on-the-moon-standard.

93   "Jack Dorsey Has No Clue": Ashley Feinberg, "Jack Dorsey Has No Clue What He Wants," *HuffPost*, January 28, 2019, https://www.huffingtonpost.com /entry/jack-dorsey-twitter-interview_us_5c3e2601e4b01c93e00e2a00.

93   "I haven't done enough": "Twitter CEO: 'I Haven't Done Enough' to Be Transparent," CNN, August 18, 2018, https://money.cnn.com/video/technology /2018/08/18/jack-dorsey-twitter-ceo-brian-stelter-transparency-shadowbanning -politics.cnnmoney/index.html.

93   short-listed Coogler for its 2018 Person of the Year: Eliana Dockterman, "The Short List No. 6 Person of the Year 2018: Ryan Coogler," *Time*, accessed March 19, 2019, http://time.com/person-of-the-year-2018-ryan-coogler-runner-up/.

94   wore a purity ring: "9 Celebrities Who've Worn Purity Rings," *Huffington Post*, July 2, 2013, https://www.huffingtonpost.com/2013/07/02/celebrities-purity -rings_n_3535439.html.

94   people you can trust around your daughter: Frank Swertlow, "Miley Cyrus' Mom Safeguards Her Career," Reuters, October 27, 2009, https://www.reuters .com/article/us-kids/miley-cyrus-mom-safeguards-her-career-idUSTRE59R0 C520091028.

95   hired Larry Rudolph: Hollie McKay, "Is Miley Cyrus' Manager Behind Her Sexed Up Transformation?," Fox News, April 13, 2016, https://www.foxnews.com /entertainment/is-miley-cyrus-manager-behind-her-sexed-up-transformation.

95   "It could not have gone better": Joyce Chen, "Miley Cyrus MTV VMA Performance 'Could Not Have Gone Better,' Her Manager Says," *Us Weekly*, August 28, 2013, https://www.usmagazine.com/celebrity-news/news/miley-cyrus -mtv-vma-performance-could-not-have-gone-better-her-manager-says-2013288/.

95   "she's been murdered": Stephanie Webber, "Miley Cyrus Saturday Night Live: Singer Says Hannah Montana Has Been Murdered, Will Not Apologize for VMA Performance," *Us Weekly*, October 6, 2013, https://www.usmagazine.com /entertainment/news/miley-cyrus-saturday-night-live-singer-says-hannah-montana -has-been-murdered-will-not-apologize-for-vma-performance-2013610/.

96   "I went from people just thinking": Jon Caramanica, "Miley Cyrus on Her Jump to Sexy Twerker," *New York Times*, December 26, 2013, https://www. nytimes.com/2013/12/29/arts/music/miley-cyrus-on-her-jump-to-sexy-twerker. html.

97   wished she could erase Hannah Montana's music: Matt Diehl, "Miley Cyrus 2.0: The Billboard Cover Story," *Billboard*, June 14, 2013, https://www .billboard.com/articles/columns/pop-shop/1567023/miley-cyrus-20-the-bill board-cover-story.

97   founded the Happy Hippie Foundation: Ramin Setoodeh, "Miley Cyrus Stands Up for Homeless Youth," *Variety*, October 11, 2016, https://variety

.com/2016/music/news/miley-cyrus-happy-hippe-foundation-homeless-youth
-1201884032/.

97   homeless children: Ibid.

Chapter 6: The Foundation Traits: Authenticity and Relatability

99   record-breaking 495 scripted original shows: Lesley Goldberg, "Peak TV
Update: Scripted Originals Hit Yet Another High in 2018," *Hollywood Reporter*,
December 13, 2018, https://www.hollywoodreporter.com/live-feed/peak-tv-up
date-scripted-originals-hit-high-2018-1169047.

99   871 films released in the U.S. and Canada: "Number of Movies Released in
the United States and Canada from 2000 to 2018," Statista, accessed March 21, 2019,
https://www.statista.com/statistics/187122/movie-releases-in-north-america
-since-2001/.

99   estimated 2.6 billion social media users around the world: "Number of Social Media Users Worldwide from 2010 to 2021 (in Billions)," Statista, accessed
March 21, 2019, https://www.statista.com/statistics/278414/number-of-world
wide-social-network-users/.

102   lick one of the donuts: Randee Dawn, "Ariana Grande Says She's Sorry After
Licking Doughnuts, Saying 'I Hate America,'" Today, July 9, 2015, https://www
.today.com/popculture/ariana-grande-apologizes-doughnut-lick-i-hate-america
-t31006.

102   "What the fuck is that?": "Ariana Grande Bails on MLB Concert . . . 'I
Hate America' Backlash to Blame?," TMZ, July 8, 2015, https://www.tmz.com
/2015/07/08/ariana-grande-i-hate-americans-donut-shop-video/.

102   tabloid television program TMZ: Ibid.

102   quickly released a videotaped apology: Jason Lipshutz, "Ariana Grande
Apologizes for 'I Hate America' Video: 'I Am Extremely Proud to Be an American,'" *Billboard*, July 8, 2015, https://www.billboard.com/articles/columns/pop
-shop/6620378/ariana-grande-apology-donut-video-america.

103   mockery of Serge Kovaleski: Daniel Arkin, "Donald Trump Criticized After He Appears to Mock Reporter Serge Kovaleski," NBC News, November 26,
2015, https://www.nbcnews.com/politics/2016-election/donald-trump-criticized
-after-he-appears-mock-reporter-serge-kovaleski-n470016.

104   "very pro-choice": Philip Bump, "Donald Trump Took 5 Different Positions on
Abortion in 3 Days," *Washington Post*, April 3, 2016, https://www.washingtonpost.com
/news/the-fix/wp/2016/04/03/donald-trumps-ever-shifting-positions-on-abortion/.

104   amending the Civil Rights Act: "Donald Trump's Advocate Interview Where He Defends Gays, Mexicans," *Advocate*, September 28, 2015, https://www.advocate.com/election/2015/9/28/read-donald-trumps-advocate-interview-where-he-defends-gays-mexicans.

104   "ban on assault weapons": Callum Borchers, "Bannon's Warning to Trump on Gun Control: Don't Even Think About It," *Washington Post*, October 4, 2017, https://www.washingtonpost.com/news/the-fix/wp/2017/10/04/bannons-warning-to-trump-on-gun-control-dont-even-think-about-it/?utm_term=.50106ac8ad0f.

104   proposed a one-time tax of 14.25 percent: Jonathan Karl, "Donald Trump Once Proposed the Biggest Tax Hike Ever," ABC News, August 6, 2015, https://abcnews.go.com/Politics/donald-trump-proposed-biggest-tax-hike/story?id=32926722.

105   make public statements that Bill Cosby: "Why Are Old Assault Claims Against Bill Cosby Back?," NBC News, November 17, 2014, https://www.nbcnews.com/pop-culture/celebrity/why-are-old-assault-claims-against-bill-cosby-back-n250161.

105   Cosby was convicted: Erin Durkin, "Bill Cosby Sentenced to Three to 10 Years in Prison for Sexual Assault," *Guardian*, September 25, 2018, https://www.theguardian.com/world/2018/sep/25/bill-cosby-sentence-sexual-assault-judge.

106   adopted a plushier lifestyle: Zack O'Malley Greenburg, "Bruce Springsteen's Net Worth: $460 Million in 2016," *Forbes*, December 14, 2016, https://www.forbes.com/sites/zackomalleygreenburg/2016/12/14/bruce-springsteens-net-worth-460-million-in-2016/#5f89a82d1eaf.

106   "walked in silence": "Leonardo DiCaprio Had to Convince Daniel Day-Lewis to Make Gangs of New York," *Daily Express*, February 23, 2014, https://www.express.co.uk/celebrity-news/461393/Leonardo-DiCaprio-had-to-convince-Daniel-Day-Lewis-to-make-Gangs-of-New-York.

107   "Authenticity in Political Discourse": Ben Jones, "Authenticity in Political Discourse," *Ethical Theory and Moral Practice* 19, no. 2 (2016): 489–504.

109   "authentic objects, persons, and collectives": Charles Lindholm, *Culture and Authenticity* (Malden, MA: Blackwell Publishing, 2008), 2.

110   "so that others can create": Sarah Green Carmichael, "Microsoft's CEO on Rediscovering the Company's Soul," *Harvard Business Review*, September 28, 2017, https://hbr.org/ideacast/2017/09/microsofts-ceo-on-rediscovering-the-companys-soul.html.

110   most valuable public U.S. company: Jordan Novet, "Microsoft Closes Out 2018 as the Top Public Company," CNBC, December 31, 2018, https://www.cnbc.com/2018/12/31/microsoft-finishes-2018-as-the-top-public-company.html.

110   highest box office earners: "People Index," Box Office Mojo, accessed March 19, 2019, https://www.boxofficemojo.com/people/?view=Actor&sort =sumgross&order=DESC&p=.htm.

111   Lawrence tripped and fell: Dhani Mau, "Jennifer Lawrence Falls Elegantly in Dior Couture, Responds Hilariously," *Fashionista*, February 25, 2013, https:// fashionista.com/2013/02/jennifer-lawrence-dior-couture-fall-oscars.

111   ordered McDonald's: Kevin P. Sullivan, "Jennifer Lawrence Orders Mc-Donald's for Oscars Broadcast," MTV News, February 24, 2013, http://www .mtv.com/news/1702506/oscars-jennifer-lawrence-mcdonalds/.

111   frank and candid answers: Dhani Mau, "Jennifer Lawrence Falls Elegantly in Dior Couture, Responds Hilariously," *Fashionista*, February 25, 2013, https:// fashionista.com/2013/02/jennifer-lawrence-dior-couture-fall-oscars.

111   number of people viewed Lawrence: Masha Tupitsyn, "The Acting Personality: Just How 'Authentic' Is Jennifer Lawrence?," *IndieWire*, March 4, 2013, https://www.indiewire.com/2013/03/the-acting-personality-just-how-authentic -is-jennifer-lawrence-133844/.

112   "relation between the two": Ibid.

112   temporarily suspended: Heidi Parker, "Rihanna's Instagram Account BACK UP After It Was Suspended for Posting Racy Photo of Her Naked Derriere," *Daily Mail*, May 5, 2014, https://www.dailymail.co.uk/tvshowbiz/article-2620673/Rihan nas-Instagram-account-BACK-UP-suspended-sharing-photo-naked-derriere.html.

112   bad-girl persona: Plum Sykes, "The Rihanna Effect: Fashion's Most Exciting Muse, on Her Third *Vogue* Cover," *Vogue*, February 17, 2014, https://www .vogue.com/article/rihanna-fashions-most-exciting-new-muse.

112   if she'd like to set up the meeting: Gregory Krieg and Ashley Killough, "Trump Asks African-American Reporter to Set Up Meeting with Black Lawmakers," CNN, February 16, 2017, https://www.cnn.com/2017/02/16/politics /donald-trump-april-ryan-congressional-black-caucus/index.html.

113   Ryan responded during an interview: "April Ryan to Trump: I'm Not a Loser," CNN, YouTube, November 9, 2018, https://www.youtube.com/watch ?v=0t6UEwZxdNs.

114   eats like a six-year-old: Patricia Sellers, "Warren Buffett's Secret to Staying Young: 'I Eat Like a Six-Year-Old,'" *Fortune*, February 25, 2015, http://fortune .com/2015/02/25/warren-buffett-diet-coke/.

114   ordered Dairy Queen: Stephanie Smith, "Warren Buffett Ordered Dairy Queen, a Coke at Four Seasons," *New York Post*, April 24, 2014, https://pagesix .com/2014/04/24/warren-buffet-ordered-dairy-queen-a-coke-at-four-seasons/.

115   "I have everything I want": "Warren Buffett on Cell Phones, Email, and Material Goods," *Piers Morgan Live*, CNN, November 8, 2013, http://piers morgan.blogs.cnn.com/2013/11/08/warren-buffett-on-cell-phones-email-and -material-goods-2/.

115   tap dances into his office: Alex Crippen, "Warren Buffett Shares His Secret: How You Can 'Tap Dance to Work,'" CNBC, December 2, 2012, https://www .cnbc.com/id/49918773.

115   he got rejected from Harvard Business School: Kathleen Elkins, "Warren Buffett: Getting Rejected by Harvard Was the 'Best Thing That Ever Happened to Me,'" CNBC, January 31, 2017, https://www.cnbc.com/2017/01/31/hbs-rejec tion-was-the-best-thing-that-ever-happened-to-warren-buffett.html.

115   she took Will and Jada Pinkett Smith: "Tiffany Haddish Took Will & Jada Pinkett Smith on a Groupon Swamp Tour," *Jimmy Kimmel Live*, YouTube, July 19, 2017, https://www.youtube.com/watch?v=C2PneBztZ3g.

115   Groupon's 2018 Super Bowl ad: Kristina Monllos, "Girls Trip's Tiffany Haddish Will Star in Groupon's Super Bowl Commercial," *Adweek*, January 15, 2018, https://www.adweek.com/brand-marketing/girls-trips-tiffany-haddish-will -star-in-groupons-super-bowl-commercial/.

115   "Yes this happened": "Yes this happened. I wish it was better Miami. I prayed on it and I have a strong feeling this will never happened again," (@Tiffany Haddish, January 1, 2019), https://twitter.com/tiffanyhaddish/status/108015586 1173948418.

116   Nyong'o said the following: "Black Girl Magic Flashback: Watch the Lupita Nyong'o Speech Heard Around the World," *Essence*, February 28, 2014, https://www.essence.com/awards-events/red-carpet/black-women-hollywood /lupita-nyongo-delivers-moving-black-women-hollywood-acceptance-speech/.

117    $9 billion worldwide: "Tom Hanks," *Numbers*, accessed March 19, 2019, https://www.the-numbers.com/person/650401-Tom-Hanks#tab=summary

117   "modern era of moviemaking": "Tom Hanks," TMZ, accessed March 19, 2019, https://www.tmz.com/person/tom-hanks/.

117   bio for his official Twitter account: "Tom Hanks," (@tomhanks), Twitter, accessed March 19, 2019, https://twitter.com/tomhanks.

117   "embody the Everyman": "*Captain Phillips* Director Paul Greengrass: 'Tom Hanks Embodies the Everyman Like No One Else,'" *Parade*, September 21, 2013, https://parade.com/157700/parade/captain-phillips-director-paul-greengrass -tom-hanks-embodies-the-everyman-like-no-one-else/.

118   The Nicest Guy in Showbiz: Josh Eells, "A League of His Own: Tom

Hanks, American Icon," *Rolling Stone*, December 10, 2012, https://www.rolling stone.com/movies/movie-news/a-league-of-his-own-tom-hanks-american-icon -244988/.

118   interacting with an autistic fan: "As if You Needed Any More Proof That Tom Hanks Is the Nicest Guy," *Huffington Post*, October 24, 2013, https://www .huffingtonpost.com/2013/10/24/tom-hanks-nice-guy_n_4157363.html.

118   public figure commits a blunder: Elliot Aronson, Ben Willerman, and Jo-anne Floyd, "The Effect of a Pratfall on Increasing Interpersonal Attractiveness," *Psychonomic Science* 4, no. 6 (1966): 227–28.

119   sexted a photo that included his four-year-old son: Barbara Ross and Larry McShane, "Anthony Weiner's Sext Photo with 4-Year-Old Son Triggers City Children's Services Investigation," *New York Daily News*, August 31, 2016, https:// www.nydailynews.com/news/politics/anthony-weiner-sext-photo-son-triggers -city-probe-article-1.2773357.

119   chance to have dinner with Barack and Michelle: Meredith Rizzo, "Living While Obama: Dinner with Contest Winners," *Root*, March 9, 2012, https://www .theroot.com/living-while-obama-dinner-with-contest-winners-1790890406.

119   suspicious similarities to the speech Michelle Obama delivered: Cooper Allen, "Was Melania Trump's Speech Plagiarized from Michelle Obama?," *USA Today*, July 19, 2016, https://www.usatoday.com/story/news/politics/on politics/2016/07/19/melania-trump-republican-convention-speech-plagiarism /87278088/.

120   public housing project on Manhattan's Lower East Side: "Ursula M. Burns," Lean In, accessed March 20, 2019, https://leanin.org/stories/ursula-burns.

120   "When we're in the family": Adam Bryant, "Xerox's New Chief Tries to Redefine Its Culture," *New York Times*, February 20, 2010, https://www.nytimes .com/2010/02/21/business/21xerox.html.

121   most popular with their own employees: "Top CEOs 2018: Employee's Choice," Glassdoor, accessed March 20, 2019, https://www.glassdoor.com/Award /Top-CEOs-LST_KQ0,8.htm.

121   "Bring Your Parents To Work Day": "LinkedIn Bring in Your Parents to Work Day is back on 11/6." (@jeffweiner, September 17, 2014), https://twitter.com /jeffweiner/status/512269015960403968.

121   Microsoft bought LinkedIn for $26.2 billion: Nick Wingfield, "Microsoft Buys LinkedIn for $26.2 Billion, Reasserting Its Muscle," *New York Times*, June 13, 2016, https://www.nytimes.com/2016/06/14/business/dealbook/micro soft-to-buy-linkedin-for-26-2-billion.html.

121   become more authentic and relatable: Herminia Ibarra, "The Authenticity Paradox," *Harvard Business Review*, January–February 2015, https://hbr.org /2015/01/the-authenticity-paradox.

121   report feeling engaged: Steve Crabtree, "Worldwide, 13% of Employees Are Engaged at Work," Gallup, October 8, 2013, https://news.gallup.com /poll/165269/worldwide-employees-engaged-work.aspx.

122   sneakily participated in a massive Secret Santa exchange: Sarah Berger, "Billionaire Bill Gates Was This Craft-Lover's Reddit Secret Santa—Here's the Epic Haul of Gifts He Gave," CNBC, December 21, 2018, https://www.cnbc .com/2018/12/21/what-bill-gates-gave-his-reddit-secret-santa-match-in-2018 .html.

122   liked Weiner's leadership: "Highest Rated CEOs 2014 Employees' Choice," Glassdoor, accessed March 20, 2019, https://www.glassdoor.com/Award/Highest -Rated-CEOs-2014-LST_KQ0,23.htm.

123   "You know people who lost their jobs": Sabrina Siddiqui, "Bill Clinton Won 1992 Town Hall Debate by Engaging with One Voter," *Huffington Post*, October 16, 2012, https://www.huffingtonpost.com/2012/10/16/bill-clinton -debate_n_1971685.html.

124   revealed her inner thoughts: Hillary Rodham Clinton, *What Happened* (New York: Simon & Schuster, 2017), 136.

124   forge the photo of them: Jenna Fratello, "Michelle Obama, George W. Bush Share a Moment at the National Museum of African American History and Culture," *Today*, September 25, 2016, https://www.today.com/news/michelle -obama-george-w-bush-share-moment-national-museum-african-t103254.

125   President Bush and I are forever seatmates: Erin Kelly, "Michelle Obama: George W. Bush Is 'My Partner in Crime' and 'I Love Him to Death,'" *USA Today*, October 11, 2018, https://www.usatoday.com/story/news/politics/onpolitics /2018/10/11/michelle-obama-george-w-bush-my-partner-crime/1603296002/.

125   announced on Facebook: "Facebook's Mark Zuckerberg Takes Up Challenge to Tour US," BBC News, January 3, 2017, https://www.bbc.com/news/busi ness-38503437.

126   she wrote on Twitter: "Thanks so much for all the well wishes everybody . . . I'll be alright . . . might just take some time . . . glad I've got the best hubby in the world to take care of me." (@carrieunderwood, November 12, 2017), https:// twitter.com/carrieunderwood/status/929739381300236288?lang=en.

126   wrote a letter to her fan club: Emily Yahr, "Carrie Underwood Warns Fans She 'Might Look a Bit Different' After 'Gruesome' Injury," *Washington Post*,

January 2, 2018, https://www.washingtonpost.com/news/arts-and-entertainment
/wp/2018/01/02/carrie-underwood-warns-fans-she-might-look-a-bit-different-after
-gruesome-injury/?utm_term=.297c3060e7ce.

126   "usual glamorous self": Emily Yahr, "Carrie Underwood Reveals Details
of Accident, Says Hype over Her Face Was Unintentional," *Washington Post*,
April 19, 2018, https://www.washingtonpost.com/news/arts-and-entertainment
/wp/2018/04/19/carrie-underwood-reveals-details-of-accident-says-hype-over
-her-face-was-unintentional/?utm_term=.e841a0724e81.

126   "Do I sound the same?": Ree Hines, "Carrie Underwood Reveals It Was
'Physically Impossible' to Sing After Injury," *Today*, November 9, 2018, https://
www.today.com/popculture/carrie-underwood-it-was-physically-impossible
-sing-after-injury-t141661.

127   "until further notice": "Comedy Central Suspends Show," *New York Times*,
May 5, 2005, https://www.nytimes.com/2005/05/05/business/comedy-central
-suspends-show.html.

127   worth $50 million: Dan Hyman, "Dave Chappelle on Trump, Cosby
and His Netflix Deal," *New York Times*, March 17, 2017, https://www.nytimes
.com/2017/03/17/arts/television/dave-chappelle-on-trump-cosby-and-his-netflix
-deal.html.

127   "Let me tell you the things I can do here": "On the Beach with Dave
Chappelle," *Time*, May 15, 2005, http://content.time.com/time/arts/article
/0,8599,1061415,00.html.

127   Chappelle appeared on *Oprah:* "Chappelle's Story," Oprah.com, February
3, 2006, https://www.oprah.com/oprahshow/chappelles-story/all.

128   the opposite of "America's sweetheart": Mary Pols, "Country Strong: Why
Paltrow Isn't America's Sweetheart," *Time*, January 7, 2011, http://content.time
.com/time/magazine/article/0,9171,2041086,00.html.

128   the most hated celebrity in America: Lauren Le Vine, "Gwyneth Paltrow
Wonders How She's a More Hated Celebrity Than Chris Brown," *Vanity Fair*,
June 30, 2016, https://www.vanityfair.com/style/2016/06/gwyneth-paltrow-most
-hated-celebrity.

129   focus on her kids: Lily Harrison, "Gwyneth Paltrow's Post-Split Plans:
Actress Reveals She's Taking a Break from Acting to Focus on Her Kids," E! News,
March 26, 2014, https://www.eonline.com/news/525210/gwyneth-paltrow-s
-post-split-plans-actress-reveals-she-s-taking-a-break-from-acting-to-focus-on
-her-kids.

130   took the bait: "Gwyneth Paltrow's Recipes 'Cost $300 a Day,'" news

.com.au, April 7, 2013, https://www.news.com.au/entertainment/celebrity-life
/gwyneth-paltrows-recipes-cost-300-a-day/news-story/7298606f65a5d0a41
5c3b11019309790.

130   "How Much It Costs to Buy Everything": John Boone, "This Is How
Much It Costs to Buy Everything on Gwyneth Paltrow's 2014 Goop Gift
Guide," Entertainment Tonight, November 13, 2014, https://www.etonline.com
/news/153908_this_is_how_much_it_costs_to_buy_everything_on_gwyneth
_paltrow_2014_goop_gift_guide.

131   emailed a gaggle of her celebrity friends: Roy Greenslade, "Vanity Fair Editor Graydon Carter: Why I Spiked Gwyneth Paltrow Article," *Guardian*, February 18, 2014, https://www.theguardian.com/media/greenslade/2014/feb/18
/graydon-carter-gwynethpaltrow.

131   described Paltrow: Elizabeth Day, "Gwyneth Paltrow: Loved, Loathed,
but Never Ignored," *Guardian*, May 4, 2013, https://www.theguardian.com/the
observer/2013/may/05/profile-gwyneth-paltrow.

131   published a profile on Paltrow: Taffy Brodesser-Akner, "How Goop's Haters Made Gwyneth Paltrow's Company Worth $250 Million," *New York Times
Magazine*, July 25, 2018, https://www.nytimes.com/2018/07/25/magazine/big
-business-gwyneth-paltrow-wellness.html.

Chapter 7: The Clincher Traits: Protectiveness and Reliability

136   rank as the least trustworthy: "Honesty/Ethics in Professions," Gallup, accessed
March 17, 2019, https://news.gallup.com/poll/1654/honesty-ethics-professions.aspx.

136   "I can hear you!": Kenneth T. Walsh, "George W. Bush's 'Bullhorn' Moment," *U.S. News & World Report*, April 25, 2013, https://www.usnews.com
/news/blogs/ken-walshs-washington/2013/04/25/george-w-bushs-bullhorn
-moment.

137   hovered around 87 percent: "Presidential Approval Ratings—George W.
Bush," Gallup, accessed March 20, 2019, https://news.gallup.com/poll/116500
/presidential-approval-ratings-george-bush.aspx.

137   branded Kerry a liar: Jim Rutenberg and Kate Zernike, "The 2004 Campaign: Advertising; Veterans' Group Had G.O.P. Lawyer," *New York Times*, August 25, 2004, https://www.nytimes.com/2004/08/25/us/the-2004-campaign
-advertising-veterans-group-had-gop-lawyer.html.

138   first daytime program in about a decade: Matthew DiLallo, "What Is Judge
Judy's Net Worth?," Motley Fool, June 26, 2015, https://www.fool.com/invest
ing/general/2015/06/26/what-is-judge-judys-net-worth.aspx.

138   "only about three percent": "Behind the Scenes with Judge Judy," WDRB News, October 30, 2012, https://www.wdrb.com/news/behind-the-scenes-with -judge-judy/article_2436b646-6662-5cdc-9ad7-0c9c2dea6711.html.

138   10 percent of recent college graduates: Daniella Diaz, "Report: 10% of College Graduates Think Judge Judy Is on the Supreme Court," CNN, January 19, 2016, https://www.cnn.com/2016/01/19/politics/judge-judy-supreme-court-poll /index.html.

138   fired a software engineer: Daisuke Wakabayashi, "Google Fires Engineer Who Wrote Memo Questioning Women in Tech," *New York Times*, August 7, 2017, https://www.nytimes.com/2017/08/07/business/google-women-engineer -fired-memo.html.

139   "harmful gender stereotypes": Ibid.

139   "inclusive environment for all": Tom Warren, "Read Google CEO's Email to Staff About Engineer'sInflammatory Memo," *Verge*, August 8, 2017, https:// www.theverge.com/2017/8/8/16111724/google-sundar-pichai-employee-memo -diversity.

139   "Ken Frazier: The Strongest Man in the World": Jeffrey Sonnenfeld, "Ken Frazier: The Strongest Man in the World," *Fortune*, August 15, 2017, http:// fortune.com/2017/08/15/merck-ceo-ken-frazier/.

140   "on many sides": Dan Merica, "Trump Condemns 'Hatred, Bigotry and Violence on Many Sides' in Charlottesville," CNN, August 13, 2017, https://www .cnn.com/2017/08/12/politics/trump-statement-alt-right-protests/index.html.

140   released a statement: Adam Edelman, "Merck CEO Quits Advisory Council over Trump's Charlottesville Remarks," NBC News, August 14, 2017, https:// www.nbcnews.com/politics/donald-trump/merck-ceo-quits-advisory-council -over-trump-s-charlottesville-remarks-n792416.

140   lashed out at Frazier: Jena McGregor, "Trump Fires Back After the CEO of Merck Resigned from His Manufacturing Council," *Washington Post*, August 14, 2017, https://www.washingtonpost.com/news/on-leadership/wp/2017 /08/14/trump-fires-back-after-the-ceo-of-merck-resigned-from-his-manufacturing -council.

140   followed his lead and withdrew: Adam Edelman and Stephanie Ruhle, "Trump Dissolves Business Advisory Councils as CEOs Quit," NBC News, August 16, 2017, https://www.nbcnews.com/politics/donald-trump/trump-dis solves-business-advisory-councils-after-ceos-depart-n793216.

140   African-American CEOs of Fortune 500 companies: Grace Donnelly, "The Number of Black CEOs at Fortune 500 Companies Is at Its Lowest Since

2002," *Fortune*, February 28, 2018, http://fortune.com/2018/02/28/black-history
-month-black-ceos-fortune-500/.

140   "taking a stand": Andrew Ross Sorkin, "Outraged in Private, Many C.E.O.s
Fear the Wrath of the President," *New York Times*, August 14, 2017, https://www
.nytimes.com/2017/08/14/business/dealbook/merck-trump-charlottesville-ceos.html.

140   bump up in consumer perception: Ted Marzilli, "Merck Gets Notable
Bump After CEO Quits Trump Council," YouGov, August 22, 2017, https://today
.yougov.com/topics/politics/articles-reports/2017/08/22/merck-gets-notable
-bump-after-ceo-quits-trump-coun.

141   world's youngest female leader: "The World's Youngest Female Leader Takes
Over in New Zealand," *Economist*, October 26, 2017, https://www.economist.com
/asia/2017/10/26/the-worlds-youngest-female-leader-takes-over-in-new-zealand.

141   "social media around the world": Charlotte Graham-McLay, "Jacinda Ardern's Progressive Politics Made Her a Global Sensation. But Do They Work at
Home?," *New York Times*, September 26, 2018, https://www.nytimes.com/2018/09
/26/world/asia/jacinda-ardern-un-new-zealand.html.

141   held baby Neve: Eleanor Ainge Roy, "Jacinda Ardern Makes History with
Baby Neve at UN General Assembly," *Guardian*, September 24, 2018, https://
www.theguardian.com/world/2018/sep/25/jacinda-ardern-makes-history-with
-baby-neve-at-un-general-assembly.

141   "we have achieved something": Ibid.

141   makeshift UN identification card: "Because everyone on twitter's been
asking to see Neve's UN id, staff here whipped one up," (@NZClarke, September 24, 2018), https://twitter.com/NZClarke/status/1044252770268672000.

141   Entertainer of the Year: Associated Press, "Tina Fey Is AP Entertainer of
the Year," *Variety*, December 23, 2008, https://variety.com/2008/biz/awards
/tina-fey-is-ap-entertainer-of-the-year-1117997736/.

141   World's Most Influential People: Alec Baldwin, "Tina Fey," *Time*, April 30,
2009, http://content.time.com/time/specials/packages/article/0,28804,1894410
_1893836_1893831,00.html.

141   Hollywood Walk of Fame: Michael Schneider, "Oprah, Neil Patrick Harris, Tina Fey to Get Hollywood Walk of Fame Stars," *Variety*, June 17, 2010,
https://variety.com/2010/tv/opinion/oprah-neil-patrick-harris-tina-fey-to-get
-hollywood-walk-of-fame-stars-14889/.

142   "it is the truth": A.J. Jacobs, "The Real Tina Fey," *Esquire*, April 13, 2010,
https://www.esquire.com/entertainment/a7244/tina-fey-funny-quotes-040710/.

142   Bill Cosby's history of rape allegations: Eliana Dockterman, "Watch Tina

Fey Joke About Bill Cosby Rape Allegations on SNL in 2005," *Time*, December 5, 2014, http://time.com/3620097/tina-fey-bill-cosby-rape-allegations-snl/.

142   first woman to lead a global automaker: Dale Buss, "GM Taps Mary Barra Next CEO; Will Be First Woman Car Chief," *Forbes*, December 10, 2013, https://www.forbes.com/sites/dalebuss/2013/12/10/gm-taps-mary-barra-next-ceo-will-be-first-woman-car-chief/#cbefb0a462f7.

142   "dress appropriately": Geoff Colvin, "Mary Barra's (Unexpected) Opportunity," *Fortune*, September 18, 2014, http://fortune.com/2014/09/18/mary-barra-general-motors/.

142   "smallest biggest change": Richard Feloni, "GM CEO Mary Barra Explains How Shrinking the Dress Code to 2 Words Reflects Her Mission for the Company," Business Insider, March 27, 2015, https://www.businessinsider.com/gm-ceo-mary-barra-on-changing-gms-dress-code-2015-3.

143   history of this behavior: Tim Higgins, "GM's Barra Cuts Costs, Emerges as CEO Contender," *Automotive News*, June 14, 2013, https://www.autonews.com/article/20130614/OEM02/306149956/gm-s-barra-cuts-costs-emerges-as-ceo-contender.

143   ran ads highlighting his votes: Anne E. Kornblut, "Bush Ad Plays on Kerry Windsurfing," Boston.com, September 23, 2004, http://archive.boston.com/news/nation/articles/2004/09/23/bush_ad_plays_on_kerry_windsurfing/.

143   "before I voted against it": "Kerry Discusses $87 Billion Comment," CNN, September 30, 2004, http://www.cnn.com/2004/ALLPOLITICS/09/30/kerry.comment/.

143   "Whichever way the wind blows": Anne E. Kornblut, "Bush Ad Plays on Kerry Windsurfing," Boston.com, September 23, 2004, http://archive.boston.com/news/nation/articles/2004/09/23/bush_ad_plays_on_kerry_windsurfing/.

144   "no place for grudges": Jacques Steinberg, "Whoopi Goldberg Joins 'The View,'" *New York Times*, August 2, 2007, https://www.nytimes.com/2007/08/02/arts/television/02view.html.

144   "you deal with it—afterward": Ibid.

144   got heated with guest Jeanine Pirro: Mara Siegler, "Whoopi Goldberg and Jeanine Pirro Get into Explosive Argument Backstage at 'The View,'" *New York Post*, July 19, 2018, https://pagesix.com/2018/07/19/whoopi-goldberg-and-jeanine-pirro-get-into-explosive-argument-at-the-view/.

145   "things I try not to be on this show": Ibid.

145   "designated adult": Soraya Nadia McDonald, "What Happened to Whoopi Goldberg?," *Washington Post*, October 22, 2015, https://www.washingtonpost.com/news/arts-and-entertainment/wp/2015/10/22/what-happened-to-whoopi-goldberg.

145   top grades for trust: Dorothy Pomerantz, "Morgan Freeman Tops Our List of the Most Trustworthy Celebrities," *Forbes*, August 15, 2012, https://www.forbes.com/sites/dorothypomerantz/2012/08/15/morgan-freeman-tops-our-list-of-the-most-trustworthy-celebrities/#62b13f46335c.

145   "than male voices with a higher pitch": Mandy Oaklander, "Science Explains Why You Love Morgan Freeman's Voice," *Time*, February 23, 2016, http://time.com/4233926/morgan-freeman-voice-waze-science/.

145   replaced Walter Cronkite: Leo Standora, "CBS Drops Walter Cronkite for Morgan Freeman as Voice of 'CBS Evening News,'" *New York Daily News*, January 5, 2010, https://www.nydailynews.com/entertainment/tv-movies/cbs-drops-walter-cronkite-morgan-freeman-voice-cbs-evening-news-article-1.460134.

145   most trusted man in America: David Folkenflik, "Walter Cronkite, America's 'Most Trusted Man,' Dead," NPR, July 18, 2009, https://www.npr.org/templates/story/story.php?storyId=106770499.

145   third in *Forbes*'s 2014 list: Dorothy Pomerantz, "Tom Hanks Tops Our List of the Most Trustworthy Celebrities," *Forbes*, February 12, 2014, https://www.forbes.com/sites/dorothypomerantz/2014/02/12/tom-hanks-tops-our-list-of-the-most-trustworthy-celebrities/#29a36ef94d54.

146   movie star at the ripe age of fifty: "Actor Morgan Freeman Receives AARP's Movies For Grownups® Career Achievement Award," AARP, February 1, 2017, https://press.aarp.org/2017-02-01-Actor-Morgan-Freeman-Receives-AARPs-Movies-For-Grownups-R-Career-Achievement-Award.

146   "everyone could rely on": Luis Gomez, "Interview: Timeless Advice from the Peerless Morgan Freeman," *Chicago Tribune*, June 8, 2014, https://www.chicagotribune.com/entertainment/ct-xpm-2014-06-08-chi-morgan-freeman-interview-20140608-story.html.

147   accusing Freeman of sexual harassment: An Phung and Chloe Melas, "Women Accuse Morgan Freeman of Inappropriate Behavior, Harassment," CNN, May 28, 2018, https://www.cnn.com/2018/05/24/entertainment/morgan-freeman-accusations/index.html.

147   Chipotle Mexican Grill was in trouble: Roberto A. Ferdman and Abha Bhattarai, "There's a Crisis at Chipotle," *Washington Post*, December 9, 2015, https://www.washingtonpost.com/news/wonk/wp/2015/12/09/chipotle-food-outbreak-ecoli-reputation.

147   Sales sank: John Kell, "Chipotle's Sales Decline Sharply for Fourth Straight Quarter," *Fortune*, October 25, 2016, http://fortune.com/2016/10/25/chipotle-sales-decline-again/.

147   meaning more advertising: Sarah Halzack, "Chipotle's New CEO Is Saying the Right Things," *Bloomberg*, April 26, 2018, https://www.bloomberg.com
/opinion/articles/2018-04-26/chipotle-earnings-new-ceo-says-the-right-things.

147   "remind people why they love Chipotle": Sarah Whitten, "After Blowout
Earnings, Chipotle's New CEO Says This Is Job Number One," CNBC, April 26,
2018, https://www.cnbc.com/2018/04/26/chipotle-shares-jump-20-percent-in-its
-second-best-trading-day.html.

147   "Saying the Right Things": Sarah Halzack, "Chipotle's New CEO Is Saying the Right Things," *Bloomberg*, April 26, 2018, https://www.bloomberg.com
/opinion/articles/2018-04-26/chipotle-earnings-new-ceo-says-the-right-things.

147   launched a new ad campaign: "Chipotle Launches New 'For Real' Campaign Placing Its Real Ingredients in the Spotlight," Chipotle, September 24, 2018,
https://ir.chipotle.com/2018-09-24-Chipotle-Launches-New-For-Real-Campaign
-Placing-Its-Real-Ingredients-In-The-Spotlight.

147   on television, on billboards, in print and on social media: Jessica Wohl,
"Chipotle Says It's for Real in New Campaign from New CMO," *Ad Age*, September 24, 2018, https://adage.com/article/cmo-strategy/chipotle-real-campaign
-cmo/315036/.

148   "noticeable" jump in sales: "Chipotle Mexican Grill Inc (CMG) Q3 2018
Earnings Conference Call Transcript," Motley Fool, October 26, 2018, https://
www.fool.com/earnings/call-transcripts/2018/10/26/chipotle-mexican-grill
-inc-cmg-q3-2018-earnings-co.aspx.

148   best annual performers on the S&P 500: Michael Sheetz, "Here Are the
Best and Worst Performing Stocks of This Tough and Volatile Year for the Market," CNBC, December 31, 2018, https://www.cnbc.com/2018/12/31/2018
-stocks-sp-500-best-and-worst-performers-in-a-volatile-year.html.

148   CEO of the year: Paul R. La Monica, "Why Chipotle's Brian Niccol Is the
CEO of the Year," CNN, December 21, 2018, https://www.cnn.com/2018/12/21
/investing/chipotle-brian-niccol/index.html.

148   "looking for a reason to be offended": Kevin Fitzpatrick, "No, Dwayne
Johnson Didn't Really Criticize 'Generation Snowflake,'" *Vanity Fair*, January 12, 2019, https://www.vanityfair.com/style/2019/01/dwayne-johnson-snow
flake-quote-fabricated.

148   set the record straight: "Settin' the Record Straight," (@therock, January 11, 2019), https://www.instagram.com/p/BsgwnjgBFyK/.

149   "that's not what we do": Ibid.

149   rambling speech to an empty chair: Travis M. Andrews, "Clint East-

wood Explains—and Regrets—His Speech to an Empty Chair," *Washington Post*, August 4, 2016, https://www.washingtonpost.com/news/morning-mix/wp /2016/08/04/clint-eastwood-explains-and-regrets-his-speech-to-an-empty-chair.

149   told *Esquire* magazine: Tom Junod, "The Eastwood Conundrum," *Esquire*, September 20, 2012, https://www.esquire.com/entertainment/movies/interviews /a15877/clint-eastwood-profile-1012/.

149   crashed into the ocean: Tatiana Siegel, "How Clint Eastwood Surviving a Plane Crash Led Him to Direct 'Sully,'" *Hollywood Reporter*, November 17, 2016, https://www.hollywoodreporter.com/features/how-clint-eastwood-surviving-a -plane-crash-led-him-to-direct-sully-947346.

150   first female CEO of a Fortune 500 company: Julia Carpenter, "Women in the Fortune 500: 64 CEOs in Half a Century," CNN Money, August 7, 2017, https://money.cnn.com/interactive/pf/female-ceos-timeline/.

150   "history of women in this century": Nora Ephron, "Paper Route," *New York Times*, February 9, 1997, https://archive.nytimes.com/www.nytimes.com /books/97/02/09/reviews/970209.09ephront.html.

151   "always protect people and stick by the reporters": "Kay Graham: Pillar of the Post and Press," CNN, July 23, 2001, http://www.cnn.com/2001/US/07/22 /graham.journalism/.

151   "queen in her own field": Ibid.

151   "sickening thing I ever heard": Katharine Graham, "The Watergate Watershed: A Turning Point for a Nation and a Newspaper," *Washington Post*, January 28, 1997, https://www.washingtonpost.com/wp-srv/national/longterm/water gate/stories/graham.htm.

152   issue five subpoenas: Bob Woodward and Carl Bernstein, *All the President's Men* (New York: Simon & Schuster, 2014), 260.

152   "There might be a revolution": Ibid.

152   "would maintain the principles Katharine Graham did": "Interview Carl Bernstein," PBS *Frontline*, February 13, 2007, https://www.pbs.org/wgbh/pages /frontline/newswar/interviews/bernstein.html.

152   most successful solo artists of all time: Isha Thorpe, "15 Times Beyoncé Broke Records And Made History," iHeartRadio, February 13, 2019, https:// www.iheart.com/content/2018-02-12-15-times-beyonce-has-broken-records-and -made-history/.

153   cover of *Sports Illustrated*'s swimsuit edition: Bryan Curtis, "The Sports Illustrated Swimsuit Issue," *Slate*, February 14, 2007, https://slate.com/news-and

-politics/2007/02/the-sports-illustrated-swimsuit-issue-an-intellectual-history
.html.

153   "It takes a lot of guts": *People* Staff, "Beyoncé: SI's Swimsuit Covergirl," *People*,
February 14, 2007, https://people.com/celebrity/beyonc-sis-swimsuit-covergirl/.

153   People accused her of lip-synching: "Beyonce Admits Inauguration Day
Lip Sync, Says She'll 'Absolutely Be Singing Live' at Super Bowl," CBS News,
January 31, 2013, https://www.cbsnews.com/news/beyonce-admits-inauguration
-day-lip-sync-says-shell-absolutely-be-singing-live-at-super-bowl/.

153   "When Beyonce tells you to stand, YOU STAND": "Beyoncé Sings the Na-
tional Anthem | Super Bowl XLVII Halftime Show Press Conference," NFL, You-
Tube, February 6, 2016, https://www.youtube.com/watch?v=tQxHSHsCpGo.

153   a cappella rendition of the Star-Spangled Banner: Ibid.

154   "the last man standing": Jen Wieczner, "Commanders in Chief: The Women
Building America's Military Machine," *Fortune*, September 24, 2018, http://
fortune.com/longform/lockheed-martin-boeing-women-defense-ceos-trump/.

154   just twenty-four companies on the Fortune 500: Zameena Mejia, "Just 24
Female CEOs Lead the Companies on the 2018 Fortune 500—Fewer than Last
Year," CNBC, May 21, 2018, https://www.cnbc.com/2018/05/21/2018s-fortune
-500-companies-have-just-24-female-ceos.html.

154   shareholder return has been 309 percent: Dan Bigman, "Lockheed Martin's Marillyn Hewson: 2018 CEO Of The Year," *Chief Executive*, July 16, 2018,
https://chiefexecutive.net/lockheed-martin-marillyn-hewson-ceo-year/.

154   cost of $400 billion: Christopher Drew, "Lockheed Chief Pledges Lower Costs
for F-35 Fighter Jet and Add 1,800 Jobs," *New York Times*, January 13, 2017, https://
www.nytimes.com/2017/01/13/business/lockheed-martin-ceo-trump-f-35.html.

154   2018 CEO of the Year: Dan Bigman, "Lockheed Martin's Marillyn Hewson: 2018 CEO Of The Year," *Chief Executive*, July 16, 2018, https://chiefexec
utive.net/lockheed-martin-marillyn-hewson-ceo-year/.

155   Best-Performing CEOs in the World: *Harvard Business Review* Staff, "The
Best-Performing CEOs in the World 2018," *Harvard Business Review*, November-
December 2018, https://hbr.org/2018/11/the-best-performing-ceos-in-the-world
-2018.

155   "One of the most important things for women": Jan Gillis, "How to Succeed in Business," *James Madison University News*, November 26, 2018, http://
www.jmu.edu/news/2018/04/24-mm-spsm18-warden.shtml.

155   "consequences for failing to perform": Carla Anne Robbins, "The Spy in

General Dynamics' Corner Office," *Fortune*, September 11, 2015, http://fortune .com/2015/09/11/phebe-novakovic-general-dynamics/.

155   focused as a "laser beam": Andrea Shalal-Esa, "Charge, Government Spending Cuts Hammer General Dynamics Results," Reuters, January 23, 2013, https:// www.reuters.com/article/us-generaldynamics-results/charge-government-spend ing-cuts-hammer-general-dynamics-results-idUSBRE90M1D920130123.

155   CEO turnaround experts: Leslie P. Norton, "World's Best CEOs: Turn-around Experts," *Barron's*, May 26, 2018, https://www.barrons.com/articles /worlds-best-ceos-turnaround-experts-1527308318.

155   beat the competition: James Langford, "Boeing Wins $805 Million Contract for Navy's First Carrier-Based Drone," *Washington Examiner*, August 30, 2018, https://www.washingtonexaminer.com/business/boeing-wins-805-million -contract-for-drones-to-refuel-navy-fighter-jets.

156   "At the end of the day": Christian Davenport, "Does Another Woman in Charge Signal a Cultural Shift in the Defense Industry?," *Washington Post*, July 13, 2018, https://www.washingtonpost.com/business/economy/does-another -women-in-charge-signal-a-cultural-shift-in-the-defense-industry/2018/07 /13/3333cedc-86be-11e8-8f6c-46cb43e3f306_story.html.

156   "Every one of these incredible women": David Brown, "How Women Took Over the Military-industrial Complex," *Politico*, January 2, 2019, https://www .politico.com/story/2019/01/02/how-women-took-over-the-military-industrial -complex-1049860.

156   "Their roles are not ornamental": Jeffrey A. Sonnenfeld, "Women Leaders Ascend in the Aerospace and Defense Industry," *Yale Insights*, Yale School of Management, July 19, 2018, https://insights.som.yale.edu/insights/women-leaders -ascend-in-the-aerospace-and-defense-industry.

156   "than the public part": *Los Angeles Times* Staff, "Transcript: Hillary Clinton's DNC Speech, Annotated," *Los Angeles Times*, July 28, 2016, https://www .latimes.com/politics/la-na-pol-hillary-clinton-convention-speech-transcript -20160728-snap-htmlstory.html.

157   how she developed those likeability traits: Marillyn Hewson, "A Mother's Resilience," *Politico*, September 19, 2013, https://www.politico.com/story /2013/09/marillyn-hewson-women-rule-a-mothers-resilience-097019.

Chapter 8: The Conscience Traits: Perceptiveness and Compassion

160   President Barack Obama sang: Sarah L. Kaufman, "Why Obama's Singing of 'Amazing Grace' Is So Powerful," *Washington Post*, June 26, 2015, https://

www.washingtonpost.com/news/arts-and-entertainment/wp/2015/06/26/why
-obamas-singing-of-amazing-grace-is-so-powerful.

161   sought to define "EQ": Peter Salovey and John D. Mayer, "Emotional Intelligence," *Imagination, Cognition and Personality* 9, no. 3 (1990): 185–211.

161   overwhelmingly more positive reviews: "Steven Spielberg," Rotten Tomatoes, accessed March 21, 2019, https://www.rottentomatoes.com/celebrity/steven
_spielberg.

162   more than $4.5 billion dollars: "Top Grossing Director at the Domestic
Box Office," Numbers, accessed March 21, 2019, https://www.the-numbers.com
/box-office-star-records/domestic/lifetime-specific-technical-role/director.

162   "Steven does this incredible thing": Yelena Shuster, "Tom Hanks and Steven Spielberg Still Crazy for Each Other After All These Years," Vulture, *New
York Magazine*, October 5, 2015, https://www.vulture.com/2015/10/hanks-and
-spielberg-still-love-working-together.html.

163   "because I am the audience": Brian Tallerico, "The Audience Man: 'Steven Spielberg Director's Collection,'" Rogerebert.com, October 31, 2014, https://
www.rogerebert.com/demanders/the-audience-man-steven-spielberg-directors
-collection.

163   "Most Trustworthy Celebrity": Dorothy Pomerantz, "Tom Hanks Tops
Our List of the Most Trustworthy Celebrities," *Forbes*, February 12, 2014, https://
www.forbes.com/sites/dorothypomerantz/2014/02/12/tom-hanks-tops-our-list
-of-the-most-trustworthy-celebrities/#5ca0ccc14d54.

163   "This is horseshit": Nancy Tartaglione, "Tom Hanks Retraces a Life in
Pictures, Talks Pitfalls of Comedy & Freedom from Self-consciousness at BAFTA
Event," *Deadline Hollywood*, October 19, 2013, https://deadline.com/2013/10
/tom-hanks-bafta-captain-phillips-saving-mr-banks-615942/.

164   cracked several jokes: "Kumail Nanjiani Standup Monologue—SNL,"
Saturday Night Live, YouTube, October 14, 2017, https://www.youtube.com
/watch?v=z2X0TaXknVE.

164   "Let's get to the reason": Ryan Broderick, "Martha Stewart's Set at the Justin Bieber Roast Proves She Is Still the Baddest Bitch of All," BuzzFeed, March 31,
2015, https://www.buzzfeed.com/ryanhatesthis/martha-stewarts-set-at-the-justin
-bieber-roast-proves-she-is.

164   "Martha Stewart's Performance": Daniel D'Addario, "Martha Stewart's
Performance at the Justin Bieber Roast Was Worth Celebrating," *Time*, March 31,
2015, http://time.com/3765113/martha-stewart-justin-bieber/.

165   "the most important person": Bob Thompson, "Take a Tip from Bezos:

Customers Always Need a Seat at the Table," *Entrepreneur*, May 28, 2016, https://www.entrepreneur.com/article/234254.

165   "earth's most customer-centric company": Robert Lenzner, "Amazon Celebrates 20 Years of Stupendous Growth as 'Earth's Most Customer-Centric Company,'" *Forbes*, April 24, 2018, https://www.forbes.com/sites/robertlenzner/2018/04/24/amazon-celebrates-20-years-of-stupendous-growth-as-earths-most-customer-centric-company/#7d8dcb644dc6.

165   "Customer Experience Bar Raisers": George Anders, "Jeff Bezos's Top 10 Leadership Lessons," *Forbes*, April 4, 2012, https://www.forbes.com/sites/georgeanders/2012/04/04/bezos-tips/#32eee0cd2fce.

165   consistently ranks among the top companies: "Trader Joe's and Costco Top Amazon in Customer Satisfaction, ACSI Data Show," American Customer Satisfaction Index, February 26, 2019, https://www.theacsi.org/news-and-resources/press-releases/press-2019/press-release-retail-and-consumer-shipping-2018-2019.

165   more than 100 million Prime members: Heather Kelly, "Amazon Reveals It Has More Than 100 Million Prime Members," CNN, April 19, 2018, https://money.cnn.com/2018/04/18/technology/amazon-100-million-prime-members/index.html.

165   more than 50,000 employees: Jodi Kantor and David Streitfeld, "Inside Amazon: Wrestling Big Ideas in a Bruising Workplace," *New York Times*, August 15, 2015, https://www.nytimes.com/2015/08/16/technology/inside-amazon-wrestling-big-ideas-in-a-bruising-workplace.html.

166   "cry at their desk": Ibid.

166   new six-week-paid-leave policy: Rachel Emma Silverman, "Joining Tech Rivals, Amazon Adds Paternity Leave, More Paid Time Off for Mothers," *Wall Street Journal*, November 2, 2015, https://www.wsj.com/articles/joining-tech-rivals-amazon-adds-paternity-leave-more-paid-time-off-for-mothers-1446503585.

166   World's Greatest Leader: "World's Greatest Leaders," *Fortune*, accessed March 21, 2019, http://fortune.com/worlds-greatest-leaders/2016/.

166   "put in your shopping cart": Russell Glass, "Using Data to Better Understand Customers and Pursue Prospects," LinkedIn, December 16, 2015, https://www.linkedin.com/pulse/using-data-better-understand-customers-pursue-prospects-russell-glass/.

167   record-breaking sixteen Tony Award nominations: Steven Zeitchik, "'Hamilton' Breaks Tonys Record with 16 Nominations," *Los Angeles Times*, May 3, 2016, https://www.latimes.com/entertainment/arts/culture/la-et-cm-tony-nominations-20160502-snap-story.html.

167   "The first Broadway show ever": Michael Paulson, "'Hamilton' Leads a Record-Breaking Holiday Week on Broadway," *New York Times*, January 2, 2019, https://www.nytimes.com/2019/01/02/theater/broadway-grosses-hamilton-record.html.

168   "intensely curious": Gordon Cox, "'Hamilton' Star Lin-Manuel Miranda Is Ready for His Next Coup," *Variety*, September 27, 2016, https://variety.com/2016/legit/features/lin-manuel-miranda-hamilton-next-projects-1201870498/.

168   "always attracted to": Ibid.

168   "pulse of the American mood": Sabrina Siddiqui, "Bill Clinton Won 1992 Town Hall Debate By Engaging with One Voter," *Huffington Post*, October 16, 2012, https://www.huffingtonpost.com/2012/10/16/bill-clinton-debate_n_1971685.html.

169   "As thrilled as I am": Kit Eaton, "Tim Cook, Apple CEO, Auburn University Commencement Speech 2010," *Fast Company*, August 26, 2011, https://www.fastcompany.com/1776338/tim-cook-apple-ceo-auburn-university-commencement-speech-2010.

169    $8.3 billion fortune: Andrew Ross Sorkin, "The Mystery of Steve Jobs's Public Giving," *New York Times*, August 29, 2011, https://dealbook.nytimes.com/2011/08/29/the-mystery-of-steve-jobss-public-giving/.

169   "most influential product of Silicon Valley": David Montgomery, "The Quest of Laurene Powell Jobs," *Washington Post*, June 11, 2018, https://www.washingtonpost.com/news/style/wp/2018/06/11/feature/the-quest-of-laurene-powell-jobs.

169   worth an estimated $20 billion: Ibid.

169   Apple gave away $100 million: John Aidan Byrne, "Apple Tries to Fix Rep as 'Stingest' Company," *New York Post*, September 2, 2012, https://nypost.com/2012/09/02/apple-tries-to-fix-rep-as-stingest-company/.

170   focusing on Apple's charitable contributions: Nilay Patel, "Tim Cook Boasts About Apple's Charitable Contributions During Internal All-Hands Meeting," *Verge*, February 2, 2012, https://www.theverge.com/2012/2/2/2766403/tim-cook-apple-charity-project-red-stanford.

170   charitable corporate-matching program: Brian Caulfield, "Apple to Match Employees' Charitable Contributions," *Forbes*, September 8, 2011, https://www.forbes.com/sites/briancaulfield/2011/09/08/apple-to-match-employees-charitable-contributions/#2b9e52cc47d2.

170   earned a terrible reputation: Sam Levin, "Uber's Scandals, Blunders and PR Disasters: The Full List," *Guardian*, June 27, 2017, https://www.theguardian.com/technology/2017/jun/18/uber-travis-kalanick-scandal-pr-disaster-timeline.

170   "humble personality at ease": Drew FitzGerald, "Meet Uber's Choice for CEO: Dara Khosrowshahi," *Wall Street Journal*, August 17, 2017, https://www.wsj.com/articles/meet-ubers-choice-for-ceo-dara-khosrowshahi-1503889860.

170   launched a new ad campaign: "Moving Forward: Uber," Uber, YouTube, May 17, 2018, https://youtu.be/4l5vGcuhtaQ.

171   adopt a "learn-it-all" attitude: Justin Bariso, "Microsoft's CEO Just Gave Some Brilliant Career Advice. Here It Is in 1 Sentence," *Inc.*, April 24, 2017, https://www.inc.com/justin-bariso/microsofts-ceo-just-gave-some-brilliant-career-advice-here-it-is-in-one-sentence.html.

171   "generated more than $250 billion in market value": Harry McCracken, "Satya Nadella Rewrites Microsoft's Code," *Fast Company*, September 18, 2017, https://www.fastcompany.com/40457458/satya-nadella-rewrites-microsofts-code.

171   "Fueled a Humble Comeback": Adam Lashinsky, "How Microsoft CEO Satya Nadella Fueled a Humble Comeback," *Fortune*, January 15, 2019, http://fortune.com/2019/01/15/microsoft-comeback-satya-nadella-humble/.

172   "dial up your mom": Tierney McAfee, "McDonald's Super Bowl 2015 Ad: Families Pay for Burgers with Hugs," *Hollywood Life*, January 30, 2015, https://hollywoodlife.com/2015/01/30/mcdonalds-super-bowl-commercial-2015-pay-with-lovin-ad/.

172   "the world is what we make it": "Coca-Cola Super Bowl 2015 TV Commercial, 'Big Game,'" iSpot.tv, accessed March 21, 2019, https://www.ispot.tv/ad/7xYD/coca-cola-super-bowl-2015-big-game.

172   secondary sales of tickets: Jesse Lawrence, "Global Citizen Festival Tickets Averaging More Than $1,000 on Secondary Market," *Street*, August 13, 2015, https://www.thestreet.com/story/13253527/1/global-citizen-festival-tickets-averaging-more-than-1000-on-secondary-market.html.

173   "Money has no utility to me": Neil Tweedie, "Bill Gates Interview: I Have No Use for Money. This Is God's Work," *Telegraph*, January 18, 2013, https://www.telegraph.co.uk/technology/bill-gates/9812672/Bill-Gates-interview-I-have-no-use-for-money.-This-is-Gods-work.html.

173   total over $29 billion: Dan Alexander, "Warren Buffett Toasts the World's Two Greatest Philanthropists, Bill And Melinda Gates," *Forbes*, June 4, 2015, https://www.forbes.com/sites/danalexander/2015/06/04/warren-buffett-toasts-the-worlds-two-greatest-philanthropists-bill-and-melinda-gates/#50c6675a4e01.

173   single $50 million gift: Associated Press, "Gates Foundation Charity to Spend $50m on Fighting Ebola in West Africa," *Guardian*, September 10, 2014,

https://www.theguardian.com/society/2014/sep/10/gates-charity-60m-donation
-ebola-fight-west-africa.

173   $80 million to close the "data gap": Michela Tindera, "Gates Foundation
Pledges $80 Million to Close the Gender 'Data Gap,'" *Forbes*, May 17, 2016,
https://www.forbes.com/sites/michelatindera/2016/05/17/gates-foundation
-pledges-80-million-to-close-the-gender-data-gap/#304f8e762f50.

173   lifetime donations totaling $21.5 billion: Emmie Martin and Tanza
Loudenback, "The 20 Most Generous People in the World," Business Insider,
October 12, 2015, https://www.businessinsider.com/most-generous-people-in-the
-world-2015-10.

173   gave away $2.6 billion: Alex Morrell, "Buffett Donates $2.6 Billion in
Berkshire Hathaway Shares to Gates Foundation, Other Charities," *Forbes*,
July 8, 2013, https://www.forbes.com/sites/alexmorrell/2013/07/08/buffett
-donates-2-6-billion-in-berkshire-hathaway-shares-to-gates-foundation-other
-charities/#3c50f333b4be.

173   donated $2.8 billion: Alex Morrell, "Buffett Donates $2.8 Billion, Breaks
Personal Giving Record," *Forbes*, July 15, 2014, https://www.forbes.com/sites
/alexmorrell/2014/07/15/buffett-donates-2-8-billion-breaks-personal-giving
-record/#5336d5e46547.

173   donations totaling $2.84 billion: Alex Morrell, "Warren Buffett Unleashes
Another $2.8 Billion Donation," *Forbes*, July 6, 2015, https://www.forbes.com
/sites/alexmorrell/2015/07/06/warren-buffett-unleashes-another-2-8-billion
-donation/#27583f2b75a1.

173   "as long as we see an increase in philanthropic projects": Geoffrey A.
Fowler, "More Billionaires Sign On to Giving Money Away," *Wall Street Journal*,
September 19, 2012, https://www.wsj.com/articles/SB100008723963904439956
04578003043533208534.

174   net worth of $6.5 billion: Bloomberg, "Salesforce's Marc Benioff Is Buying
Time Magazine, Boosting His Influence," *Los Angeles Times*, September 17, 2018,
https://www.latimes.com/business/la-fi-time-magazine-benioff-20180917-story.html.

174   "To be truly successful": Dan Pontefract, "The Top 15 CEO Quotes About
Operating with a Higher Purpose," *Forbes*, May 3, 2016, https://www.forbes
.com/sites/danpontefract/2016/05/03/the-top-15-ceo-quotes-about-operating
-with-a-higher-purpose/#252f78ca3e72.

174   1-1-1 system: "Take the Pledge," salesforce.org, accessed March 21, 2019,
https://www.salesforce.org/pledge-1/.

174   bought *Time* for $190 million: Julia Waldow, "Marc Benioff: 'I Want Time Magazine to Be Unshackled,'" CNN, October 4, 2018, https://www.cnn .com/2018/10/04/media/marc-benioff-time-magazine/index.html.

174   "I'm not going to be operationally involved": Ibid.

175   "gender gap": "Feminist Majority Foundation President Eleanor Smeal," feminist.org, accessed March 21, 2019, http://www.feminist.org/welcome/esbio .html.

176   "a thousand points of light": Danny Clemens, "President George HW Bush's 'Thousand Points of Light' Legacy of Service, Volunteerism," Eyewitness News, ABC7NY, December 2, 2018, https://abc7ny.com/politics/thousand -points-of-light-and-bush-41s-legacy-of-volunteerism/4814168/.

176   "compassionate conservative": "President George W. Bush on Compassionate Conservatism," *Catalyst, a Journal of Ideas from the Bush Institute*, Fall 2018, https://www.bushcenter.org/catalyst/opportunity-road/george-w-bush-on-com passionate-conservatism.html.

177   no less than $70,000 per year: Patricia Cohen, "One Company's New Minimum Wage: $70,000 a Year," *New York Times*, April 13, 2015, https://www .nytimes.com/2015/04/14/business/owner-of-gravity-payments-a-credit-card -processor-is-setting-a-new-minimum-wage-70000-a-year.html.

177   "It's not about making money": Scott Stump, "CEO Raising Workers' Minimum Pay to $70K: 'It's About Making a Difference,'" *Today*, April 15, 2015, https://www.today.com/money/gravity-payments-ceo-dan-price-raising-minimum -pay-70k-t15246.

177   "You're ripping me off": Paul Keegan, "Here's What Really Happened at That Company That Set a $70,000 Minimum Wage," *Inc.*, November 2015, https://www.inc.com/magazine/201511/paul-keegan/does-more-pay-mean-more -growth.html.

177   "felt horrible": Ibid.

178   forcibly removed from his seat: Camila Domonoske, "Passenger Forcibly Removed from United Flight, Prompting Outcry," NPR, April 10, 2017, https:// www.npr.org/sections/thetwo-way/2017/04/10/523275494/passenger-forcibly -removed-from-united-flight-prompting-outcry.

178   released a statement: Lauren Thomas, "United CEO Says Airline Had to 'Re-Accommodate' Passenger, and the Reaction Was Wild," CNBC, April 10, 2017, https://www.cnbc.com/2017/04/10/united-ceo-says-airline-had-to-re-ac commodate-passenger-and-twitter-is-having-a-riot.html.

178   "Swift cultivates a gawky adorkability": Nancy Jo Sales and Jessica Diehl,

"Taylor Swift's Telltale Heart," *Vanity Fair*, March 15, 2013, https://www.vanity
fair.com/hollywood/2013/04/taylor-swift-cover-story.

179   "23 Times Taylor Swift": Ellie Woodward, "23 Times Taylor Swift Was So
Adorably Awkward You Wished She Was Your BFF," BuzzFeed, August 26, 2014,
https://www.buzzfeed.com/elliewoodward/times-taylor-swift-was-so-adorably
-awkward-you-wished-she.

179   #5 (Twitter followers): "Twitter: Most Followers," Friend or Follow, accessed March 21, 2019, https://friendorfollow.com/twitter/most-followers/.

179   #8 (Instagram followers): Avery Hartmans, "The 50 Most Followed Instagram Accounts in 2018," Business Insider, December 31, 2018, https://www
.businessinsider.com/instagram-top-50-people.

179   "17 Times Ed Sheeran": Christina Garibaldi, "17 Times Ed Sheeran Made
Us Laugh Until We Cried," MTV, June 18, 2015, http://www.mtv.com/news
/2190173/ed-sheeran-17-laugh-until-we-cried/.

179   "14 Times Ed Sheeran": Sophie Gadd, "14 Times Ed Sheeran Was Literally
the Nicest Man in Show Buisiness," BuzzFeed, July 21, 2015, https://www.buzz
feed.com/sophiegadd/14-times-ed-sheeran-was-actually-the-nicest-man-in
-show-busi.

180   "just as sweet as you thought": Erin Strecker, "Stop What You're Doing &
Watch Ed Sheeran's Too-Cute 'Sesame Street' Appearance," *Billboard*, April 1, 2015,
https://www.billboard.com/articles/news/6517217/ed-sheeran-sesame-street-song.

180   vial of his blood around her neck: Nicholas Hautman, "Billy Bob Thornton Says Ex Angelina Jolie Is 'Still a Friend,' Explains Their Infamous Blood
Necklaces," *Us Weekly*, June 13, 2018, https://www.usmagazine.com/celebrity
-news/news/billy-bob-thornton-explains-blood-necklaces-with-angelina-jolie/.

180   role model for celebrities: Rachel Simon, "7 Reasons Angelina Jolie Is
Hollywood's Best Role Model for Women, Because the Actress' Life Is Incredibly Inspiring," *Bustle*, March 24, 2015, https://www.bustle.com/articles/71653-7
-reasons-angelina-jolie-is-hollywoods-best-role-model-for-women-because-the
-actress-life-is.

180   special envoy to the United Nations: "UNHCR Special Envoy Angelina
Jolie Begins Visit to Bangladesh, Host to Nearly 1 Million Rohingya Refugees,"
UNHCR, February, 4, 2019, https://www.unhcr.org/news/press/2019/2/5c
57b8ea4/unhcr-special-envoy-angelina-jolie-begins-visit-bangladesh-host-nearly
.html.

180   "Humanitarian of the Year": "Angelina Jolie: Humanitarian," *Time*,
June 12, 2014, http://time.com/2865972/angelina-jolie-humanitarian/.

180 donated more than $8 million: Lesley Messer and Stephen M. Silverman, "Brad Pitt & Angelina Jolie Gave $8 Mil to Charity," *People*, March 21, 2008, https://people.com/celebrity/brad-pitt-angelina-jolie-gave-8-mil-to-charity/.

181 announced that the company was giving: Rose Marcario, "Our Urgent Gift to the Planet," LinkedIn, November 28, 2018, https://www.linkedin.com/pulse /our-urgent-gift-planet-rose-marcario/.

184 "let them know you love them": Joe Azbell, "Blast Rocks Residence of Bus Boycott Leader," Stanford, Martin Luther King, Jr. Research and Education Institute, accessed March 21, 2019, https://kinginstitute.stanford.edu/king-papers /documents/blast-rocks-residence-bus-boycott-leader-joe-azbell.

184 "decades before the concept had a name": Robin Stern and Diana Divecha, "Dr. Martin Luther King, Jr., His Emotions and Beliefs Moved a Country," Yale Center for Emotional Intelligence, accessed March 21, 2019, http://ei.yale.edu /emotions-beliefs-moved-country/.

Chapter 9: Public Prejudice and the Perception of Likeability

189 "Donald Trump's latest nemesis": Talya Zax, "Meet Trump's Latest Nemesis—Steven Goldstein from the Anne Frank Center," *Forward*, February 23, 2017, https://forward.com/culture/qa/363959/meet-steven-goldstein-director-of -the-anne-frank-center-and-nemesis-of-the/.

190 Baldwin allegedly punched a cameraman: Nicholas Riccardi, "Alec Baldwin Arrested in Battery on Photographer: Privacy: Cameraman Claims He Was Punched by the Actor, Who Asked Him Not to Videotape the Homecoming of His and Kim Basinger's Baby Girl," *Los Angeles Times*, October 27, 1995, http:// articles.latimes.com/1995-10-27/local/me-61811_1_alec-baldwin.

190 he left an infamous voice mail: "Alec Balwin Phone Call to Daughter," savonna lessley, YouTube, April 29, 2007, https://www.youtube.com/watch?v=8J0 -ZatDHug.

190 kicked off an American Airlines flight in Los Angeles: Erin Calabrese, "Alec Baldwin Thrown off AA Flight at LAX for 'Playing Game' on Phone," *New York Post*, December 6, 2011, https://nypost.com/2011/12/06/alec-baldwin-thrown -off-aa-flight-at-lax-for-playing-game-on-phone/.

190 He punched one: Janon Fisher and Larry McShane, "Alec Baldwin Punches Daily News Photographer After Obtaining Marriage License in New York with Fiancee Hilaria Thomas," *New York Daily News*, June 20, 2012, https://www .nydailynews.com/new-york/alec-baldwin-punches-daily-news-photographer -obtaining-marriage-license-fiancee-hilaria-thomas-new-york-article-1.1098387.

190   ended up calling another: "Alec Baldwin Explodes on Another Photog," TMZ, June 29, 2012, https://www.tmz.com/2012/06/29/alec-baldwin-paparazzi-attack-explodes-new-york-threat/.

190   Baldwin chased a photographer: "Alec Baldwin: Fine, I Did Use a Homophobic Slur," TMZ, November 15, 2013, https://www.tmz.com/2013/11/15/alec-baldwin-homophobic-slur-twitter/.

190   Baldwin was arrested for assault and harassment: Michael R. Sisak, "Alec Baldwin Charged with Assault in Alleged Parking Dispute," Associated Press, November 2, 2018, https://www.apnews.com/a3c752c6f816439691d5254bbb180354.

192   "And we can count on Fox News": "President Obama's Anger Translator," C-SPAN, YouTube, April 25, 2015, https://www.youtube.com/watch?v=HkAK9QRe4ds.

192   When Trump admitted: Stephen Collinson and Jeremy Diamond, "Trump Finally Admits It: 'President Barack Obama Was Born in the United States,'" CNN, September 16, 2016, https://www.cnn.com/2016/09/15/politics/donald-trump-obama-birther-united-states/index.html.

192   "built his career around being": Greg Farrell, "American Express Built on Value of Nice Guys Finishing First," USA Today, April 25, 2005, https://www.deseretnews.com/article/600128960/American-Express-built-on-value-of-nice-guys-finishing-first.html.

193   "Be mad as hell": Alex Shephard, "Brett Kavanaugh's Strategy Is to Be Mad as Hell," New Republic, December 21, 2018, https://newrepublic.com/minutes/151431/brett-kavanaughs-strategy-mad-hell.

193   "I don't know, have you?": Allyson Chiu, "Brett Kavanaugh Likes Beer, but Not Questions About His Drinking Habits," Washington Post, September 28, 2018, https://www.washingtonpost.com/news/morning-mix/wp/2018/09/28/brett-kavanaugh-likes-beer-but-not-questions-about-his-drinking-habits.

193   "might have been too emotional at times": Brett M. Kavanaugh, "I Am an Independent, Impartial Judge," Wall Street Journal, October 4, 2018, https://www.wsj.com/articles/i-am-an-independent-impartial-judge-1538695822.

194   African-American males accounted for: John Sullivan, Zane Anthony, Julie Tate, and Jennifer Jenkins, "Police Fatally Shot Nearly 1,000 People, and 46 Officers Were Killed, Nationwide in 2017," Chicago Tribune, January 6, 2018, https://www.chicagotribune.com/news/nationworld/ct-nationwide-police-fatal-shootings-2017-20180106-story.html.

194   "the risk of being killed by police": Kim Eckart, "New Study Finds Police-Related Fatalities May Occur Twice as Often as Reported," University of Wash-

ington News, August 28, 2018, https://www.washington.edu/news/2018/08/28
/new-study-finds-police-related-fatalities-may-occur-twice-as-often-as-reported/.

194   "I am not going to stand": Steve Wyche, "Colin Kaepernick Explains Why
He Sat During National Anthem," NFL, August 27, 2016, http://www.nfl.com
/news/story/0ap3000000691077/article/colin-kaepernick-explains-protest-of
-national-anthem.

195   other players around the NFL began: Mark Sandritter, "A Timeline of
Colin Kaepernick's National Anthem Protest and the Athletes Who Joined Him,"
SBNation, September 25, 2017, https://www.sbnation.com/2016/9/11/12869726
/colin-kaepernick-national-anthem-protest-seahawks-brandon-marshall-nfl.

195   The president tweeted about it: John Fritze, "NFL: Trump's Toughest
Tweets Knocking Players for Kneeling During National Anthem," *USA Today*,
September 9, 2018, https://www.usatoday.com/story/news/politics/2018/09/09
/donald-trumps-toughest-tweets-kneeling-during-national-anthem/1248196002/.

195   Haters burned Kaepernick's jersey: "49ers Fans Burning Kaepernick's Jersey to the National Anthem," (@BlackSchefter, August 27, 2016), https://twitter
.com/BlackSchefter/status/769687104477548545.

195   cover of *Time*: Sean Gregory, "All Across the Country, Athletes Are Fueling
a Debate About How America Defines Patriotism," *Time*, September 22, 2016,
http://time.com/magazine/us/4503993/october-3rd-2016-vol-188-no-13-u-s/.

195   the first white NFL player: Chris Chavez, "Why Browns Tight End Seth
DeValve Decided to Protest During the National Anthem," *Sports Illustrated*,
August 22, 2017, https://www.si.com/nfl/2017/08/22/seth-devalve-national
-anthem-protest-cleveland-browns.

195   "Proud of My Husband": Erica Harris DeValve, "I'm Proud of My Husband for Kneeling During the National Anthem, but Don't Make Him a White
Savior," *Root*, August 24, 2017, https://verysmartbrothas.theroot.com/i-m-proud
-of-my-husband-for-kneeling-during-the-anthem-1798374605.

196   received praise for defending: Jemele Hill, "Beto O'Rourke Grabbed a Political Third Rail—and Electrified His Campaign," *Atlantic*, October 27, 2018,
https://www.theatlantic.com/ideas/archive/2018/10/beto-orourke-grabbed-a
-political-third-railand-electrified-his-campaign/574057/.

196   lost by only two and a half points: "Texas Senate Election Results: Beto
O'Rourke vs. Ted Cruz," *New York Times*, January 28, 2019, https://www.ny
times.com/elections/results/texas-senate.

197   Americans started to hate: Alex Williams, "Do We Really Hate Anne Ha-

thaway?," *New York Times*, April 5, 2013, https://www.nytimes.com/2013/04/07
/fashion/what-is-anne-hathaway-doing-wrong.html.

197   most lambasted Oscar hosts: *THR* Staff, "Oscar Reviews: What the Critics
Thought About James Franco, Anne Hathaway," *Hollywood Reporter*, February 27,
2011, https://www.hollywoodreporter.com/news/oscar-reviews-what-critics-thought
-162253.

197   "The 83rd Annual Academy Awards will likely be": Tim Goodman, "83rd Annual Academy Awards: Television Review," *Hollywood Reporter*, February 27, 2011,
https://www.hollywoodreporter.com/review/franco-bombs-at-oscars-makes-162234.

197   "Hathaway worked her derriere off": Hank Stuever, "TV Review: At Oscars,
the Kids Were All Right and the 'Speech' Was Well-Prepared," *Washington Post*,
February 28, 2011, https://www.washingtonpost.com/lifestyle/style/tv-review
-oscars-tk-tk-tk/2011/02/25/ABUgFlJ_story.html?utm_term=.f595da9956b7.

198   "1.5 million search results": Kevin Fallon, "The Cult of Hathahaters:
Will It Hurt Anne Hathaway's Oscar Chances?," *Daily Beast*, January 20, 2013,
https://www.thedailybeast.com/the-cult-of-hathahaters-will-it-hurt-anne-hatha
ways-oscar-chances.

198   "Why Do People Hate Anne Hathaway?": Louis Peitzman, "Why Do
People Hate Anne Hathaway?," BuzzFeed, December 6, 2012, https://www.buzz
feed.com/louispeitzman/why-do-people-hate-anne-hathaway.

198   "Hollywood's most polarizing star": Daniel D'Addario, "Anne Hathaway:
Hollywood's Most Polarizing Star," Salon, February 27, 2013, https://www.salon
.com/2013/02/26/anne_hathaway_hollywoods_most_polarizing_star/.

198   overcompensating "theater kid": Brian Moylan, "Why Does Everyone Hate
Anne Hathaway?," Hollywood.com, accessed March 18, 2019, http://www.holly
wood.com/celebrities/why-do-people-hate-anne-hathaway-60231034/.

198   Most Annoying Celebrity of 2013: Mick LaSalle, "The Most Annoying
Celebrity of 2013 . . . Anne Hathaway," SFGate, March 8, 2013, https://blog
.sfgate.com/mlasalle/2013/03/28/the-most-annoying-celebrity-of-2013-anne
-hathaway/.

198   first encountered Hathahate: Laura Brown, "Kiss & Make Up with Anne
Hathaway: We Dare You," *Harper's Bazaar*, October 9, 2014, https://www.harp
ersbazaar.com/culture/features/a3888/anne-hathaway-interview-1114/.

199   Hathahate was finally over: Sara Stewart, "The Hatha-hate Is Finally Over,"
New York Post, August 21, 2015, https://nypost.com/2015/08/21/the-hatha-hate
-is-finally-over/.

201   "public" part more difficult: "Transcript: Hillary Clinton's Speech at the Democratic Convention," *New York Times*, July 28, 2016, https://www.nytimes .com/2016/07/29/us/politics/hillary-clinton-dnc-transcript.html.

201   "Fluency in English": Jennifer Earl, "George H.W. Bush's Biographer Jon Meacham Draws Laughs from Bush Kids During Eulogy," Fox News, December 5, 2018, https://www.foxnews.com/politics/george-h-w-bush-biographer-jon -mecham-draws-laughs-from-bush-kids-during-eulogy.

201   "vision thing": Robert Ajemian, "Where Is the Real George Bush?," *Time*, January 26, 1987, http://content.time.com/time/magazine/article/0,9171,96334 2,00.html.

201   remain Hillary Rodham: Michael Kruse, "The Long, Hot Summer Hillary Became a Politician," *Politico*, April 14, 2015, https://www.politico.com/maga zine/story/2015/04/hillary-clinton-2016-arkansas-116939.

201   "married to an ardent feminist": David A. Graham, "A Short History of Hillary (Rodham) (Clinton)'s Changing Names," *Atlantic*, November 30, 2015, https://www.theatlantic.com/politics/archive/2015/11/a-short-history-of-hillary -rodham-clintons-name/418029/.

201   "Mrs. Frank White": Michael Kelly, "Again: It's Hillary Rodham Clinton. Got That?," *New York Times*, February 14, 1993, https://www.nytimes.com /1993/02/14/us/again-it-s-hillary-rodham-clinton-got-that.html.

201   "I learned the hard way": Amy Chozick, "Times Drops 'Rodham' in Referring to Hillary Clinton," *New York Times*, November 30, 2015, https://www .nytimes.com/politics/first-draft/2015/11/30/times-drops-rodham-in-referring -to-hillary-clinton/.

202   Mr. and Mrs. Bill Clinton: Michael Kelly, "Again: It's Hillary Rodham Clinton. Got That?," *New York Times*, February 14, 1993, https://www.nytimes .com/1993/02/14/us/again-it-s-hillary-rodham-clinton-got-that.html.

202   "the little brown ones": Associated Press, "Bush Defends 'Little Brown Ones' Term for Grandchildren, Tells 'Pride and Love,'" *Los Angeles Times*, August 17, 1988, http://articles.latimes.com/1988-08-17/news/mn-655_1_pride.

203   "little woman standin' by my man": Michael Kruse, "The TV Interview That Haunts Hillary Clinton," *Politico*, September 23, 2016, https://www.politico .com/magazine/story/2016/09/hillary-clinton-2016-60-minutes-1992-214275.

203   "could have stayed home": Ted Koppel, "Making Hillary Clinton an Issue," *Nightline*, March 26, 1992, https://www.pbs.org/wgbh/pages/frontline/shows /clinton/etc/03261992.html.

204 Clinton's low likeability ratings: David Brooks, "Why Is Clinton Disliked?," *New York Times*, May 24, 2016, https://www.nytimes.com/2016/05/24/opinion/why-is-clinton-disliked.html.

204 *Glamour* responded: Krystal Marie Ball, "Male Pundit Accidentally Lays Out the Sexist Reasoning Behind Hillary Clinton's Likability Problem," *Glamour*, May 26, 2016, https://www.glamour.com/story/male-pundit-accidentally-lays-out-the-sexist-reasoning-behind-hillary-clintons-likeabilty-problem.

204 Kate McKinnon played Hillary: "Hillary Actually—SNL," *Saturday Night Live*, YouTube, December 18, 2016, https://www.youtube.com/watch?v=IAhF8tPqafQ.

205 "The Making of Hillary 5.0": Philip Rucker and Anne Gearan, "The Making of Hillary 5.0: Marketing Wizards Help Re-imagine Clinton Brand," *Washington Post*, February 21, 2015, https://www.washingtonpost.com/politics/the-making-of-hillary-50-marketing-wizards-help-reimagine-clinton-brand/2015/02/21/bfb01120-b919-11e4-aa05-1ce812b3fdd2_story.html.

205 "Fighting the 'Wimp Factor'": Margaret Garrard Warner, "George H.W. Bush's Greatest Campaign Challenge: Revisit Newsweek's 1987 Cover Story, 'The Wimp Factor,'" *Newsweek*, December 3, 2018, https://www.newsweek.com/newsweek-1987-cover-story-george-hw-bush-wimp-factor-1241611.

205 combat the public perception: Stephen Battaglio, "How I Survived Roger Ailes' Wrath in 1988: 'He Wanted to Beat You Up a Little Bit,'" *Los Angeles Times*, May 19, 2017, https://www.latimes.com/business/hollywood/la-fi-ct-ailes-bush-20170519-story.html.

205 Bush being pulled out of the Pacific Ocean: "George Bush Rescued at Sea by the USS Finback—02 September 1944," TheBushLibrary, YouTube, December 5, 2016, https://www.youtube.com/watch?v=N8ZYv2TFnZg.

205 Bush got angry on national television: Peter J. Boyer, "Rather's Questioning of Bush Sets Off Shouting on Live Broadcast," *New York Times*, January 26, 1988, https://www.nytimes.com/1988/01/26/us/rather-s-questioning-of-bush-sets-off-shouting-on-live-broadcast.html.

206 show off his toughness: Mark O. Hatfield, "Vice Presidents of the United States," Senate.gov, accessed: March 18, 2019, https://www.senate.gov/artand history/history/resources/pdf/george_bush.pdf.

206 had their likeability analyzed and bashed: Maggie Astor, "'A Woman, Just Not That Woman': How Sexism Plays Out on the Trail," *New York Times*, February 11, 2019, https://www.nytimes.com/2019/02/11/us/politics/sexism-double-standard-2020.html.

208   awful reviews: "Freeheld," Rotten Tomatoes, accessed: March 18, 2019, https://www.rottentomatoes.com/m/freeheld_2015.

208   wound up being $573,000: "Freeheld," Box Office Mojo, accessed: March 18, 2019, https://www.boxofficemojo.com/movies/?id=freeheld.htm.

Chapter 10: Scandals, Killer Scandals, and Likeability Comebacks

212   gouged the price of the drug Daraprim: Andrew Pollack, "Drug Goes from $13.50 a Tablet to $750, Overnight," *New York Times*, September 20, 2015, https://www.nytimes.com/2015/09/21/business/a-huge-overnight-increase-in-a-drugs-price-raises-protests.html.

212   "the most hated man in America": Phil McCausland, "Fraud Trial for Martin Shkreli, 'Most Hated Man in America,' Begins Monday," NBC News, June 25, 2017, https://www.nbcnews.com/news/us-news/fraud-trial-martin-shkreli-most-hated-man-america-begins-monday-n776581.

212   drunken rampage of anti-Semitism: Audrey Gillan, "Mel Gibson Apologises for Anti-semitic Abuse," *Guardian*, July 31, 2006, https://www.theguardian.com/world/2006/jul/31/arts.usa.

212   Roseanne Barr's racism: John Koblin, "After Racist Tweet, Roseanne Barr's Show Is Canceled by ABC," *New York Times*, May 29, 2018, https://www.nytimes.com/2018/05/29/business/media/roseanne-barr-offensive-tweets.html.

213   "'stop that's gay'": Travis M. Andrews, "Kevin Hart Says He's out as Oscars Host After Outrage over Homophobic Tweets," *Washington Post*, December 7, 2018, https://www.washingtonpost.com/arts-entertainment/2018/12/06/kevin-harts-homophobic-tweets-resurface-after-he-is-announced-oscars-host/?utm_term=.cbeea5a706ea.

214   "personal responsibility and care for their lives": David Corn, "SECRET VIDEO: Romney Tells Millionaire Donors What He REALLY Thinks of Obama Voters," *Mother Jones*, September 17, 2012, https://www.motherjones.com/politics/2012/09/secret-video-romney-private-fundraiser/.

214   poll numbers plunged: Andy Kroll, "New Polls Show Majority of Americans Don't Like Romney's '47 Percent' Remarks," *Mother Jones*, September 26, 2012, https://www.motherjones.com/politics/2012/09/new-polls-show-majority-americans-dont-romneys-47-percent-remarks/.

214   "basket of deplorables": Amy Chozick, "Hillary Clinton Calls Many Trump Backers 'Deplorables,' and G.O.P. Pounces," *New York Times*, September 10, 2016, https://www.nytimes.com/2016/09/11/us/politics/hillary-clinton-basket-of-deplorables.html.

215   less likely to support Romney: Frank Newport, "Voters' Reaction to Romney's '47%' Comments Tilts Negative," Gallup, September 19, 2012, https://news .gallup.com/poll/157544/voters-reaction-romney-comments-tilts-negative.aspx.

215   "There was one moment": Diane Hessan, "Understanding the Undecided Voters," *Boston Globe*, November 21, 2016, https://www.bostonglobe.com/opinion /2016/11/21/understanding-undecided-voters/9EjNHVkt99b4re2VAB8ziI /story.html.

217   win the Masters Tournament: "Tiger Woods Biography," Biography.com, accessed March 19, 2019, https://www.biography.com/people/tiger-woods-9536492.

217   won fourteen championships: Christine Brennan, "For Tiger Woods, Winning His Next Major Might Not Be That Far Off," *USA Today*, September 24, 2018, https://www.usatoday.com/story/sports/christinebrennan/2018/09/24/tiger -woods-winning-15th-major/1411308002/.

217   offered a public apology: "Tiger Woods' Apology: Full Transcript," CNN, February 19, 2010, http://www.cnn.com/2010/US/02/19/tiger.woods.transcript /index.html.

217   seven consecutive Tour de France titles: "A Timeline of Lance Armstrong's Cycling Career," Associated Press, April 19, 2018, https://www.apnews .com/93540f296e244bafb5dbf7f2d2b79c89.

218   "most sophisticated, professionalized": Serena Dai, "Lance Armstrong Ran the 'Most Sophisticated' Doping Ring Ever," *Atlantic*, October 10, 2012, https:// www.theatlantic.com/national/archive/2012/10/lance-armstrong-ran-most-so phisticated-doping-ring-ever/322680/.

218   officials stripped Armstrong: Juliet Macur, "Armstrong Cuts Official Ties with Livestrong Charity," *New York Times*, November 12, 2012, https://www .nytimes.com/2012/11/13/sports/cycling/armstrong-cuts-officials-ties-with-his -livestrong-charity.html.

218   confessed to doping: "Lance Armstrong's Confession," OWN, YouTube, January 17, 2013, https://www.youtube.com/watch?v=N_0PSZ59Aws.

220   peak of the sitcom's popularity: Michael V. Tueth, *Laughter in the Living Room: Television Comedy and the American Home Audience* (New York: Peter Lang, 2005), 165.

220   2017–18 television season: Tony Maglio, "NBC Wins 2017–18 Nielsen TV Season in Ratings; CBS Tops Total Viewers," *Wrap*, May 22, 2018, https://www .thewrap.com/nbc-wins-2017-18-nielsen-tv-season-in-ratings-cbs-tops-total-viewers/.

220   Cosby had sexually assaulted them: Chris Francescani and Luchina Fisher, "Bill Cosby: A Timeline of His Fall from 'America's Dad' to a 'Sexually Violent

Predator,'" ABC News, September 26, 2018, https://abcnews.go.com/Entertain
ment/bill-cosby-trial-complete-timeline-happened-2004/story?id=47799458.

220   judge sentenced Cosby: Erin Durkin, "Bill Cosby Sentenced to Three to 10
Years in Prison for Sexual Assault," *Guardian*, September 25, 2018, https://www
.theguardian.com/world/2018/sep/25/bill-cosby-sentence-sexual-assault-judge.

220   Spacey made a sexual advance: Adam B. Vary, "Actor Anthony Rapp:
Kevin Spacey Made a Sexual Advance Toward Me When I Was 14," BuzzFeed,
October 30, 2017, https://www.buzzfeednews.com/article/adambvary/anthony
-rapp-kevin-spacey-made-sexual-advance-when-i-was-14#.ua6BnqYYLy.

220   "I honestly do not remember the encounter": Daniel Victor, "Kevin Spacey
Criticized for Using Apology to Anthony Rapp to Come Out," *New York Times*,
October 30, 2017, https://www.nytimes.com/2017/10/30/arts/kevin-spacey-reac
tion.html.

221   #1 in the ratings: Paul Farhi, "NBC Suspends Brian Williams as Its Lead
Anchor for Six Months," *Washington Post*, February 10, 2015, https://www.wash
ingtonpost.com/lifestyle/style/nbc-suspends-brian-williams-as-its-lead-anchor
-for-six-months/2015/02/10/bc6b79d0-b187-11e4-827f-93f454140e2b_story.html
?utm_term=.c069a6844351.

222   "I don't know what screwed up": Erik Wemple, "NBC News's Brian Williams Recants Story about Taking Incoming Fire During Iraq War Coverage,"
Washington Post, February 4, 2015, https://www.washingtonpost.com/blogs
/erik-wemple/wp/2015/02/04/nbc-newss-brian-williams-recants-story-about
-taking-incoming-fire-during-iraq-war-coverage.

222   tops in the ratings: Stephen Battaglio, "Matt-Lauer-free 'Today' Is Still
Top-rated Morning Show, but NBC's Lead Is Shrinking," *Los Angeles Times*, December 27, 2017, https://www.latimes.com/business/hollywood/la-fi-ct-today
-ratings-lauer-20171227-story.html.

222   Lauer's having gotten Ann Curry fired: Lesley Messer and Liz McNeil,
"Ann Curry: Her Surprising Exit," *People*, July 16, 2012, https://people.com
/archive/ann-curry-her-surprising-exit-vol-78-no-3/.

222   NBC fired Lauer: Stephanie Merry, "Matt Lauer Breaks Silence: 'To the
People I Have Hurt, I Am Truly Sorry,'" *Washington Post*, November 30, 2017,
https://www.washingtonpost.com/news/arts-and-entertainment/wp/2017/11/30
/to-the-people-i-have-hurt-i-am-truly-sorry-matt-lauer-releases-statement-to
-today/?utm_term=.136492f44dbf.

223   "America's First Family": Joe Hagan, "Long Night at Today," *New York*

Magazine, March 24, 2013, http://nymag.com/news/features/today-show-hosts
-2013-4/.

223   near-instant cancellation of her show: John Koblin, "After Racist Tweet,
Roseanne Barr's Show Is Canceled by ABC," *New York Times*, May 29, 2018,
https://www.nytimes.com/2018/05/29/business/media/roseanne-barr-offensive
-tweets.html.

224   delivered an anti-Semitic rant: Audrey Gillan, "Mel Gibson Apologises for
Anti-Semitic Abuse," *Guardian*, July 31, 2006, https://www.theguardian.com
/world/2006/jul/31/arts.usa.

224   audio recordings of Gibson surfaced: "Audio Captures Gibson Death
Threat Against Ex-Girlfriend," CNN, July 13, 2010, http://www.cnn.com/2010
/SHOWBIZ/celebrity.news.gossip/07/12/mel.gibson.rant/index.html.

225   women came forward accusing Freeman: An Phung and Chloe Melas,
"Women Accuse Morgan Freeman of Inappropriate Behavior, Harassment,"
CNN, May 28, 2018, https://www.cnn.com/2018/05/24/entertainment/morgan
-freeman-accusations/index.html.

225   "Anyone who knows me": Jocelyn Noveck, "Morgan Freeman Apologizes
in Wake of Harassment Accusations," Associated Press, May 24, 2018, https://
apnews.com/f10507a1739a4f1886435acbed1733e5.

Chapter 11: The Global Turn-On: Comparing Eight World Leaders

227   friendship that saved the world: Arthur Herman, "Friendships That Saved
the World," *Wall Street Journal*, March 22, 2017, https://www.wsj.com/articles
/friendships-that-saved-the-world-1490221982.

228   Barack Obama flew to Berlin: Jonathan Freedland, "US Elections: Obama
Wows Berlin Crowd with Historic Speech," *Guardian*, July 24, 2008, https://
www.theguardian.com/global/2008/jul/24/barackobama.uselections2008.

228   Crimeans wanted to unite with Russia: Paul Roderick Gregory, "Inside Putin's Campaign of Social Media Trolling and Faked Ukranian Crimes," *Forbes*,
May 11, 2014, https://www.forbes.com/sites/paulroderickgregory/2014/05/11
/inside-putins-campaign-of-social-media-trolling-and-faked-ukrainian-crimes/#2b
2906927140.

228   Twitter hashtag #CrimeaIsUkraine: "Twitter Verifies Account of Russia's
MFA in Crimea, Ukraine Files Complaint," UNIAN (Ukrainian news agency),
January 11, 2019, https://www.unian.info/society/10404918-twitter-verifies
-account-of-russia-s-mfa-in-crimea-ukraine-files-complaint.html.

228   Trump tweeted: "Why would Kim Jong-un insult me by calling me 'old,' when I would NEVER call him 'short and fat?,'" (@realDonaldTrump, November 11, 2017), https://twitter.com/realdonaldtrump/status/929511061954297857.

229   turned to coercion: "North Korean Leader Kim Jong Un just stated that the 'Nuclear Button is on his desk at all times.'" (@realDonaldTrump, January 2, 2018), https://twitter.com/realdonaldtrump/status/948355557022420992?lang=en.

229   bases much of his leadership: *WSJ* Staff, "Modi Says His Fashion Sense Is a Gift from God," *Wall Street Journal*, March 17, 2015, https://blogs.wsj.com/indiarealtime/2015/03/17/modi-says-his-fashion-sense-a-gift-from-god/.

229   world's most popular democratically elected leader: Bruce Stokes, Dorothy Manevich, and Hanyu Chwe, "Three Years in, Modi Remains Very Popular," Pew Research Center, November 15, 2017, http://www.pewglobal.org/2017/11/15/india-modi-remains-very-popular-three-years-in/.

230   changes his bold and colorful outfits: "Narendra Modi's Image Factory," *Economist*, August 9, 2018, https://www.economist.com/asia/2018/08/09/narendra-modis-image-factory.

230   other leaders in India: Bruce Stokes, Dorothy Manevich, and Hanyu Chwe, "Three Years in, Modi Remains Very Popular," Pew Research Center, November 15, 2017, http://www.pewglobal.org/2017/11/15/india-modi-remains-very-popular-three-years-in/.

230   India has overtaken China: Prabhjote Gill, "India Overtakes China to Become the World's Fastest Growing Economy in Q1 2018," Business Insider, September 3, 2018, https://www.businessinsider.in/india-overtakes-china-to-become-the-worlds-fastest-growing-economy-in-q1-2018/articleshow/65653486.cms.

230   implemented deregulation, ending many barriers: Arvind Panagariya, "Modinomics at Four," *Foreign Affairs*, June 22, 2018, https://www.foreignaffairs.com/articles/india/2018-06-22/modinomics-four.

230   high poverty and income inequality remain: Soutik Biswas, "Why Inequality in India Is at Its Highest Level in 92 Years," BBC News, September 12, 2017, https://www.bbc.com/news/world-asia-india-41198638.

230   bases his charisma: Joanna Slater, "India's Modi Has a Strategy for Dealing with Controversies: Silence," *Washington Post*, November 28, 2018, https://www.washingtonpost.com/world/asia_pacific/indias-modi-has-a-strategy-for-dealing-with-controversies-silence/2018/11/27/ce7f6946-ed02-11e8-8b47-bd0975fd6199_story.html.

231   "God has gifted me the sense": *WSJ* Staff, "Modi Says His Fashion Sense Is a Gift from God," *Wall Street Journal*, March 17, 2015, https://blogs

.wsj.com/indiarealtime/2015/03/17/modi-says-his-fashion-sense-a-gift-from
-god/.

231 based on a simple foundation: Ibid.

231 trademarked the term "Modi Kurta": Vanessa Friedman, "Narendra Modi,
the Prime Minister of India: A Leader Who Is What He Wears," *New York Times*,
June 3, 2014, https://runway.blogs.nytimes.com/2014/06/03/narendra-modi-a
-leader-who-is-what-he-wears/.

231 "Make America Great Again": Heather Long, "Donald Trump Trademarks
'Make America Great Again,'" CNN Business, October 8, 2015, https://money
.cnn.com/2015/10/08/investing/donald-trump-make-america-great-again-trade
mark/index.html.

231 "Narendra Modi's image factory": "Narendra Modi's Image Factory,"
Economist, August 9, 2018, https://www.economist.com/asia/2018/08/09/nar
endra-modis-image-factory.

232 used 3-D holographic technology: Lance Price, "The Modi Effect: How India Elected a Hologram," *New Statesman America*, March 27, 2015, https://www
.newstatesman.com/books/2015/03/modi-effect-how-india-elected-hologram.

232 appeared simultaneously at 1,400 rallies: Ibid.

232 "just like the Hindu mythology": Tom Lasseter, "India's Top Candidate
Went Full Tupac, Campaigned Via Hologram," *Bloomberg Businessweek*, May 20,
2014, https://www.bloomberg.com/news/articles/2014-05-13/narendra-modi
-indias-election-frontrunner-had-help-from-his-hologram.

232 substantially thinner version: Haresh Pandya, "Meet 'Virtual Modi,' Gu-
jarat Chief Minister's Latest Tech Push," *New York Times*, November 23, 2012,
https://india.blogs.nytimes.com/2012/11/23/meet-virtual-modi-gujarat-chief
-ministers-latest-tech-push/.

233 embraced a severely disfigured man: Faith Karimi, "Pope Francis' Embrace
of a Severely Disfigured Man Touches World," CNN, November 7, 2013, https://
www.cnn.com/2013/11/07/world/europe/pope-francis-embrace/index.html.

233 papal name Francis: Caleb Bell, "What's in a Name? For a New Pope,
Quite a Bit," *Washington Post*, March 12, 2013, https://www.washingtonpost
.com/national/on-faith/whats-in-a-name-for-a-new-pope-quite-a-bit/2013
/03/12/edd6ff2a-8b4c-11e2-af15-99809eaba6cb_story.html.

233 taking on wealth inequality: Zachary A. Goldfarb and Michelle Boor-
stein, "Pope Francis Denounces 'Trickle-Down' Economic Theories in Sharp
Criticism of Inequality," *Washington Post*, November 26, 2013, https://www
.washingtonpost.com/business/economy/pope-francis-denounces-trickle

-down-economic-theories-in-critique-of-inequality/2013/11/26/e17ffe4e-56b6
-11e3-8304-caf30787c0a9_story.html.

233   climate change: Jim Yardley and Laurie Goodstein, "Pope Francis, in Sweeping Encyclical, Calls for Swift Action on Climate Change," *New York Times*, June 18, 2015, https://www.nytimes.com/2015/06/19/world/europe/pope-francis -in-sweeping-encyclical-calls-for-swift-action-on-climate-change.html.

233   his own institution: Lucy Pawle and Susannah Cullinane, "Pope Francis Attacks 'Diseases' of Vatican in Curia Address," CNN, December 22, 2014, https://www.cnn.com/2014/12/22/world/pope-francis-curia/index.html.

233   to remove the child: "Cute Kid Won't Leave Pope Francis Alone," CNN, October 30, 2013, http://religion.blogs.cnn.com/2013/10/30/cute-kid-wont-leave -pope-francis-alone/.

233   Person of the Year in 2013: Howard Chua-Eoan and Elizabeth Dias, "Pope Francis, the People's Pope," *Time*, December 11, 2013, http://poy.time.com /2013/12/11/person-of-the-year-pope-francis-the-peoples-pope/.

233   World's 50 Greatest Leaders: *Fortune* Editors, "The World's 50 Greatest Leaders (2014)," *Fortune*, March 20, 2014, http://fortune.com/2014/03/20/worlds -50-greatest-leaders/.

233   "enjoys broad support": "Pope Francis' Image Positive in Much of World," Pew Research Center, December 11, 2014, http://www.pewglobal.org/2014/12/11 /pope-francis-image-positive-in-much-of-world/.

233   even atheists liked the guy: Daniel Burke, "Even Atheists Love This Pope," CNN, November 7, 2013, http://religion.blogs.cnn.com/2013/11/07/atheists-who -really-loooove-this-pope/.

234   first to include women: Philip Pullella, "Pope Includes Women for First Time in Holy Thursday Rite," Reuters, March 28, 2013, https://ca.reuters.com /article/topNews/idCABRE92R0B020130328?sp=true.

234   integrated into society: "Pope Francis: Who Am I to Judge Gay People?" BBC News, July 29, 2013, https://www.bbc.com/news/world-europe -23489702.

234   Person of the Year: Lucas Grindley, "The Advocate's Person of the Year: Pope Francis," *Advocate*, December 16, 2013, https://www.advocate.com/year -review/2013/12/16/advocates-person-year-pope-francis.

234   follow his conscience: Lizzy Davies, "Pope Francis Tells Atheists to Abide by Their Own Consciences," *Guardian*, September 11, 2013, https://www.the guardian.com/world/2013/sep/11/pope-francis-atheists-abide-consciences.

234   declined dramatically: "Confidence in Pope Francis Down Sharply in U.S.," Pew Research Center, October 2, 2018, http://www.pewforum.org/2018/10/02 /confidence-in-pope-francis-down-sharply-in-u-s/.

235   accused the pope: Carlo Maria Viganò, "Testimony," DocumentCloud.org, August 22, 2018, https://assets.documentcloud.org/documents/4784141/TESTI MONYXCMVX-XENGLISH-CORRECTED-FINAL-VERSION.pdf.

235   two-year investigation of sexual abuse: Laurie Goodstein and Sharon Otterman, "Catholic Priests Abuses 1,000 Children in Pennsylvania, Report Says," *New York Times*, August 14, 2018, https://www.nytimes.com/2018/08/14/us /catholic-church-sex-abuse-pennsylvania.html.

235   rated Pope Francis favorably: Laurie Goodstein, "Pope Francis' Once-Soaring Popularity Has Dropped Dramatically, New Poll Says," *New York Times*, October 2, 2018, https://www.nytimes.com/2018/10/02/us/pope-francis-popularity.html.

235   pope expelled Archbishop McCarrick: Elizabeth Dias and Jason Horowitz, "Pope Defrocks Theodore McCarrick, Ex-Cardinal Accused of Sexual Abuse," *New York Times*, February 16, 2019, https://www.nytimes.com/2019/02/16/us /mccarrick-defrocked-vatican.html.

236   power since 1953: "Coronation of Queen Elizabeth II," History, February 9, 2010, https://www.history.com/this-day-in-history/coronation-of-queen -elizabeth-ii.

236   longest-serving monarch: Suyin Haynes, "Queen Elizabeth II Is Now the World's Longest-Reigning Monarch," *Time*, October 13, 2016, http://time.com /4529695/queen-elizabeth-longest-reigning-monarch/.

236   knight Paul McCartney: Chris Payne, "The Beatles' Top 5 Queen Elizabeth Moments: From Protests to Paul Becoming Sir Paul," *Billboard*, April 21, 2016, https://www.billboard.com/articles/columns/rock/7341528/beatles-queen -elizabeth-ii-paul-mccartney-john-lennon-jubilee-birthday.

237   estimated to be $530 million: Deniz Cam, "As Queen Elizabeth II Turns 90, a Look into Her Fortune and Her Multi-Billion Dollar Lifestyle," *Forbes*, April 18, 2016, https://www.forbes.com/sites/denizcam/2016/04/18/as-queen -elizabeth-ii-turns-90-a-look-into-her-fortune-and-multi-billion-dollar-lifestyle /#7e4c2c582418.

237   doubled to £76.1 million: Sarah Berger, "Here's How Much Money the Queen Gets (Spoiler: She Got a Big 'Raise')," CNBC, July 3, 2018, https://www .cnbc.com/2018/07/02/sovereign-grant-report-how-much-money-the-uk-gives -queen-elizabeth-ii.html.

237   15 percent of the profit: "Crown Estate Makes Record £304m Treasury Payout," BBC News, June 28, 2016, https://www.bbc.com/news/uk-36643314.

237    $9.4 million from horse racing: Maria Puente, "Queen Elizabeth II Rakes in Whopping $9M Racing Her Beloved Horses," *USA Today*, March 7, 2018, https://www.usatoday.com/story/life/2018/03/07/queen-elizabeth-ii-rakes-whopping-9-m-racing-her-beloved-horses/400888002/.

237   "can fall victim to tribalism": "The Queen's Christmas Message 2018: In Full," BBC, December 25, 2018, https://www.bbc.com/news/av/uk-46680354/the-queen-s-christmas-message-2018-in-full.

237   hundreds of others like it: Mehera Bonner, "Twitter Is Super Pissed About the Queen's Completely Extra Gold Piano," *Cosmopolitan*, December 26, 2018, https://www.cosmopolitan.com/entertainment/a25683473/queen-gold-piano-twitter-reactions/.

239   five days after Princess Diana's death: Warren Hoge, "Elizabeth Returns to London to Bury, and Praise, Diana," *New York Times*, September 6, 1997, https://www.nytimes.com/1997/09/06/world/elizabeth-returns-to-london-to-bury-and-praise-diana.html.

239   "annus horribilis": "A Speech by the Queen on the 40th Anniversary of Her Succession (Annus Horribilis Speech)," Royal.uk, November 24, 1992, https://www.royal.uk/annus-horribilis-speech.

240   caught fire: Celeste Allen, "25 Years Ago, the Queen of England Was Having Her Worst Year Ever," *Timeline*, August 31, 2017, https://timeline.com/british-royal-family-worst-year-1992-4c2092210ed6.

240   Xi ordered Chinese comfort food: Mia Li, "Divining China's Direction by What Xi Ate," *New York Times*, December 30, 2013, https://sinosphere.blogs.nytimes.com/2013/12/30/divining-chinas-direction-by-what-xi-ate/.

240   Bill Clinton set the standard: Marian Burros, "Bill Clinton and Food: Jack Sprat He's Not," *New York Times*, December 23, 1992, https://www.nytimes.com/1992/12/23/garden/bill-clinton-and-food-jack-sprat-he-s-not.html.

241   stopped at a Chipotle: Matthew Yglesias, "Hillary Clinton, the Chipotle Burrito, and the Dumbest Media Frenzy of 2016 (So Far)," *Vox*, April 17, 2015, https://www.vox.com/2015/4/17/8445471/hillary-clinton-chipotle.

241   ordered lunch at a bakery: Helena Andrews-Dyer, "Barack Obama and Joe Biden Grab Lunch in Georgetown," *Washington Post*, July 30, 2018, https://www.washingtonpost.com/news/reliable-source/wp/2018/07/30/barack-obama-and-joe-biden-grab-lunch-in-georgetown-and-the-crowd-goes-wild/.

241   Chairman of Everything: Javier C. Hernandez, "China's 'Chairman of

Everything': Behind Xi Jinping's Many Titles," *New York Times*, October 25, 2017, https://www.nytimes.com/2017/10/25/world/asia/china-xi-jinping-titles -chairman.html.

242 "in touch with common concerns": Laurie Burkitt and Yang Jie, "Xi Jinping's Buns Are All the Rage," *Wall Street Journal*, December 29, 2013, https:// blogs.wsj.com/chinarealtime/2013/12/29/xis-buns-are-all-the-rage/.

242 Big Daddy Xi: Tom Phillips, "Xi Jinping: Does China Truly Love 'Big Daddy Xi'—or Fear Him?," *Guardian*, September 19, 2015, https://www.theguardian. com/world/2015/sep/19/xi-jinping-does-china-truly-love-big-daddy-xi-or-fear-him.

242 as if they know him personally: "Who Is Xi Dada?," *People's Daily*, China, YouTube, September 22, 2015, https://www.youtube.com/watch?v=PnRo9AMT 8FI&feature=youtu.be.

242 portrays Xi as a Confucian father: Chris Buckley, "Xi Jinping Thought Explained: A New Ideology for a New Era," *New York Times*, February 26, 2018, https://www.nytimes.com/2018/02/26/world/asia/xi-jinping-thought-explained -a-new-ideology-for-a-new-era.html.

243 banned poor Pooh on social media: Javier C. Hernandez, "China Censors Winnie-the-Pooh on Social Media," *New York Times*, July 17, 2017, https://www .nytimes.com/2017/07/17/world/asia/china-winnie-the-pooh-censored.html.

243 portrayal of Vladimir Putin: "Vladimir Putin Sketches," NBC, accessed March 19, 2019, http://www.nbc.com/saturday-night-live/cast/beck-bennett-15 166/impersonation/vladimir-putin-285102.

243 rides shirtless on horses: Mail Foreign Service, "On Holiday with Vladimir: Putin Takes a Dip, Climbs a Tree, and Loses His Shirt—again—in Back-to-Basics Siberia Vacation," *Daily Mail*, August 5, 2009, https://www.dailymail.co.uk /news/article-1204250/Vladimir-Putin-takes-dip-climbs-tree-makes-basics-Siberia -vacation.html.

243 hunting and shooting an endangered tiger: "Raw Video: Putin Shoots Tiger with Tranquilizer," Associated Press, YouTube, September 1, 2008, https:// www.youtube.com/watch?v=Hkt5G0uHO0g.

243 Putin saved the lives of the TV crew: Our Foreign Staff, "Vladimir Putin the Hero 'Saves TV Crew from Tiger Attack,'" *Telegraph*, August 31, 2008, https://www.telegraph.co.uk/news/worldnews/europe/russia/2658077/Vladimir -Putin-the-hero-saves-TV-crew-from-tiger-attack.html.

243 whole ordeal was a fraud: Miriam Elder, "Putin's Fabled Tiger Encounter Was PR Stunt, Say Environmentalists," *Guardian*, March 15, 2012, https://www .theguardian.com/world/2012/mar/15/putin-tiger-pr-stunt.

243   scuba diving in the Black Sea: Andrew Osborn, "Vladimir Putin Diving Discovery Was Staged, Spokesman Admits," *Telegraph*, October 5, 2011, https://www.telegraph.co.uk/news/worldnews/europe/russia/8808689/Vladimir-Putin-diving-discovery-was-staged-spokesman-admits.html.

244   Putin as Hercules: Steve Rosenberg, "In Pictures: The 12 Labours of . . . Putin," BBC News, October 7, 2014, https://www.bbc.com/news/world-europe-29513589.

244   black belt in Judo: *Daily Mail* Reporter, "What Do You Mean They Let Me Win? Macho Man Putin Shows Off the Judo Moves That Won Him a Black Belt," *Daily Mail*, December 3, 2010, https://www.dailymail.co.uk/news/article-1341038/Vladimir-Putin-shows-judo-moves-won-black-belt.html.

244   coauthored a book on Judo: Vladimir Putin, Vasily Shestakov, and Alexy Levitsky, *Judo: History, Theory, Practice* (Berkeley, CA: North Atlantic Books, 2004).

244   instructional DVD: *Let's Learn Judo with Vladimir Putin*, IMDb, October 6, 2008, https://www.imdb.com/title/tt1734102/.

244   shown only taking down people: "'Judo Knight' Putin Shows Off Martial Arts Skills in Wrestling Bout," RT, YouTube, December 23, 2010, https://www.youtube.com/watch?v=0lxMglj8LuM.

244   "Who needs bodyguards": "Putin & Co to Teach You Judo," RT, YouTube, October 7, 2008, https://www.youtube.com/watch?v=C7yjCaCQPO8.

244   song that hit YouTube in 2016: "Девушка супер спела песню "Такого, как Путин," Злачное Место Продакшн, YouTube, April 19, 2016, https://www.youtube.com/watch?v=m3doQKa1BNg.

244   sang about a young woman: Damien Sharkov, "Russians Go Wild for Song About Loving 'Someone Like Putin,'" *Newsweek*, April 21, 2016, https://www.newsweek.com/russians-go-wild-hit-about-loving-someone-putin-450578.

245   represented 14 percent: "Did More Russians or Americans Die in World War II?," National WWII Museum, September 17, 2018, https://www.nationalww2museum.org/war/articles/did-more-russians-or-americans-die-world-war-ii.

245   as high as 3.3 million: English translation: Julie Gratz, "World War I Casualties," Reperes, accessed March 19, 2019, http://www.centre-robert-schuman.org/userfiles/files/REPERES%20–%20module%201-1-1%20-%20explanatory%20notes%20–%20World%20War%20I%20casualties%20–%20EN.pdf.

245   estimated 5 million Russians: Lewis Siegelbaum, "Famine of 1921–22," Seventeen Moments in Soviet History, accessed March 19, 2019, http://soviethistory.msu.edu/1921-2/famine-of-1921-22/.

245   as many as 14 million Russians: Bruce Pannier, "Kazakhstan: The Forgotten Famine," RadioFreeEurope RadioLiberty, December 28, 2007, https://www.rferl.org/a/1079304.html.

245   call his boss a "strongman": Anton Troianovski, "Branding Putin," *Washington Post*, July 12, 2018, https://www.washingtonpost.com/graphics/2018/world/putin-brand.

245   forget their economy ranks eleventh in the world: "Projected GDP Ranking (2018–2023)," Statistics Times, June 9, 2018, http://statisticstimes.com/economy/projected-world-gdp-ranking.php.

246   through a photo seen around the world: Amy B Wang, "The G-7 Summit, Summed Up in One Photo," *Washington Post*, June 9, 2018, https://www.washingtonpost.com/news/worldviews/wp/2018/06/09/the-g-7-summit-summed-up-in-one-photo/.

246   PhD in quantum chemistry: Aine Cain, "Angela Merkel Will Serve 4 More Years as the Chancellor of Germany—Here's How 'the New Leader of the Free World' Got Where She Is Today," Business Insider, September 25, 2017, https://www.businessinsider.com/angela-merkel-early-career-2017-9.

247   "There is no image consultant": Rosemary Goring, "Rosemary Goring: Angela Merkel's Unflashy Appearance Is a Winning Tactic," *Herald*, December 13, 2015, https://www.heraldscotland.com/opinion/columnists/rosemary_goring/14142929.Rosemary_Goring__Angela_Merkel_s_unflashy_appearance_is_a_winning_tactic/.

247   taken by her official photographer: Martin Pengelly, "Merkel's G7 Photo Says Everything About Trump's Diplomacy—or Does It?," *Guardian*, June 10, 2018, https://www.theguardian.com/world/2018/jun/10/angela-merkel-photo-donald-trump-diplomacy.

247   post it on social media: "Zweiter Tag des G7-Gipfels in Kanada," (@bundeskanzlerin, June 9, 2018), Instagram, https://www.instagram.com/p/Bjz0RKtAMFp/?taken-by=bundeskanzlerin.

247   Other photos of the event: "One scene—four different perspectives #G7," (@fabreinbold, June 9, 2018), https://twitter.com/fabreinbold/status/1005533097549598726/photo/1.

247   she has issued stern warnings: "Merkel Says German Multicultural Society Has Failed," BBC News, October 17, 2010, https://www.bbc.com/news/world-europe-11559451.

247   Germans call her *Mutti*: Olga Khazan, "Why Is Merkel Still So Popular?," *Atlantic*, September 22, 2013, https://www.theatlantic.com/international/archive/2013/09/why-is-merkel-still-so-popular/279887/.

247   call her the Decider: Eric Westervelt, "Can Angela Merkel Fix Europe's Economic Crisis?," NPR, December 8, 2011, https://www.npr.org/2011/12/08/143292255/can-angela-merkel-save-europe.

248   marathon meeting: Patrick Wintour and Ben Doherty, "Vladimir Putin Leaves G20 After Leaders Line Up to Browbeat Him over Ukraine," *Guardian*, November 16, 2014, https://www.theguardian.com/world/2014/nov/16/vladimir-putin-leaves-g20-after-leaders-line-up-to-browbeat-him-over-ukraine.

248   featured only Merkel's hands: Kate Connolly, "'Merkel Diamond' Takes Centre Stage in German Election Campaign," *Guardian*, September 3, 2013, https://www.theguardian.com/world/german-elections-blog-2013/2013/sep/03/angela-merkel-diamond-german-election-campaign.

248   *Brigitte* magazine: "Angela Merkel: Der BRIGITTE—Talk im Video," *Brigitte*, May 3, 2013, https://www.brigitte.de/aktuell/brigitte-live/brigitte-live--angela-merkel--der-brigitte-talk-im-video-10694910.html.

249   party won a clear majority: Veronica Hoyo and William M. Chandler, "Emmanuel Macron Just Won a Majority in France's National Assembly. Here Is Why It Matters," *Washington Post*, June 20, 2017, https://www.washingtonpost.com/news/monkey-cage/wp/2017/06/20/emmanuel-macron-just-won-a-majority-in-frances-national-assembly-here-is-why-it-matters.

250   resigned as Hollande's minister of the economy: Angelique Chrisafis, "Resignation of French Minister Macron Fuels Presidential Bid Rumors," *Guardian*, August 30, 2016, https://www.theguardian.com/world/2016/aug/30/frances-economy-minister-emmanuel-macron-resigns.

250   prefers equality to freedom if given the choice: Marion Van Renterghem, "Riots, Low Ratings . . . Where Did It All Go Wrong for Emmanuel Macron?," *Guardian*, November 28, 2018, https://www.theguardian.com/commentisfree/2018/nov/28/emmanuel-macron-populism-french-president.

250   "loves holding my hand!": Maggie Haberman, "Trump and Macron: From White Knuckles to 'He Loves Holding My Hand," *New York Times*, July 19, 2017, https://www.nytimes.com/2017/07/19/us/politics/trump-macron-holding-hands.html.

251   arranged for a private dinner: Maggie Haberman, "Trump and Macron Cement Unlikely Friendship in Bastille Day Visit," *New York Times*, July 14, 2017, https://www.nytimes.com/2017/07/14/world/europe/trump-macron-frendship-france-bastille-day-parade.html.

251   borrowing ideas from the left and the right: David A. Bell, "For Emmanuel

Macron, How Did Things Get So Bad So Fast?," *Nation*, December 13, 2018, https://www.thenation.com/article/emmanuel-macron-yellow-vest-france/.

251   president of the rich: Adam Nossiter, "Emmanuel Macron's Unwanted New Title: 'President of the Rich,'" *New York Times*, November 1, 2017, https://www .nytimes.com/2017/11/01/world/europe/france-emmanuel-macron.html.

252   YouTube video in 2018: "Emmanuel Macron Scolds Teenager for Calling Him 'Manu,'" *Guardian* News, YouTube, June 18, 2018, https://www.youtube .com/watch?time_continue=33&v=102vFxWl-Ls.

252   another viral video: "Macron Tells Young Jobseeker: 'I Can Find You a Job by Crossing the Road,'" BBC News, September 16, 2018, https://www.bbc.com /news/world-europe-45541697.

252    $31,000 of taxpayers' money on cosmetics: Benoit Morenne, "Macron Has Spent $31,000 to Keep Looking Young Since Taking Office," *New York Times*, August 25, 2017, https://www.nytimes.com/2017/08/25/world/europe/france -president-macron-makeup-expenses.html.

252   dipped to 29 percent: Dominique Vidalon, "Macron's Popularity Falls Further in September: Polls," Reuters, September 23, 2018, https://www.reuters .com/article/us-france-macron-poll/macrons-popularity-falls-further-in-septem ber-polls-idUSKCN1M307G.

252   tens of thousands: Michel Rose and Luke Baker, "No Leader, Lots of An-ger: Can France's 'Yellow Vests' Become a Political Force?," Reuters, December 6, 2018, https://www.reuters.com/article/us-france-protests-future/no-leader-lots-of -anger-can-frances-yellow-vests-become-a-political-force-idUSKBN1O51ON.

253   Trudeau-versus-Trump comparisons: Steve Scherer, "Canada's Trudeau Uses Trump Card to Attack Main Political Rival," Reuters, November 16, 2018, https://www.reuters.com/article/us-canada-politics/canadas-trudeau-uses-trump -card-to-attack-main-political-rival-idUSKCN1NL23W.

254   Justin Trudeau's reintroduction: Justin Trudeau, "Je t'aime, Papa: Justin Trudeau's Eulogy to His Father," *Globe and Mail*, October 23, 2015, https://www .theglobeandmail.com/news/politics/jetaimepapa-justin-trudeaus-2000-eulogy /article26923529/.

254   performed a striptease: "Justin Trudeau: Striptease Raises Money for Liver Disease at What a Girl Wants Gala," *Huffington Post*, November 18, 2011, https:// www.huffingtonpost.ca/2011/11/18/justin-trudeau-striptease_n_1101153.html.

254   attack ad: Josh Visser, "'In Over His Head': Conservatives Launch First Attack Ad at Justin Trudeau, Set to Circus Music and Striptease," *National Post*,

April 15, 2013, https://nationalpost.com/news/politics/in-over-his-head-conser
vatives-launch-first-attack-ad-at-justin-trudeau-complete-with-circus-music-and
-striptease.

254   Trudeau recorded a video: "Prime Minister Trudeau Delivers a Message on
Pink Shirt Anti-Bullying Day," Justin Trudeau—Prime Minister of Canada, You-
Tube, March 15, 2016, https://www.youtube.com/watch?v=HJB_fBUMBWg.

255   planeload of 163 Syrian refugees: Rebecca Joseph, "1st Planeload of Syrian
Refugees Land on Canadian Soil," Global News, December 10, 2015, https://
globalnews.ca/news/2394286/live-blog-toronto-set-to-welcome-feds-first-syrian
-refugees-to-canada/.

255   Trudeau cried: Andrea Janus, "'I'm Proud to Be Here': Syrian Refugee
Has Tearful Reunion with Justin Trudeau," CBC, December 5, 2016, https://
www.cbc.ca/news/canada/toronto/programs/metromorning/metro-morning
-justin-trudeau-refugee-reunion-1.3880485.

255   Trudeau cried in public: Gary Mason, "Politics and Tears: For Trudeau, It
Works," *Toronto Globe and Mail*, November 30, 2017, https://www.theglobeand
mail.com/opinion/politics-and-tears-for-trudeau-it-works/article37145320/.

256   indigenous Canadians: Amy Smart, "Trudeau Apologizes to B.C. Indigenous Community for 1864 Hanging of Chiefs," *Globe and Mail*, November 2,
2018, https://www.theglobeandmail.com/canada/article-trudeau-to-apologize-to
-bc-indigenous-community-for-1864-hanging-of/.

256   LGBTQ Canadians: Dan Levin, "Canada Offers $85 Million to Vic-
tims of Its 'Gay Purge,' as Trudeau Apologizes," *New York Times*, November 28,
2017, https://www.nytimes.com/2017/11/28/world/canada/canada-apology-gay
-purge-compensation.html.

256   Jewish refugees: "Trudeau to Apologize Wednesday for 1939 Decision to
Turn Back Jewish Refugee Ship," CBC, November 1, 2018, https://www.cbc.ca
/news/politics/st-louis-apology-to-come-wednesday-1.4888076.

256   "Why I'm Raising My Kids to Be Feminists": Justin Trudeau, "Why I'm
Raising my Kids to Be Feminists," *Marie Claire*, October 11, 2017, https://www
.marieclaire.com/politics/a12811748/justin-trudeau-raising-kids-feminist/.

INDEX

STEVEN GOLDSTEIN is a civil rights leader who began his career as a television news producer, winning ten Emmys, before becoming a producer for Oprah Winfrey. He worked as a lawyer for the U.S. House Judiciary Committee and as a communications director in the U.S. Senate before becoming a strategist for leaders in politics, business, and entertainment. He was the founding executive director of Garden State Equality, New Jersey's statewide organization for LGBTQ equality, where his work was chronicled in an Academy Award–winning documentary. He later served as the executive director of the Anne Frank Center for Mutual Respect, the national civil and human rights organization. He is a graduate of Brandeis University, Harvard's John F. Kennedy School of Government, the Columbia School of Journalism, and Columbia Law School. He has taught law and political science at Rutgers University and is currently studying for the rabbinate at the Academy for Jewish Religion in New York.